CHEAPSIDE—Recent developments are restoring Cheapside to its former grandeur. Once London's show street, the one wide market street of the mediæval walled City. It was named after the market held in the centre, Anglo-Saxon *céap*, meaning barter or purchase. With imposing houses, it formed part of the Monarch's route to Guildhall. Joustings were held there. The balcony (still to be seen) in the tower of St. Mary-le-Bow, church of the famous Bow Bells, accommodated spectators.

CAMOMILE STREET. There is a mystery about this street name of a medicinal plant used for alleviating skin troubles. How did the thoroughfare get its name? Your guess is as good as ours. This short street has associations with part of the old Wall of London. No mention of it was made by John Stow, Elizabethan tailor and antiquary, on whose quaint writings all subsequent histories of London are based.

Was it named after a resident merchant, a City benefactor, a builder or the humble herb? We do not know. Tall, modern buildings dominate the Camomile Street of 1962.

CATHERINE WHEEL ALLEY

THE last of the old galleried inns in London, City's Bishopsgate, which was partly destroyed by fire in 1895 and later demolished, gave its name to this thoroughfare.

When street names were only partially used, houses of all kinds were known by signs over the doors or projecting into the road. Fleet Street, for instance, was celebrated for its inns and signboards. Apart from public houses, this form of address ceased when street numbering came in. Some sign names were perpetuated in the name of the street.

D0279700

ELY PLACE

HERE is an atmosphere of peace and quiet in strange contrast to the traffic-filled, bustling streets in the immediate neighbourhood of Hatton Garden and Holborn. Bishops of Ely formerly lived in this ancient spot, whose earliest mention is towards the close of the 13th century. The strawberries which once grew in the gardens of its houses are mentioned by William Shakespeare.

FLEET STREET

IF you were asked to name one of the mos famous streets in the world, you would be saf in mentioning Fleet Street. This is equally well known as "The Street of Ink", or just "The Street"

The name of this centre of the nation's newspape industry can be traced as far back as 1274. It get its name from the once navigable Fleet Rivee This is now converted into an enclosed sewee which flows into the Thames at Blackfriars Bridge

GRACECHURCH STREET—John Stow records a herb market was once held in this busy City street. Corn and fodder were also sold. It has been known by a variety of spellings, suggesting antiquity, including Graces and Gracious Street, the name being derived from that of a nearby church. It got its present name after the Great Fire. Foundations of public buildings erected during the Roman occupation of London have been found there.

GOPHIR LANE. Here is an interestingly unusual street name. So different from its former appellation—Cross Lane. Harben in his *Dictionary of London* has a note about it, in which he records the name as Gopher and Gofair Lane and Gofairlane. He says it was mentioned in several wills of the 14th century, and also in an Indenture of Mortgage in 170 where it is described as "Goefair alias Cro Lane". There was an Elias Gofaire who h rents in the parish of St. Swithin in "Candeliu strate" in 1309-10, so that the street was probab named originally after this family.

HOUNDSDITCH—Formerly a defensive feature and called the City or Town Ditch. Nearby houses made it pestilential by clogging it with their filth, rubbish, dead cats and dogs, thus endangering the citizens' health. Old London, overcrowded and unwholesome, was not a pleasant place to live in. The records contain many suggestions for stopping up, cleansing and converting the Ditch into public gardens.

HOLBORN VIADUCT—This is one of the City's most interesting engineering feats, opened in 1869 and costing £2,500,000, a lot of money in those days. The Viaduct crossed the Fleet valley to continue the main thoroughfare from Holborn to Newgate Street at the same level. It removed some steep inclines, which caused great difficulty in days of horse-drawn vehicles.

LONDON WALL

THIS important business thoroughfare was first mentioned in 1388 and parts of the Roman wall are still to be seen.

Among the major post-war works undertaken by the City Corporation has been the making of Route 11, and New London Wall is the first section of this modern west to east traffic route, in one of the worst blitzed areas of the City. With the acquisition of the land, it cost almost £1,000,000. It has a dual carriageway with an overall width of 86 feet and a total length of about 1,800 feet.

Beneath it is a public car park for 250 cars which was built at a cost of £350,000.

MARRYAT STREET, HAMMERSMITH

NAMED after Capt. Frederick M. Marryat (1792-1848), who lived in the district and was the famous author of adventure yarns like *Midshipman Easy*. He was a boisterous youth, who ran away from school on many occasions, always with the idea of going to sea. He finished as a captain in the Navy and later became an editor and novelist.

LONDON STONE

In 1961, for the first time for centuries, Londoners were able to see in its entirety the mysterious London Stone, removed from the site of St. Swithun's, Cannon Street, and exhibited at Guildhall Museum. Although the Stone baffles experts in some respects, they now agree that it came from between Dorset and the Wash and not Troy. Stow's survey (1598) said that the London Stone, then in the middle of Cannon Street, was so deeply embedded, that if a cart collided with it the cart suffered.

MIDDLESEX STREET.—"Going down the Lane" is a Cockney expression referring to Petticoat Lane (formerly Hogg Lane) and called Middlesex Street since about 1830. It is one of the City's show places, with its open air market, jostling crowds and loquacious stall-holders. People still refer to Petticoat Lane, probably so called because of clothing which has been sold there for centuries. It is hard to realise it once housed foreign ambassadors and was lined with trees.

Mulberry Walk, Chelsea, is a reminder of the days when a brave attempt was made to start a silk industry in Chelsea. A number of mulberry trees were planted in the district, the silk worms having a marked preference for this tree. Alas, the venture did not fulfil expectations, but a pleasant name remained.

NEWGATE STREET. The name Newgate is as redolent of City history as an old English garden is of fragrance. Newgate Gaol was a notorious House of Correction, formerly a prison over the gate. The gaol served the City and Middlesex and was very big. It was pulled down in 1902 to make room for the Central Criminal Court, better known as the Old Bailey. This was badly damaged during the blitz, but has now been completely restored. It has been the scene of many famous murder trials.

PUDDING LANE. As every schoolboy knows, the Great Fire of London started at a baker's shop in Pudding Lane, near London Bridge, on 2nd September, 1666, leaving only one fifth of the City standing. But what kind of pudding is commemorated in the name? One authority says: "Now commonly called Pudding Lane, because the Butchers of Eastcheape have their skalding House for Hogges there, and their puddings with other filth of Beastes are voided down that way to theyr dung boates on the Thames".

PICCADILLY

HOW Piccadilly got its name is a mystery. It may have been borrowed from the Piccadilly Hall, a place of amusement. This was named after the ruffs, called "pickadils" or "peccadillos"—the stiffened points of which resembled spear heads—worn by many of the gallants of James I's reign.

PRINCE CONSORT ROAD in Kensington, although only short, is London's best lighted street, having 34 lamp posts. This is because a child was run over by a cab when the street was poorly lighted and the mother left a legacy for the erection of more lamps.

PALISSY STREET

THIS street in Bethnal Green, is named after a French potter and enameller Bernard Palissy, who died in 1589. The streets on the estate have names of Huguenot origin on account of the association of the locality with those Protestant refugees who came from France in the 16th century.

PATERNOSTER ROW

MANY City street names are reminders of former days. Fleet Street and Walbrook commemorate erstwhile waterways, while Aldgate and Bishopsgate tell of the old City gates. Whereas streets like Hosier Lane and Ironmonger Lane recall specific trades carried on there, Paternoster Row was connected with religious processions. The site of Paternoster Row will now be lost in a new and large-scale development of St. Paul's Cathedral precincts, based on the plan prepared by the eminent architect, Sir William Holford. The scheme includes a piazza, shops, colonnades, arcades and terraces at various levels above a car park.

SADLER'S WELLS

MR. Sadler, a highway surveyor, discovered a chalybeate spring in the wooded garden of a music house he had opened in Islington in 1863. The Wells soon became famous and fashionable, and gout and rheumatism sufferers flocked there. According to tradition, it was a place of public entertainment as early as Elizabeth I's reign.

THE TEMPLE—Something of the indefinable charm that is the Spirit of London is found in places like the Temple. This habitat of lawyers lies between the busy Strand and Embankment. In its cloistered byeways are encountered barristers in their wigs and gowns on their way to the nearby Law Courts or returning to their chambers.
One is reminded of the epitaph:
> Here lie the bodies of John and Ben,
> Lawyers both, but honest men;
> God works His wonders now and then.

Tyburn—the place where executions took place in public in former times—was in the Oxford Road, not far from where Marble Arch now stands. The execution was preceded by a procession from notorious Newgate Gaol, in the City, to Tyburn, the criminal being drawn in a cart. The practice was abolished in 1783, after which this salacious entertainment was provided outside Newgate. This, too, had ceased before Newgate Gaol was demolished in the year 1902.

UPPER THAMES STREET

THE City's only theatre—The Mermaid—(it has no cinema, of course) stands at the Blackfriars end of the street. This, obviously, is the City's theatre-land, for not only was an attempt made in 1616 to rebuild a theatre on this site which was frustrated by the City authorities, but in 1596-1655 the Blackfriars Theatre attracted its patrons to the same area.
Times changed, for in 1958 the Lord Mayor laid as a symbolic foundation of the Mermaid Theatre to be built within the walls of a blitzed warehouse, a brick from a bombed London dock and one from the bedroom where Mozart was born in Salzburg.

WOOD STREET.—It is interesting to note the names of streets running off Cheapside, such as Bread Street, Honey Lane, Milk Street and Wood Street, where these commodities were sold or in the great market of adjacent Cheap, better known to us as Cheapside.
Mrs. Beeton, (1836-1865) famous cookery writer, lived in Wood Street. At the corner where it joins Cheapside is a solitary giant plane tree which towers over three two-roomed shops, examples, but not originals, of two-storey houses permitted by the Rebuilding Act, 1667, after the Great Fire.

CITIES OF ENCHANTMENT

LONDON

by

IVOR BROWN

Illustrated by
FELIX KELLY

NEWNES : LONDON

First published 1960

Text set in 12 point Garamond, 1 point leaded

Made and printed in Great Britain by
The Garden City Press Limited, Letchworth, Hertfordshire
for George Newnes Limited, Tower House
Southampton Street, Strand, W.C.2

Contents

I

Magnetic Monster

I have often amused myself with thinking how different a place London is to different people. They, whose narrow minds are contracted to the consideration of some one particular pursuit, view it only through that medium. A politician thinks of it merely as the seat of government in its different departments; a grazier, as a vast market for cattle; a mercantile man, as a place where a prodigious deal of business is done upon 'Change; a dramatick enthusiast, as the grand scene of theatrical entertainments; a man of pleasure, as an assemblage of taverns, and the great emporium for ladies of easy virtue. But the intellectual man is struck with it as comprehending the whole of human life in all its variety, the contemplation of which is inexhaustible.

James Boswell

1

THE praise of London has been constant in English prose and poetry. No early salute was more eloquent and generous than that of the Scottish poet Dunbar, who, somewhere about the year 1500, called London his sovereign city, seemliest in sight, gem of all joy, and jasper of jocundity. He could hardly sing fairer than that. It is curious that he used what is now a medical term in further describing London as "a most mighty carbuncle of virtue and valour." The oddness lies in the coincidence that when William Cobbett was damning London for being too large he called it " The Wen." A wen, like a carbuncle, is an ugly kind of tumour. But Dunbar was not thinking of bodily blotches: the word which he used had two meanings. His carbuncle was a precious stone. It had various meanings and might be ruby, emerald, or sapphire: essentially it was gay and glittering: he was repeating with emphasis his vision of a "jasper of jocundity." And for a long time London was especially lauded for its geniality of spirit. To Edmund Spenser, following Dunbar, it was " merry London, my most kindly nurse."

Kindly it has been, a ready hostess of the native invader, from Scotland, Wales, and the North. Its social life is rich in Societies of these strangers, the men from the rest of Britain who dine and wine and proclaim the splendours of their countries and counties and then go back to their London homes and earn their London livings. London has gained much, it is true, by its acceptance of the exile. It was the Welsh Tudors who ended the baronial brawling of the Middle Ages and the Wars of the Roses and gave the land unity, discipline, and civil peace, with the glories of Elizabethan England to come. The Flemings and Huguenots brought their crafts; the Scots their mastery of architecture, through the brothers Adam: it was a king from Scotland, James the Sixth and First, and an adventurous " developer " from Wales who provided London with its first decent water supply. Through many centuries the willingness to offer a refuge for the unwanted and the persecuted has brought the brains of the Jews and the talents of political refugees to quicken the native faculties and enliven the solid merits of the aboriginals. But the charity in the first place came from the heart. It was an impulse before it was an investment.

In our own time, as the result of wars and terrors and persecutions in Europe, London has conspicuously added to its cosmopolitan quality. In such an essentially Londonish region as Camden Town I have recently observed, as a wayfarer, that the Mediterranean and the Caribbean seas have abundantly flowed into the Thames. I have been in a bus, going from Hampstead to central London, whose passengers were mainly talking in Italian, in a tongue which I took to be Cypriot-Greek, and in the English of the West Indians. New York was for a long time " the melting-pot " of the nations and the races. London is catching up in the performance of that function. And certainly the coloured folk are adding to what Dunbar called its jocundity. Coming from the sun into our greyness of weather, they bring their laughter with them—and, astonishingly, keep it.

The writer's praise continued. It was tempered by censure of the crowding. The township by the Thames became in time a monster; it had its magic, as the writers testified. But with the crowds came crimes. To the poet Cowper London was his " freckled fair," in which he saw

> " Much that I love and more that I admire
> And all that I abhor."

No city can be stainless and the bigger the city the more chance of spots on its face. To the satirists, whose

contribution to any literature is large in proportion to its wit,
London was a natural target for indictment. But popular
sentiment was against the sneers of the clever; the town
remained a magnet. In song and melodrama the lights of
London made a beckoning flare. The illusion of streets
paved with gold might lead to disillusion and even disaster,
but those lamps were warm and mellow in the general mind.
Still the carbuncle was a jewel and not a pestilence.

Against that praise of tolerance and good temper there
can easily be set ugly instances of the opposite, outbreaks of
racial street-warfare and the violence of young hooligans
who became known as " Teddy Boys " because they strangely
affected the masculine costumes of half a century ago. But
it has always to be remembered, when these examples of
scoundrelism are reported and discussed, that vice is " news "
and virtue is not. It is a melancholy, but universal, fact that
the public's pence will not be attracted by the Press nor its
shillings won by the cinema if it is shown a balanced picture
of society in which decency is as much featured as debauch-
ery and kindliness is as prominent as cruelty. That is true
of any nation or of any city. But for every Londoner who is
surly or even actively hostile to the immigrant or savagely
violent in a gang war of youngsters who bring their knives
to the party there are hundreds of thousands who are
maintaining the old spirit of acceptance and hospitality.

The jocundity takes various forms as fashions change.
When I was a boy London's factory girls danced in the street
on public holidays to native tunes ground out by a barrel-
organ, a piece of London life that has vanished, like the
muffin-man with his bell and unlike the Punch and Judy
puppet-show which has managed to survive. That was the
hilarity when their boys were really Teddy Boys in all
chronological accuracy. Now the granddaughters of those
who kicked up their heels to a " hurdy-gurdy " in the street
frequent dance-halls for rocking and rolling to imported
" off-beat " rhythms supplied by musicians with an orgi-

astic fury. Those who gave a copper to the barrel-organist have silver now for dance-hall entrance money. That is at least a form of economic progress. So jocundity has changed its tune and most elderly people will think the change is for the worse. But elderly people never do like change, whether of music or morals, and the senior Londoners are always regretting the town that was; this has occurred in every great city that ever existed.

The vogues in merry-making may alter less rapidly than in the composition of a wardrobe. But alter they do, and I do not doubt that before long the rock-and-rollers will have discovered the simple animations of the polka, the suave pleasures of the waltz, or even be deciding to tread the stately measure of a pavane or a minuet. It is a long-established custom to regard the dancing of a period as a particular sign of its decadence. John Selden, author of *Table Talk,* wrote of the downward slide of London's jocundity in the reign of Charles I.

" The Court of England has much altered. Att a Solemne dancing, first you have the grave measures, then the Corantoes and the Galliards, and all this is kept upp with ceremony, att length they fell to Trenchmore, and so to the Cushion Dance, Lord and Groome, Lady and Kitchen Maid, no distinction: So in our Court. In Queen Eliz: time, Gravitie and state was kept upp. In King James time things were pretty well. But in K. Charles time there has binn nothing but Trenchmore and the Cushion Dance, Omnium gatherum, tolly polly, hoyte come toyte."

The London of today and tomorrow will doubtless have plenty of " tolly polly and hoyte come toyte." But that does not mean that its average citizen has declined into a debauchee. The jocund is a constantly changing article, like the aspect of the city in which the gaiety is pursued.

The face of London is being altered radically as I write.

A walk in the West End shows me a sky flecked with
gigantic cranes; we are at last filling up the craters of
bomb damage and we are not only filling them up but
soaring out of them. (The delay in central reconstruction
was caused by the well-justified insistence that the appalling
dearth of homes for the people after the war should make
domestic housing the first target of our social policy.
When that primary need had been satisfied as far as could
be, we might set to work on different things.) London will
never scrape the sky as some other cities have done, but it
is beginning to brush the lower clouds not only with its
office blocks in the middle but with its rebuilding of the
poorer suburbs to the east and south, where the London
County Council has encouraged its architects to replace
the space wastage of the small house with the space economy
of the tenement pile.

That is a policy which is thought wrong by many who
believe that London should scatter itself into New Towns,
since proper homes for family life are not flats but houses,
however much land the latter may consume. As a matter
of fact, such is the pressure of population now that the
L.C.C. is executing both policies at once. Any journey by
train or car which takes one through the old working-class
areas will show how the reconstruction is altering the entire
look of the town. Women have a " face-lift " to preserve
their looks. Whether the new " face-lift " of London's
architecture will enhance its appearance is an arguable
point. But there it is: the sky is full of gigantic cranes, and,
when the cranes have gone, it will be full of gigantic
buildings. The monster keeps growing out of its structural
clothes because so many people want to be inside it and
they do thus choose to concentrate beside the Thames
because they like it. Efforts to decant Londoners into New
Towns always meet with a considerable amount of resistance, even if it be certain that a decent living can be earned
elsewhere in conditions more spacious and airy. The lure

of London continually has its pull, and the Londoner still believes that jocundity is more attainable in an urban mass than in a rural dispersion.

It is the habit now to speak of a conurbation. In the House of Lords it has been called " a filthy word for a filthy thing." But it expresses its meaning plainly enough, at least to those who are aware that " *urbs* " is the Latin for city and " *con* " for with or together. It might have pleased that speaker better if we talked more simply of a town-cluster: but conurbation has become established in the planners' jargon and so has the thing itself, filthy or other-wise, for which it stands. London spreads and will spread further. We do our best to contain or modify the conur-bating process. We decree a Green Belt of open land on the outskirts, but we have to admit that the town crops up again beyond the Belt, much as a fat man who has tried to bind in his middle reaches soon finds a disconcerting emergence of flesh above and below the strap.

When will Greater London become Greatest? The term implies some finality, but where and when will the limit be? Presumably when the monster has lost all its attractive power, but it shows no signs of doing so.

Here is a city that has achieved the bulk and the variety of an entire province. But still it prospers, still it beckons The nation looks to it and flocks to this maze and swarming-ground, which is now neither one thing nor one place. There is no unit of organisation called London. There is a whole network of Londons. First there is the Administra-tive County of London, whose citizens, if they bother to vote at local polls (and most do not), elect the London County Council. The county covers only 117 square miles, but these include twenty-eight Metropolitan Boroughs. That would seem to be plenty, but it is a tiny matter com-pared with the surrounding region of 2,000 square miles served by the London Transport Board. The area known as the Metropolitan Police District and guarded, somewhat inadequately owing to lack of numbers and difficult recruitment, by a single Force, runs to 735 square miles; the spread of suburbs defined as Greater London by the Registrar-General contains 720 square miles. The vital supplies of water are collected and distributed by the Metropolitan Water Board serving 570 square miles.

Added to these bodies there are the London Electricity Board and the administrators of the London Postal District, each with separate and rather smaller, but still vast, territories. At the very heart is the single, historic Square Mile of the City of London. This has its own pride of independent history, its own Common Council, its own large Green Belt estates, its own considerable powers, and its own police. The Port of London Authority, on whose efficient conduct of a huge harbour so much of London's prosperity depends, has a wide reach outside London, being responsible for the navigation of 69 miles of the River Thames. For gas and hospital services Greater London is only part of a much larger area which reaches in some cases to the coast.

So what is London? A foolish thing, if you believe that the best size for a city is half a million people, for which view a case can easily be argued. A town with that population can possess a first-rate university, with the appropriate faculties and professions of medicine and law practised at the highest level. Even without the advantage of capital status, such a city can decently sustain the arts and make the visits of artists sufficiently rewarding to attract the best. It can have shops of a quality no less excellent than that of the London stores. Above all, its citizens who work in the centre can get in and out of their suburbs in less than half an hour and in many cases much less. That they can do without the pains and indignities of queueing, pushing, and even entering combat for a place on a bus or tube train. But how many Londoners, if they had a chance of removing to such a town, would take it? They are not allured by a prospect of cheaper land values and so of cheaper housing, or by the presence of country, perhaps fine country, within a few minutes' travel; moors and beaches may be at their doors or easily reached. Not for those who go elsewhere are the many miles of traffic-blocked roads along which Londoners must crawl in bumper-to-bumper motoring on holidays and at weekends, when even a Jaguar cannot outstride the snail. None the less, the chief ambition of many living well away from London is to get into London, while very few Londoners are craving for escape.

Since the fascination holds, despite all the nuisances, the magic of London must be of tremendous power. But it is a charm hard to analyse and explain. London has had a long, strange, eventful history with its last chapter its most disastrous in the destruction suffered. Though much went down in ruin, rubble, and flames many of the finest testaments of London's ancient taste and grandeur still handsomely abide. Yet how many Londoners know or care at all about the history of their city or their suburb? Some deposits of the rough, urban story are frequented as " sights " for a family or a school outing. That scene of many cruelties and horrors, the Tower of London, attracts its eager throngs to see where the heads of the mighty tumbled and the Crown jewels remain. Westminster Abbey, St. Paul's, the museums, the art galleries are there. They store the treasures of English achievement in building, in dedicated craftsmanship, and in the finest forms of human creation. Yet the footsore sightseer who said, " You can have your edifying edifices—give me a drink," was only echoing the opinion of myriads of Londoners who have lived within a bus ride of these sanctuaries and Culture Castles and have omitted to catch the bus. We are not, despite all the imposing figures of evening classes and the no less imposing sales of informative paper-backs, a studious people. But to be ignorant is not to ignore. A citizen who

cares little or nothing for his town's history or beauty may
care much, in a quiet, unexplicit way, for the place as a
part of his existence.

So we are ready to celebrate in song and pay tribute with
a chorus. When a lusty baritone proclaims his pride in
" Dear Old London Town " he plays upon and stimulates
a feeling which is as genuine as it is common. The people
who roar the words may have been overcrowded and
badly housed all their lives and rescued from blitz-burial
during the war while their bits and pieces of domestic
property were fuel for the fires of German hate and triumphant glee. The assault could only increase the affection
and strengthen the people's pride and joy in the mighty
mess that was their home-town. This love of London might
be superficially dismissed as only a Saturday-nightish and
music-hall delight. It was, indeed, the Strand and Piccadilly
and Leicester Square that made the matter of the Victorian
and Edwardian folk-songs. Whoever bellowed genially
about Whitehall and Westminster, sang a salute to the Civil
Service, or hymned the glory of County Hall? The show-
man's history in wax at Madame Tussaud's was often nearer
to public affection than was history in stone at the Tower or
in the Abbey. An intellectual could call the local patriotism
of the Londoner a shallow affection for the shallower things.
But that is itself a shallow view. The feeling has been and
remains a sturdy growth, though paving-stones are its soil.

Being a capital is, of course, a huge asset to any city,
unless it be one of those segregated Parliamentary capitals
where only politicians hive and thrive. London is both a
royal, a political, and a financial capital. It was made by its
river, which many forget, and still is fed by its shipping,
which most Londoners never see. It is the oldest as well as
much the largest of the English towns and, therefore, in the
eyes of the country it is expected to have the best of everything on view and to have it all the time. In many ways that
expectation is met.

There are the State occasions. Television conveys the pageantry, but until we have transmission of colour there is much missing on the screen that a Londoner or a London visitor can, at the cost of some physical strain, amply appreciate. There are those who find their pleasure in watching the comings and goings of politicians; to hang about the illustrious alley that is Downing Street has never been one of my pleasures. I do not deprecate the labours of our statesmen, but they are not elected to create a spectacle and, since we live in an age of industrious photography and incessant newsreels, I see little point in waiting upon the personal appearances of Ministers whose features, if striking, are sufficiently well known and, if not, are scarcely an invitation to stand and stare.

Certainly in displays of sport and recreation London gets the fullest opportunities. In cricket, it has two Test matches every summer and, though the latest methods of defensive play adopted in the higher levels of that game have made it more a matter for yawning endurance than for rapturous applause, the crowds still flow in. The two kinds of football have their major exhibitions at Twickenham and Wembley; at an international or university " rugger " match or at a " soccer " Cup Final it is not easy to be bored. It is true that television may offer a better view than does many a seat on the ground; but the crowds do not diminish.

To travel " hard " overnight in order to mill a way into these arenas remains a popular pastime of the Welsh when their fifteen comes to Twickenham or of any townsmen of the Midlands or the North when their eleven battles for the supreme honours at Wembley. They come swarming with songs on their lips, rosettes on their coats, and the complete conviction that, for a day at least, there is only one thing that counts. A leather ball, oval or round, is the centre of a ritual in one of the British religions; goal-posts are totem poles and the players demi-gods. There are

2—L

fierce celebrations of the cult all over the country; but
London on a winter or spring Saturday is turned into the
high temple of the faithful myriads. And in this worship
there are no distinctions of class.

Wimbledon is magnetic mainly to the middle class.
There again, at the end of June, the devotees of lawn tennis
will pay quite heavily and put up, on occasion, with the
broiling heat of an airless enclosure to see the champions
of many nations prove their staying-power as well as their
speed of eye and limb in the long-drawn matches that may
reduce the strongest to a limp exhaustion. There again
television provides excellent viewing from a domestic
arm-chair; but the fascination of being on the spot is
always potent enough to make the Wimbledon journey
seem worth the while.

The British have a curious passion for going in droves to
see that which can hardly be seen at all. They will line
the banks of the Thames on a day of biting March gales and
squally rain to see a tiny section of the Oxford and Cambridge boat-race and then hang about to find out which side
has won. In the last quarter of a century, with Cambridge
rowing so constantly in the ascendant, there has not often
been much doubt about that. Still, the boat-race is a
London event and thousands, who know nothing about
the technique of oar-propulsion, will face wind and weather
in order to see what can be perfectly well seen by staying at
home in warmth and comfort.

The same is true of the Derby. Without a seat on the
Epsom grand-stands, which the great majority of Derby-
goers have not, the great horse-race is something happening
behind a myriad human backs or parked vehicles. The
crowds on the hillside may have a glimpse of the start or
the finish or catch sight of the jockeys' caps as the cavalcade
whirls round Tattenham Corner. It is possible to spend
Derby Day on Epsom Downs and never see a horse (I
have done so myself). But it costs nothing and it is Derby

Day. So the multitude turns out and is delighted by the invisible event. Only in steeplechasing does London miss the chief event of the year, the Grand National, which is run at Aintree, near Liverpool. Otherwise the south-eastern conurbation has all the spectacles of greatest appeal and of the loftiest, as well as the largest, patronage. Royal Ascot is close to Windsor, where one of the Norman castles built for London's, or the Crown's, defence has grown through the centuries in grandeur and has continued to be the principal royal home outside of London. A little farther up the river is Henley, a pleasant country town at any time and especially in the autumn when its background of beech-planted hills is lit with a conflagration of October colouring. But it is the July Royal Regatta which draws the world's leading oarsmen across the Atlantic or through the Iron Curtain to compete on the Henley reach of the Thames; to be a spectator there is easy for a Londoner who has some leisure at that time.

The London " season " has for a long time lasted on until the beginning of August. Then Parliament rises for a long recess; then the Law Courts are mainly closed; then the schools begin their summer holidays and parents with families of school age are at last able to escape to the country or the coast. It is easily arguable that England, and especially London, wastes its summer by dallying so long before the general vacation. Scotland has regarded July as a holiday month and most of its schools close then, some weeks before the English pupils can lay down their books and pens and cease facing the most important and exacting examinations of the year. July is nearly always the hottest month of an English summer; if there is a heat-wave, with the thermometer rising to ninety degrees Fahrenheit, which in a humid, thundery climate can be more exhausting than a temperature of a hundred in dry heat, the arrival of the airless, oppressive weather will probably be then. Ever since I sweated my way through long July examinations, which lasted almost a fortnight, I have regarded this arrangement of dates as a major act of cruelty.

If I go to Scandinavia, in mid-June, as I like to do, I find the vacation already beginning and all educational and urban activities either closing or much reduced. The northern countries make a fine festival of their midsummer, when there is daylight for twenty hours or more. To be by, on, or in the sea is a pleasure to which all aspire and which most can well manage. Yet for another month or more, while Copenhagen and Stockholm are emptying themselves into the felicity of their adjoining waters, the English children are scribbling for their educational certificates. The relief, no doubt, is all the greater when it comes, but the habit of waiting for August seems to be foremost among England's foolish things.

I surmise that the time-table of the London season was originally dictated by considerations of sport and of the blood sports in particular. The rich had their country houses as well as their town mansions, but it was believed that a milord would find only tedium in the country unless there was something to kill. So Parliament and financial business continued until the grouse-shooting was ready on August 12th on the moors of the North and in Wales and Scotland; after the grouse came the partridge and pheasant, ready for shooting in September and October, and finally the start of fox-hunting in November. At one time there was no autumn session of Parliament; its members, except for the Irish, were all of one class although of two parties, and this class had more agreeable things to do. To tramp the heather or await the driven birds beside the coverts was a much more attractive exercise than tramping through the lobbies for a Parliamentary division of the House and the recording of a vote. The party Whips could not be expected to lay on their strict discipline of attendance when the Whips of another kind were laying on the hounds to a November scent.

That easeful life of the governing class no longer exists. Parliament reassembles before the end of October and the conduct of administration and of business life in London can no longer be conditioned by a sporting calendar. There is so much more work to be done and there are quite different people to do it. The great country houses are too expensive now to serve only as the autumn homes of those who retired there to recuperate from the luxuries as well as the labours of summer in London by sojourning with their guns and hounds and horses until Christmas. They are now, if their owners can afford to keep them at all, public museums and showpieces to which the plebeian sightseers, arriving by motor-coach, are welcome at the price of half a crown a look. Or they may be the property of the National Trust, which allows the owners to live on there if they have first endowed the upkeep of the property and are ready to admit visitors on certain days of the week. But this kind of visitation ends with September.

So the middle of September is now London's lighting-up time for its autumnal and its winter life. It always strikes me as a pity that so many of our foreign visitors to the capital have come and gone by then. Most of them, it is true, are better used to heat than we are and what we consider a sticky and a sultry July is less exhausting to those who at home would be enduring the ferocious heat then afflicting so much of the North American continent. None the less, when the freshness of May has gone from the parks and gardens and the vivid greens are dwindling into drabness, London is a poorer spectacle in July than it was two months earlier and will be two months later. The park gardeners do as well as may be all the year round, but they seem to take an especial pride and to achieve the most triumphant results in the October glory of their great beds of chrysanthemums. Their roses, too, will be facing the earliest night-frost undismayed. A little mist creeping off the ponds at dusk brings subtlety to the delicate colour schemes of London's autumn afternoons and the foreigner who can linger or come to us when summer is spent is likely to get a more delicate glimpse of the town than high summer will afford.

According to the present run of the seasonal weather, he is unlikely to meet any severity of cold until after Christmas. Fog there will be, but that, though it may be frequent after the beginning of November, is not the black and choking horror that it used to be. The importance of smoke abatement has at last been recognised and smokeless zones enforced, with the result that the autumn mists are not so thickly impregnated with soot. There remain the inevitable exhalations of a city built mainly on clay in a climate that is mostly governed by the mild, rain-carrying winds from the west. Nothing will prevent a thickish haze seeping up on winter nightfalls from the parks and suburban gardens, but the filthy mixture of smoke and fog, known as " smog," grows blessedly less.

No country-dweller would think of London as a clean town, but the place is certainly less afflicted by soot than it was. I remember that in my Hampstead boyhood to follow a tennis ball into the bushes was to have one's flannels immediately, completely, and disgustingly blackened by the dense deposit of smuts. Now the bushes will not be rurally speckless; but at least they will not turn flannels from white to black in a moment. Our predecessors with their ample supply of coal-carrying and fire-lighting domestic labour and their ignorance of smokeless fuels created, from the rosy comfort of their flaming hearths, dirt-laden skies. Below their feet was the squelch of mud which made a trade for the long-vanished crossing-sweeper; metalled roads have ended that. Above them was the kind of fog which Dickens pictured in language worthy of the fumes of hell. Perhaps it is the freedom from mud that is most encouraging to those who, like myself, are always eager to find a good word for the present, when it can properly be done. Here is a London November in Dickens's *Bleak House*:

" London. Michaelmas Term lately over, and the Lord Chancellor sitting in Lincoln's Inn Hall. Implacable November weather. As much mud in the streets, as if the waters had but newly retired from the face of the earth, and it would not be wonderful to meet a Megalosaurus, forty feet long or so, waddling like an elephantine lizard up Holborn Hill. Smoke lowering down from chimney-pots, making a soft black drizzle, with flakes of soot in it as big as full grown snow-flakes—gone into mourning one might imagine, for the death of the sun. Dogs, undistinguishable in mire. Horses, scarcely better; splashed to their very blinkers. Foot passengers, jostling one another's umbrellas, in a general infection of ill-temper, and losing their foot-hold at street-corners, where tens of thousands of other foot passengers have been slipping and sliding since the day broke (if this day ever broke), adding new deposits to the crust upon crust of mud, sticking at those points tenaciously to the pavement, and accumulating at compound interest. . . .

" Fog everywhere. Fog up the river, where it flows among green aits and meadows; fog down the river, where it rolls defiled among the tiers of shipping, and the waterside pollutions of a great (and dirty) city. Fog on the Essex marshes, fog on the Kentish heights. . . .

" Gas looming through the fog in divers places in the streets, much as the sun may, from the spongy fields, be seen to loom by husbandman and ploughboy. Most of the shops lighted two hours before their time—as the gas seems to know, for it has a haggard and unwilling look."

We have our reliefs. We have got rid of the mud. We have electricity that is less defeated and defeatist than the Victorian gas-lamps. And, furthermore, I have known some

of the most agreeable of London days in November.
Thomas Hood, who died in 1845, wrote in his own mood
and manner concerning the London that Dickens had
drenched in dirt and darkness with his tremendous prose.
Hood said that it had no sun, no moon, no noon and so
was properly called November. I am writing this four
days before Christmas. It is so warm that I have just had
to get up and let in some more night air. No birds? Black-
bird and missel-thrush have been singing in the garden to
greet the belated dawns of December. No leaves? Even
after November our oak-trees were carrying their banners,
thin but persisting, of umbered foliage. We have had, it is
true, a number of November mists and the sound of the
cough is heard in the home. The wet day now is a dark
day too, but I find London, wen, protuberance, conurbation—call it what you will—a less foolish and more fascinating thing when it is not lying drab in long hours of our so
often sulky sunshine but exchanging with a decent speed
the common light of an autumn noon for the crepuscular
witchery of five o'clock. In summer, after all, you cannot
shut out a long, soaking day: you have to go on looking at
it. But in winter you can pull the curtains with a snap of
satisfaction: or, if there is call to hospitality and to entertainment, you can feel that such escape, whatever the
weather, is proper to the season. A warm smell coming
from a restaurant is repulsive in summer, but alluring in
winter. And what is true of the eating-house is true of the
town itself. The aroma of a city alters with the seasons and
its best scents are winter scents, just as the country scents
are richest in the spring and summer.

Why London, despite its jostle and sprawl, is none the
less magnetic to millions is a mystery which I have tried
fairly to analyse, not obscuring the nuisances such as
pressure of noise and numbers on the nervous system. I
have added that my affection is for the city lamps and the
town lit up, aspects least conspicuous in the middle of the

WINTER SCENE

A London Square after snow.

year and most heartening when October comes. But in
the following chapter I endeavour to do no less justice to
London's summer offerings in the way of grass and greenery
and the various avenues of civic ventilation.

Inside the mass of London there is a healthy striving of
the midgets to preserve their personality. There is a
notable adherence, for example, to the name of village and
to the use of old as an adjective of separation from the new.
This is not done in a silly spirit of " Ye Olde "; the " Ye
Olde " public-houses are more likely to be found in newly
developed areas. To assert that this or that enclave is Old
Chelsea or Old Hampstead or Highgate Village or Dulwich
Hamlet is to make a just claim to historical status. The
inhabitants of the villages may be newcomers, but they are
proud of following the aboriginals. Furthermore they are
probably living in genuinely " period " houses whose
good looks are beyond challenge; it is also true that the
prices of these, mainly Georgian, homes are high in proportion to their age and excellence of aspect.

I see houses advertised now as being in Wimbledon
Village and these are not cottages. This claim to antiquity
can be sustained since the Wimbledon parish church of
St. Mary was founded in the fourteenth century, when
Chelsea's Old Church also was first built. London has long
been loyal to a pastoral past in many of its street names, of
which the Haymarket is the most obvious example. Piccadilly, where the Elizabethan herbalist Gerard went to
gather his " simples," was then a country lane which drew its
title from a rich clothier who had done well by the selling
of the fashionable pickadils or ruffs. His mansion was
jestingly known by the source of his wealth and Pickadil
Hall later on gave us our Piccadilly. That street leads to one
of London's central and still distinguishable villages,
Shepherd Market. This now fashionable nook was laid out
in 1734 by Edward Shepherd on part of an old fairground
used for revels and raree-shows since 1688. Here was held

the famous May Fair which gave its name to the surrounding district and became synonymous with social grandeur.

But it is not only in the historic villages that the village spirit lives on to counter the flattening process of modern development. The High Street of a suburb will now contain branches of all the chief multiple stores so that one High Street looks very much like another. But the convenience of shopping, which the well-stocked multiples provide, has not destroyed the small shop round the corner. In the side streets there are clustered small businesses conducted by one family; they manage, like the shopkeepers in a country village, to maintain a considerable assortment of miscellaneous goods, with groceries, newspapers, sweets and tobacco as the common staples. Although handicapped by their inability to make bulk purchases from the wholesalers at reduced rates as well as by lacking the size and glitter of the High Street stores, they manage to hold on. Many housewives appreciate the personal touch; they can gossip over the daily purchase; the " small man " may keep open when the large establishments shut and thus meet the need of a late purchaser. They can stand up to the brisk salesmanship of United Groceries (with its hundreds of branches) by having no appeal beyond that of friendliness and personality. It will be a great loss to London life if these assertions of the village spirit are squeezed out. Fortunately, there seems to be no immediate danger of that.

Londoners, too, are very fond of their local paper; it comes out once a week, reports the affairs of the borough, and keeps an eye on the village side of things, whether they be matrimonial or commercial. The proceedings in the police court down the road are not of so grave a nature as to be national news, but they are good food for suburban conversation. The planners of our New Towns like to use the word neighbourhood when they are speaking of a certain area to be laid out. It is an old word and a true one when applied to the London villages. On the whole London

2

Down the Strand

Down through the ancient Strand
The spirit of October, mild and boon
And sauntering, takes his way
This golden end of afternoon. . . .

Till Clements' angular and cold and staid,
Gleams forth in glamour's very stuffs arrayed;
And Bride's, her aery, unsubstantial charm
Through flight on flight of springing, soaring stone
Grown flushed and warm
Laughs into life full-mooded and fresh-blown;
And the high majesty of Paul's
Uplifts a voice of living light, and calls—
Calls to his millions to behold and see
How goodly this his London Town can be!

W. E. Henley

2

"LET's all go down the Strand" was the refrain of a popular music-hall song, attributed, without dates, by the *Oxford Dictionary of Quotations* to a lyric-writer called Harry Castling. From the same hand came a ditty which gave London one of its Edwardian catch-cries, "What-ho! She bumps." These curious phrases were a feature of my London boyhood. It became the rule for all errand-boys, at a time when errand-boys abounded, to have the current tag on their lips. "There's 'air" or "Get your 'air cut," "Does your mother know you're out?" and, thanks to Mr. Castling, "What-ho! She bumps" had replaced appeals to buy lavender among the Street Cries of London. They were pointless exclamations, as a rule, but widely popular. Numerous "Up West" revellers, either native or visiting London, must have wandered out of the public-houses at closing time singing "Let's all go down the Strand." If they stumbled on their way there would be this reference to bumping.

The second of Harry Castling's contributions to the Street Cries would have been a proper companion to the first during many centuries of English history. The Londoners who had been taking the riverside track from the City to the village of Westminster since Saxon times had long endured a very bumpy passage as they went down the Strand. When the Romans had to evacuate Britain they took away with them the art of making roads, and it is a curious fact, considering the importance of transport for conflict as well as for commerce, that this island was rather worse "roaded" in A.D. 1700 than it was in A.D. 400. To make a firm surface for traffic would not seem to be immensely difficult. The Romans managed it widely, but the Saxons, Normans, and their successors made only perfunctory efforts to maintain and extend the great " streets " which were part of the Latin legacy to England. Few things would have been more valuable to medieval Londoners than a proper causeway beside the river, but for hundreds of years the passage was a mess of swamp, shrub, and holes. The traveller in wet weather paddled and at any time bumped.

In 1315 the passage from Temple Bar to Westminster was described as being in a shocking condition. Special tolls and taxes were subsequently imposed by various kings in order to get funds for proper paving, but the work done was perishable and ill-renewed. As late as 1532 the Strand route was " full of pits and sloughs, very perilous and noisome." None the less the advantage of a site looking south across the river was seized upon by the great noblemen. There they built their town mansions and there their titles have been preserved by the naming after them of the modern Strand's tributary streets. In two cases, in York Street, Adelphi, and at Somerset House, we have relics of the watergates through which the grandees approached their sumptuous barges on the river. The Thames was the answer to their transport problem. The Strand or shore of the river was still rough, but the water itself offered smooth journeying.

Then London went about its business with the aid of oars to such an extent that the absence of a satisfactory road to the back doors of the big riparian houses was more of an inconvenience to the servants than to the masters. The amount of wheeled traffic, even in Shakespeare's time, was quite small: the average person walked the short distance necessary to reach the waterside where the number of wherrymen offering journeys either way with their cries of " Eastward ho " and " Westward ho " was very large and the trade was brisk. There was no temptation to sing

" Let's all go down the Strand ": there was every encouragement for all to sail up or down the Thames which has
given that famous street its familiar name.

So in the street list of the Strand area the great seigneurial
titles abide; running west to east they are Northumberland, Buckingham, York, Durham House, Savoy, Lancaster,
Norfolk, Arundel, and Essex. The tabards, the coats of
arms, and the mottoes of old pride have retired to a world
of pedigree-scholarship and academic heraldry; but at least
the noise of the old names is constant in the London
air.

It was inevitable that the riverside mansions would go in
time; when London grew in commercial wealth and in
possibilities of still greater wealth such sites were coveted
for development. The beginning of the end came during
the Restoration, but the agent of the change was a man who
had no royalism in his blood. He was the son of that rabid
Puritan, Praise God Barebones. As Dr. Nicholas Barbon
he abandoned the study of medicine for the smart practice
of estate agency and fire insurance. Eric de la Maré in his
book on *London's Riverside* quotes Roger North's obser-
vations on Barbon's way of going to work when he had
raised the capital to buy up one of the big houses.

" He was the inventor of this new method of building
by casting of ground into streets and small houses, and
to augment their number with as little front as possible,
and selling the ground to workmen by so much per foot
front, and what he could not sell build himself. This has
made ground rents high for the sake of mortgaging, and
others following his steps have refined and improved
upon it, and made a superfoetation of houses about
London."

Barbon was a jerry-builder and the stuff that he put up was
often collapsible. But the new pattern of the Strand had
been outlined. As de la Maré puts it:

" He was the first of the worst kind of speculative builder that our own century has known too well. His activities and influence extended all over London, but nowhere did they have so great an effect as in the area lying between the Strand and the river. Within a year the dignified abode of earls and prelates had been replaced by streets of houses, taverns and cookshops and the garden on the riverside had become a range of wharves for brewers and wood merchants."

Barbon's destructive work began near Temple Bar. Essex House, scene of Robert Devereux's futile and abortive rebellion of 1601, disappeared in 1674 and the neighbouring Arundel House in 1677. Before that Durham House, in what became the Adelphi, had made way for shops. This once episcopal mansion became the London home of Sir Walter Raleigh, the most widely gifted, the extremely intractable, and the worst treated of all the Elizabethan adventurers, explorers, fortune-hunters, inventors, and poets-militant who bestowed such brilliance on their epoch and lit the river bank with the gems on their garments and the jewels of their speech and writing. A visitor to the Tower must think of Raleigh's long languishment therein; he had tolerable conditions for a man whose mind was a kingdom, but who was without the liberty of action for which he craved. But the name of Durham House Street just as surely calls up for me the memory of that tactless courtier who, neglecting to be courtly, lived so close to Elizabeth's Whitehall and never could get near her heart. He was known as " damnable proud " and the Queen preferred some humility in her waiting gentlemen.

One imagines these great houses as a mixture of stronghold and pleasance, battlemented, narrow-windowed for defence against brawl or street fight, but spaciously halled for a banquet, a masquerade, and a visit of the players.

Down to the water ran courtyards and gardens. The river itself was broader than it is now with its banks built up to hold the tidal surge in check. On the surface was a blaze of barges manned by oarsmen in rich-coloured livery. The stream they furrowed was far cleaner than it has been for a century and a half, with the salmon coming up in an unpolluted passage to their spawning in far shallows. (There was a good run of Thames salmon till 1800.) Swans would be abounding in unsmutched whiteness—and still they do abound undismayed by dirt and ugliness; birds are not aesthetes. It was Silver Thames to the poets, but nobody can sing of it in terms of argent now. None the less the Strand's river, despite our misuse, is still a heart-lifting spectacle as the tide brings the vigour of the sea into London's heart and gives its precious lift to the barges of commerce. Drab vessels they may be now in colour, but they are symbols of the maritime being that has been so large a part of London's power to endure and also to allure.

The Somerset House which we know is in the form of Sir William Chambers's dignified classical-style building begun in 1776. This was the first home of the Royal Academy of Art. Soon the bureaucrats moved in. Today it houses the files and statistics of the Registrar-General, the wills massed in the Probate Department, and the inevitably unpopular tax-gatherers of the Board of Inland Revenue. The curious visitor may inspect any will for a fee of two shillings. Those fascinated by testamentary documents can see the dispositions of property made by many famous men including those of Shakespeare, Dr. Johnson, and Charles Dickens. In the east wing of Somerset House is King's College, one of the major units of London University.

During the seventeenth century this hive of today's official business and scholastic pursuits had been a site of royal occupation. One must use the word site because the old building, which was the home of several Stuart queens

ST. MARY-LE-STRAND

. . . one of fifty churches suggested by Queen Anne for the benefit of
London's soul. The architect James Gibbs certainly made it beneficial
to London's eyes.

and housed the bier of their enemy (Oliver Cromwell lay there in state), was wholly swept away. Later on the Thames Embankment diminished the splendour of Chambers's reconstruction by separating it from the river and so making the watergate a relic instead of the front door to a highway as it had been in the past.

Between Temple Bar and Charing Cross there are three historic churches, two of them conspicuous and one sequestered. Farthest to the east is St. Clement Danes and next to it St. Mary-le-Strand. Both have island sites and the traffic must swirl round these exquisite things, floating like buoys upon the flood. In front of both there is much-prized parking space for motor-cars, soon seized in the morning by the early drivers to work. There have been outcries that churches are an out-of-date nuisance in mid-Strand and should be destroyed to ease the traffic problem. Such monstrous vandalism can surely never happen now, since St. Clement's, heavily bombed and burned in 1941, has been finely restored and made the especial church and memorial shrine of the Royal Air Force. Here are the rolls of honour, including an American roll, of those who went " *per ardua ad astra* " and on the columns are the illuminated medallions of the various Air Force Commands. This is a Wren church of 1681, with a Gibbs spire added nearly forty years later. The antiquity of a holy building upon the spot is immense; the name refers to a Danish holding before the Norman Conquest. The famous peal of bells, chanting the summons to " Oranges and Lemons," which once called children to an annual distribution of fruit, rings out again after the silence which Goering's bombers enforced. To this finely galleried fane comes a steady flow of visitors, including relatives of airmen who gave their lives; here people look and remember; some stop and pray.

Statues at either end of St. Clement's remind us of two very different men of two different centuries. Dr. Johnson looks eastward to his home in Gough Square and Gladstone westward to Downing Street and Westminster. London's statuary, with a few exceptions, is generally derided or at least lamented by the connoisseurs, but I find some pleasure in seeing personalities, lone-standing men, amid the mechanised mass-movement all around, even if the artistry of the sculptor has fallen below the deserts of his subject.

St. Mary's was the first of fifty churches which Queen Anne suggested for the benefit of London's soul. The architect James Gibbs, who finished it after that queen's death, certainly made it beneficial to London's eyes. Its steeple is its major grace; it is rather dark within, but its coffered ceiling has elegance. The interior, with no galleries, now contrasts poorly with that of the new St. Clement's, but it has its warm admirers.

Among my friends of thirty years ago was a Fleet Street journalist, Tommy Pope, whose grace of mind and civilised wit were denied proper scope in the kind of work by which he lived. He left as one of his last wishes a memorial service in St. Mary's of the Strand. That binds the church to my affection, as St. Clement's is bound to the loyalties of all friends of the flying men.

Moving west to the few but famous acres called Savoy, we find the Strand's hidden church, entitled the Queen's Chapel of the Savoy. The Savoy Palace was one of the oldest and grandest of the riverside mansions. It took its name from the Count of Savoy who was granted land between the river and " La Straunde " by Henry III in 1246. Then it passed to " old John of Gaunt, time-honoured Lancaster." Since the monarch was the Duke of Lancaster, and so toasted when the royal health is drunk in Lancashire, the Savoy Chapel became in time an essentially royal place of worship. It is now the chapel both of the Queen and of the Royal Victorian Order. The royal pews are isolated at a small height at the west end. The present building, which looks so tiny beside the vast Savoy Hotel and the neighbouring office blocks, is mainly the product of re-building after a fire in 1864. It has a notable wooden roof blazoned with heraldic embellishments and yet there is a striking simplicity of atmosphere. The exterior is so aus-terely humble that it might be the church of a remote moorland parish.

It is a consoling and, as far as the London tumult will allow, a quiet place. There is a churchyard with seats in it and those who have found a journey up or down the Strand foot-wearisome on a sunny day can sit there on the flank of Savoy Hill and find a surprising tranquillity of spirit as well as a modest comfort for the limbs. There are windows of royal remembrance in this once private chapel, which is now open to the public; but it is strangely unregal and unpalatial in its modest crouch beside one of the largest of London's " luxury hotels." The gravestones against the wall do not speak of particularly eminent burials. One can sit and quote Gray's " Elegy." Inside the chapel there are remembered, without too much boast of heraldry, those who knew and suffered the pomp of power; outside lie the owners of the simpler annals. The Strand itself seems far away.

West of the Savoy was the mansion of the powerful Salisbury family; their name lingered on in the Savoy Hotel's one-time rival, the Cecil. I remember being taken there, after its early grandeur had passed, because it had, according to my host, the best curries in London. Not having tasted all the curries in all the hotels and restaurants of the town, I could neither support nor deny this claim to supremacy; but I felt that I was feeding finely among curry-conscious nabobs. The Cecil made way for oil. Shell-Mex House stands massively on the Salisbury land and its conspicuous clock-tower is known as Big Benzine.

There is little cause to linger today in what is still called Adelphi after the Adam brothers. They developed the Durham House site as a commercial undertaking and ran into deep financial waters, emerging, however, with success as well as making a feast of sweetly reasonable architecture for the higher domesticity of Georgian London. Near to the theatres, it drew the players and the playwrights, first David Garrick and latterly Bernard Shaw, Sir James Barrie, and John Galsworthy. Fragments of the old good taste remain to shame London for letting the Adelphi, almost a living character, a gentleman in brick, go down, and the impersonal office blocks go up. One can pay a farewell glance to the Adelphi home life at No. 7 John Street, and be struck with grateful amazement that the Royal Society of Arts has been spared by both bombs and Big Business. It holds its ground and its civil bastion of taste in John Adam Street. The hall, which can be taken for meetings by those who care to meet in old and gracious serenity, has mural paintings by James Barry, whose purpose was to depict the progress of civilisation. The irony of this survival can be acutely felt by walking out into the street and observing the architectural deposits of our own progressive century.

We are now getting back to the hub of the traffic hurly-burly at Charing Cross and to the hub of administration at Whitehall. The last of the big houses to go was in that quarter. Northumberland House survived until 1873. The castellated mansion with four turrets had passed through the hands of several families, the Earls of Northampton and Suffolk having been owners before the ducal house of Northumberland was established there. The family were bought out for half a million pounds by a public authority and the great leaden figure of a lion was sent away to the other and more remote riverside home of the Percy family, Syon House at Isleworth, which looks across the water-meadows to the far corner of Kew Gardens. The Metro-politan Board of Works made this costly deal in order to create Northumberland Avenue and open up the ways to the Thames and to Whitehall. The epoch of the Strand palaces was over and Dr. Barbon's work was done. But the M.B.W. was not making way, as Barbon did, for the erection of small and shoddy stuff. Hotels and a club of massive proportions soon covered the ducal demesne.

The only comparable structure, that is to say a private riparian mansion, was the home of the first Viscount Astor, built in Victorian Tudor style, near the Temple Underground Station in 1895. That is not the kind of architecture praised by contemporary critics, but Mr. de la Maré, usually a severe critic of such ventures, is almost kind to this experiment, admitting that " for its time this is a fine piece of pastiche." But private ownership did not survive and the Incorporated Accountants turned it into the headquarters of our financial mathematics.

Between Northumberland Avenue and Whitehall is Scotland Yard, a name familiar across the world to all readers of crime news and detective stories. Its name has been shortened in the Press to " The Yard " since the sub-editors who have to compose headlines for narrow columns must have brevity or burst. Foreign readers of newspapers may be puzzled to read, concerning some murder mystery, that " The Yard " is taking this or that action. The commonly used phrase " Yard moves " does not refer to motion over three feet of ground but to intervention by the Criminal Investigation Department.

But why Scotland? Here again we get back to the old baronial, ducal, and royal occupation of positions in the Strand. There had been a palace there before the Normans came. It was used in the Middle Ages as a state residence for Scottish kings when they came to London to do homage or negotiate with the kings and queens of England. The union of the crowns on the arrival of King James the Sixth of Scotland to be King James the First of England removed the regal function of the building and it was relegated to administrative purposes. John Milton had an office there when he was Cromwell's secretary. The roll of Strand poets, incidentally, is not a long one. The Elizabethan players and actors have been more associated with the Surrey side of the river; but the Strand had high honours with Milton in the Scottish palace, Raleigh at Durham House, and Chaucer, a pensioner of John of Gaunt's, as well as a diplomatic agent and clerk of building works, " on the strength " at the Lancastrian stronghold of the Savoy Palace.

Scotland Yard, to be more exact, New Scotland Yard, is a Norman Shaw building of 1891. The Scottish part of the name has been explained. The humble title of Yard was drawn from a wharf where colliers landed their coal. The young Charles Dickens who made his start in authorship with *Sketches by Boz*, written between the ages of twenty-one and twenty-four, has given us a vivid picture of the Yard in his time, the Yard in transition.

" When this territory was first accidentally discovered by a country gentleman who lost his way in the Strand, some years ago, the original settlers were found to be a tailor, a publican, two eating-house keepers, and a fruit-pie maker; and it was also found to contain a race of strong and bulky men, who repaired to the wharfs in Scotland Yard regularly every morning about five or six o'clock to fill heavy waggons with coal, with which they proceeded to distant places up the country, and supplied the inhabitants with fuel. When they had emptied their waggons they again returned for a fresh supply; and this trade was continued throughout the year."

Boz went on to describe the village of the wharfingers. In the eating-houses the joints were of a size and the puddings of a solidity appropriate to the appetites of coal-heavers. In the old public-house, with dark wainscoting and a huge glowing fire, the muscular patrons drank " large draughts of Barclay's best " and sang choruses which sounded out across the river.

But a new type of " Yarder " was moving in. The nearness of the House of Commons and the increase in the number of Members of Parliament made the Yard a much-used short cut from the Strand to Whitehall: the Police Commissioners settled round the corner. The innkeeper found that the incoming public were avoiding his beery and song-resounding snuggery; to attract the genteel the eating-house keepers began to put white tablecloths on their bare wooden tables. The choruses died down and the coalmen took their cargoes, along with their thirsts and appetites, elsewhere. So ended the lusty proletarian life of one of the Strand villages. The administrative middle class were taking over. The last of the barons, or in this case of the dukes, went with Northumberland House. The last of the colliers had gone in the eighteen thirties, when the barges no longer brought their grimy cargoes to this port of call. But still the name lingers, Scotland Yard, with its echo of dynastic chronicles and of the coal-wharf long ago.

My walk has been from east to west along the south side of the street, the one time river-shore, La Straunde. The return journey can be made along the north side of the road. It has less history and is more associated with modern pleasure-seeking.

" Let's all go down the Strand,
    Let's all go hand in hand.
You be leader, I shall walk behind,
    Let's look round and see what we can find."

I quote the song, no lyrical masterpiece, from boyhood memory, and with no claim to accuracy. There was a further couplet, I think.

" That's the place for fun and noise
    All among the girls and boys."

The words, whether or not they are faithful to the author's

text, sum up the old mood of Strand promenading and the quest for what Dr. Johnson called " a frisk " and has recently been " a caper."

It is difficult now to achieve much hand-in-hand perambulation, at least during the day. The pavements are not wide and the crowds are dense, especially in summertime when the visitors, British or foreign, are strolling and stopping and staring. Street-widening, begun in 1958 at the Charing Cross end, makes things easier for traffic, but the Strand will never be a convenient boulevard for strollers. Since the City expanded westward, the office block has reared its massive bulk hereabouts and supplants the old shops with a swarming-ground of office workers pouring in and out by the hundred at the rush hours. Those with no business to do are well away from Charing Cross at those times: they may be buffeted if not trampled underfoot at half-past five in the afternoon, since the homeward-bound are determined to catch the first possible train. To judge by this stampede for the suburbs the Londoners must be zealots of domesticity—or is it just that they hate their place of work? An American visitor, who may have arrived with the illusion that the British are slow movers and innocent of hustle, may get a violent surprise: the young people seem to be in training for a sprinting race and come careering with a menacing frenzy down passages and platforms. Moving stairways in the underground stations do not coax them all to accept a lift. Many charge up the steps which do not provide motion quick enough for them.

So the Strand has become increasingly a Business Street and less of the old songster's avenue for diners-out and parties seeking a spree. When the office blocks pushed their way up Fleet Street into Aldwych and the Strand, and finally into Leicester Square and St. James's, most of the famous restaurants were edged out. The youngster of title and wealth who collected his lady friend at the stage door of the Gaiety Theatre in order to sup at Romano's is a type which has vanished like Romano's itself. Instead there are the fleshpots of Simpson's, catering lavishly for the carnivorous with a nice taste in " roasts." No restaurant better deserves to be called, without disparagement, and indeed as a compliment, " a joint." A relic of the Edwardian and Bohemian period survives in Rule's, which is in the romantically entitled Maiden Lane running just north of the Strand. There, with more " period atmosphere," one can sniff the aroma of a time when there were " stage-door Johnnies " who, in their own elegant way, made the Strand part of the West End. " Playing the game in the West " was another old music-hall song. That kind of player has moved to Mayfair.

Theatres are still plentiful on the north side; there are the Adelphi, Vaudeville, Strand, and Aldwych, with the Savoy, tucked in beside the great hotel, on the south. The Gaiety, once the high temple of Victorian burlesque and of Edwardian musical comedy, is disappearing as I write; it had long been a mournful shell, bare, ruined choirs where Gertie Millar sang. The fall in the emotional temperature of the Strand was lowered when the Tivoli Music-Hall became a cinema; that site has now been lost to entertainment altogether. I can remember the " Tiv " when it was star-clustered with the leading comedians and comediennes of the time. Harry Lauder, George Robey, and Marie Lloyd were regular attractions, with the waiters serving drinks among the seats of the smoke-hazy auditorium. What an audience to play to, with these liquorish diversions and the readiness to chatter if the performer did not dominate and silence them. There was no crooning into microphones then; the unaided voice and the blaze of personality of one lonely figure had to conquer—and did.

An office block is a densely populated building and its population, as a rule, has a feminine majority, since there secretarial work, typing, and office routine need more heads and hands than does the occupation of a directive post. Thus, in the matter of shops, the Strand is no longer the " men only " or " men mainly " street that it used to be. An example of this change occurred early in 1959 when Mr. Harris, the craftsmen of hand-made and " bespoke " shoes for men, including in his clientèle types ranging from the Emperor of Abyssinia to Mr. Bob Hope, left his niche beside the Savoy Hotel in order to take up work in Oxford Street. He gave as his reason for departure, " The Strand has become a woman's street." There are still famous shirt-makers and less costly clothing stores in the street, but one expects to see the big drapers moving in to meet the lunch-time shopping of the myriads of women workers. Shops for women have sprung up in the City where the male clerks no longer make up the purchasing public and in Holborn the famous masculine store of Gamage, a great provider of sports gear and men's wear, has realised that a change of sex-appeal is inevitable and profitable in the policy of retail trade. Only a very conservative temperament would be offended by this alteration. The Strand has acquired a new form of decoration; where " gents' office-wear " gave only dark and dingy colour to its pavements, the feminine and secretarial swarm add new tints and pretty faces.

There is not much architectural distinction about the Strand of today. Yet before one begins to walk east there is a striking visual opportunity, which few, I fancy, ever bother to take. Try standing on the steps of Charing Cross main-line station, not at a rush hour, since, as I have said, you are likely to be swept off your feet. In the comparative calm of middle day the position is well worth a pensive minute's occupation. Three pinnacles of varying height are before you: in the immediate foreground is the Cross. When Queen Eleanor died at Harby in Nottinghamshire in 1290, the procession carrying her body to Westminster

Abbey made twelve stops on the way and at each a cross was erected in her memory. At the village of Charing the last of the series was set up; the Puritans destroyed it in 1643. The present Cross was erected by the London, Chatham and Dover Railway Company, who commissioned a replica based on surviving drawings of the original, with E. M. Barry as architect and Thomas Earp as sculptor. It commemorates a queen famous for charity and good works. Dr. Johnson's belief that the full tide of human existence is to be found at Charing Cross is now more true than ever; amid such press it is salutary to have this sea-mark on the flood. It cannot claim to be a genuine antique, but it is a genuine reminder of a medieval piety which left us much greater works than this. It should aptly set the spectator's foot upon the way to Westminster itself, where the Middle Ages do not whisper of a mere enchantment but proclaim their glory to the full.

On the left of the spectator who pauses on the station steps, the Nelson Monument goes stabbing at the sky. It is easy to argue that the great Corinthian column of 167 feet overreaches its tributary purpose and seems rather to send the Admiral skyrocketing than to remind the passing myriads of his presence. However, it announces eminence beyond doubt and is a pillar of salutation which no Londoner would like to see truncated.

The third pinnacle in our view, and a lovely one, is the spire of St. Martin-in-the-Fields, which is the parish church of the Lords of the Admiralty. This rises higher than does the neighbouring statue of Nelson but, because it is the crown of James Gibbs's substantial as well as elegant building, it does not seem to be so much enskied. So our vista from Charing Cross includes in replica the Middle Ages, in architecture the neo-classicism of the eighteenth century, and in the clouds the soaring Victorian tribute to the commander of the seas. It is no mean start for a walk along the Strand.

C. E. Montague, denying the accusation of ugliness in London, once wrote:

"London! London on an early autumn afternoon of quiet sunshine, when all the air is mysterious with a vaporous gold-dust of illuminated motes and the hum of the traffic seems to fall pensive and muted round the big, benign London policeman

with uplifted hand
Conducting the orchestral Strand."

A generation has passed since then and the orchestra has become more of a jazz band. It would be hard now to talk of the traffic falling to a pensive hum; the roar is continuous and the police today are not so big. Nor would benignity be the quality always applied to them when a motorist has one of those incessant differences of opinion about parking in a side street. But the policeman, though less of a giant, has still good manners and good advice for the stranger in search of guidance and information. At one time, when the traffic first began to swell, to attempt a non-stop pedestrian crossing of the Strand was as hazardous as it then was to make a non-stop flight across the ocean. But the zebra crossings are a great relief and the walker can launch out with confidence on these gangways to the other shore.

People will always indulge in melancholy about the London that is lost to us.

"What's not destroyed by Time's devouring hand,
Where's Troy and where's the Maypole in the Strand?"

That was written about 230 years ago. Since then the name of Maypole has stood for a chain of dairies and for a brand of margarine. Maypoles are still erected by Merrie England revivalists in our more cultural villages, but we hardly want one in the Strand. The annual Norwegian gift of a giant Christmas tree to twinkle with its lights in Trafalgar Square is a happy thought which illumines the Charing Cross end of our street.

It can be said in defence of our time that we do make some efforts at preservation, whereas our ancestors made none. The Elizabethans did not found a Society for the Preservation of Plantagenet England nor did the Stuarts organise campaigns to save their Tudor legacy. They took it for granted that a city will continually have its face lifted; and that it will not always be carried out with the kindly surgery of the craftsman who is now called a " beautician." The devouring hand of Time has had such a calamitous colleague in Enemy Action that we have had vast gaps to fill and we have had to execute the repairs in a way that will cover the costs by more profitable use of the holes in the street. So the architect of today must think in terms of rentable floor space; to that end he is as much a Cubist as were the advanced painters of fifty years ago.

So round about the Strand the rectangles arise, huge crates for the storage of office documents and those who write them, read them, and file them. Ungainly they are, but there are gains to be counted. The Cubists are providing well-warmed and well-lit storage for the community's business life. They serve the public health. It would be a cruel conservatism that would sustain, for antiquity's sake, the cramped and dingy offices of Victorian London. A spacious lift replaces narrow stairs; the windows are numerous and wide. Knocking structural personality away, we let a new order of cleanliness come in. Massive rectangular building is no charmer of the eye, but as citizens, if not as aesthetes, we must give it a square deal. When we restore we do it with taste and judgment, as the revived body of St. Clement Danes confirms. And, if you must snatch a glimpse of the antique, the Strand has its Roman Bath, " temporarily closed " as I write, but some day to be reopened. The insatiable destroyers of legend insist, of course, that it is not Roman at all; but at least they allow it to be a part of medieval plumbing and of its bathing arrangements. Here perhaps a medieval Earl of

Arundel coped with his problem of " personal freshness," as the advertisers of our soaps like to say.

I am not one of those mystics who, like Francis Thompson, can descry the shining traffic of

> " Jacob's ladder
> Pitched between Heaven and Charing Cross."

I find there a pagan street where one little expects to meet " the cloth." The churches of the Strand are two islands and a niche: their sanctity is confined, not emanating. Here is a work-a-day and play-a-night street with a pulse strongly beating and a fair circulation of the civic blood. The crowds who pour out from their work at lunch-time are aware of a vivacious spot. Moreover, it is none of your specialised areas where one trade or calling dominates. There is no feeling of a closed shop, no severely professional aroma, as in the highly medicated Harley-Wimpole area.

What a medley one meets emerging on a fine midday, seeking the snack or more substantial meal, professors and students from King's College, civil servants from Somerset House, broadcasters of the British Way of Life to all corners of the world from their news-and-views workshop in Bush House, lawyers at the Law Court and the Temple end, magazine journalists from Southampton Street and newspaper-men from Fleet Street! Then there are those who serve the London interests of Australia and New Zealand, workers in the new victorious industry of commercial television, and fruit merchants and cabbage-kings coming in from Covent Garden. Add to these the host of visitors staying at the sumptuous Savoy, site of a princely palace and now content to be named plain hotel, or at the less expensive Strand Palace which gives good middle-class service under its almost regal name. Here is London epitomised and concentrated, the capital packeted. If we do not sing rollicking songs about it, as our fathers did, that is not because we have lost our feeling for the place, but

4—L

because our songs are now mostly made in America and are more concerned with " the blues " of Broadway than with the conviviality of London suburbans on the spree, painting London mildly red.

A walk along the north side of the Strand ends at the Victorian substitute for Wren's Temple Bar which was removed to Theobalds Park in Hertfordshire because it obstructed the traffic. There have been demands for its return, but not to the old site: one suggestion for a new position was the end of Middle Temple Lane. But it still remains in rustication. Its successor, designed by Boehm, has a bronze griffin, one of the City's emblems, as well as statues of Queen Victoria and King Edward VII, then Prince of Wales. The Bar divides the City of London from the City of Westminster, and still the Sovereign, when he or she is driven to the City and its Guildhall, must stop there to receive admission from the Lord Mayor of London, who hands over the Sword of State. This is then returned to him; thus he upholds his City's ancient rights and symbolises, with the Sword, his protection of the Sovereign while visiting the historic enclave.

Before one reaches the Bar there are the Law Courts, a neo-Gothic pile of the eighteen-seventies. The official title is the Royal Courts of Justice and there are thirty separate courts within, including the Court of Appeal, and the divisions of Chancery and Queen's Bench. The Probate, Admiralty and Divorce division is housed on the west side of the main building. The public can watch the course of justice on any day in legal term-time between the hours of ten and four. There is no charge for admission: here is an economical way of spending a spare hour or two, but the opportunity is somewhat neglected except when there is a case which concerns notable people and is receiving some publicity.

The structure of the Law Courts is described in the cheap, handy, easily pocketable, and most informative

Penguin Guide to London as " rambling and unrealistic." I suppose the compiler meant by his choice of the adjective " unrealistic " that our Courts of Justice do not look like practical workshops of up-to-date equity. There is certainly spaciousness, and the architects apparently took the view that respect for the law would be enhanced by an atmosphere of antique and almost ecclesiastical solemnity. Suppose that you choose Divorce, turn out of the Strand up the west courtyard where cars are parked, and take the designated entrance, you will climb stone stairs to occupy a seat at the back of a chamber of considerable height. The walls are panelled half-way up and then the stone soars to a lofty ceiling. There are shelves of books, some behind wire: they are no doubt repositories of immense legal wisdom, but the learned servants of the Law appear to have come sufficiently equipped and without need of further research on the spot. For these tomes have a look of being long unused and never likely to be touched. The windows are skied and closed. Ventilation presumably is achieved through the grilles in the walls. One does not go there for a breath of fresh air.

Divorce brings to mind court scenes in stories, plays, and films with ladies of elegance in the witness-box and handsome counsel rapping out their questions to the embarrassment of these butterflies on the wheel. The judge in these fictions will be venerable of years, possibly testy of temper, and majestically out of this world. You may of course strike a *cause célèbre*, with all parties conforming to the ideals of drama and full newspaper reports. But it is unlikely. One may expect as judge a middle-aged and suavely sympathetic man who wears a black gown and a white bow-tie as though he were a schoolmaster caught half-way between his classroom and an evening party. His wig is not the grand, full-bottomed article but a small, rather half-hearted headpiece of office.

During a recent visit I found no glamorous ladies in the

box; the litigants were obviously humble folk who could never have afforded to go to court until the grant of legal aid was introduced. I listened to some undefended cases, in which the judge had to deal with the custody of the children affected or to exercise his discretion as to the granting of a decree where both parties admitted their misdeeds.

In general, there is no solemnity of method to match the "unrealistic" architecture. The judge you will find patient and easy-going both with counsel and witnesses. He may be rather like the chairman of a Marriage Guidance Council, trying to smooth things out and make the best possible arrangement for the children of these broken unions, essentially human in his probing of embarrassing distresses and dilemmas. Beneath wig and gown there is likely to be a kindly uncle.

Behind the cases of the day there will probably be the sadly familiar reappearance of the marriage without a home, which has been the curse of postwar Britain. A houseless young couple has had to live with "in-laws." To share a kitchen is to keep a pot of contention boiling: they have tried in despair a boarding-house and one of their fellow lodgers has been an acquisitive and presumably attractive young woman. The addresses of the parties suggest the greyer parts of suburbia, whose dull tints have smeared the lives in which little adventures of sex have come as a release from wretched conditions of housing. The grave and biblical word adultery will be heard, but it seems too sinister, too aweful for the kind of trespass that has been going on in the dreary confusion of inadequate and over-crowded homes.

This is all far away from the London of Dickens with its scoundrels and humbugs and ebullient characters drawn on the grand scale and coloured with the rich paint-box of prose. I think rather of George Gissing's London, shabby and depressed. Here is a drab little woman who, while seeking divorce from a husband who has left her, admits adultery on her own part, just once. One feels that great sins are not for her and she is muddled when asked for the date of her lapse. Perhaps she has imagined it, to assert herself, to keep her end up, as it were, and to show that she, though deserted, is desirable.

So it goes on. A middle-class woman has married below her station and has rapidly repented. She does not appear, but throughout the hearing there is a small boy in the background whose custody has to be settled. These divorce courts are poignantly haunted with the bewilderment of children, now living with father, now with mother, now pushed off to grandparents. There is every effort made with sympathy and wisdom on the Bench to find the best solution. Visitors who drop in and hear this kind of case conducted will find none of the stage stuff: the proceedings are slow and relaxed: they are also reassuring. At any rate the judge in the cases passing before him could not be a more discerning arbiter. Most of such cases are not sharply exciting, but to any observer of human nature they must offer an appealing spectacle. To a writer there is matter for stories and plays. To those with ears for " the still, sad music of humanity " there is abundant cause for absorbed attention.

The Courts of Queen's Bench are approached directly from the Strand. The lure of the lofty had so gone to the architect's head that the amount of stairs to be climbed to reach the Visitors' Gallery is formidable and there is no lift. The reward for the average spectator may be small. The judge is rather more romantically robed: the red sash across his gown breaks the sombreness of the scene. One may hope to encounter a breach of promise case conducted before a jury, and the presence of a jury has dramatic value, giving Counsel a very different target from that of a single judge: it also provides more faces to watch. But the greater probability is an action for damages with no jury.

Perhaps a plaintiff sues a hospital for alleged blunders in treatment. So a doctor has a long stand in the witness-box and Counsel have been schooling themselves in medical jargon in order to extract the statements they want. Or a works foreman is cross-examined about the place and circumstances of an accident. The Judge takes notes in longhand and Counsel wait upon his penmanship. The proceedings go their quiet, unforced way and the visitor who is watching from an immense height, as though he were in the gallery of a theatre, may find hearing difficult. He may remember too that going down stairs is easier than ascending and that the air is fresher in the street. In any case he has wasted no entrance money and free entertainment is better served in Probate and Divorce. A legal friend has told me that a tough probate case, with embittered relations contesting a will, makes the best viewing of all; that is if you wish to see humanity behaving like hungry dogs over a succulent bone.

So ends the Strand which often makes the news. So, at Temple Bar and the Law Courts, begins Fleet Street, which records it.

3

Green Islands

A great deal of company, and the weather and garden pleasant: and it is very pleasant and cheap going thither, for a man may go to spend what he will, or nothing, all as one. But to hear the nightingale and other birds, and hear fiddles and there a harp, and here a Jew's trump, and here laughing, and there fine people walking, is mighty divertising.

Samuel Pepys

3

" GREEN ISLANDS " is a term which the London County Council likes to give to its common-lands, parks and gardens. The Council has made an admirable short film in colour which bears that title. (I am not talking of the spoken commentary since I wrote it myself. I am thinking of the places shown and of the photography employed to show them in their richness of trees, flowers, grass, and water at the various seasons.) Amid the oceans of urban sprawl these places are genuinely islands; the name is not merely a sentimental one. They can be treasure islands for those who know how to use them. It was the L.C.C.'s complaint that far too many people knew far too little of their opportunities. They needed to be told—or shown.

Our great cities, whenever founded, were enormously enlarged in what Stanley Baldwin justly called " The Age of Anyhow." After the mechanical inventions of the Industrial Revolution and the rapid increase of population which followed the rise of the new mills and factories the towns most affected by the swirl of new riches and new poverty were developed without plan or pity. So it happened that in many great provincial cities there are no central parks: it was only when large areas had been covered with industrial premises and with the housing deemed appropriate to the workers that the city rulers began to realise that a town, as well as a man, needs lungs and that seas of brick should be islanded with occasional grass. So a belated pause was here and there permitted in the onrush of building; a lonely park was permitted. As the urban pressure drove outwards, eating up the fields, an act of civic wisdom sometimes purchased what had been milord's country mansion and saved its grounds for the health and recreation of the people. But the middle of this bricky mess had no break in the structural clutter; there was a multitude of streets and no trees in the street.

London was much luckier. One cannot say that its civic rulers were necessarily much wiser and planned better than those of other towns. Its good fortune was the fact of its being a royal city. Kings live in palaces and palaces must have grounds, even hunting grounds. These may be given away or taken over. The old Radicals used to criticise severely the extravagance of the monarchy and its parasites; they had cause enough in some cases for their criticism. But they usually forgot to mention the royal bounty which gave London so much of its green among the grey.

Hyde Park and Kensington Gardens make an open space of no less than 635 acres in the heart of London's western centre. Adjoining it on the east and south are the Green Park of fifty-three acres and St. James's Park of ninety-three acres. Thus there are nearly eight hundred acres of open land between the kingdom of the bureaucrats, which is Whitehall, the palace of the politicians, which is Westminister, the Royal Borough of Kensington, and the terraces of the now less fashionable Bayswater. This is an island indeed, and it is made up of royal pleasure-grounds that were turned over to serve the more urgent needs of common persons who could not retire to Windsor or a country estate when they wanted to stroll and bask and inhale a cooler air than close-packed streets allowed.

The Reformation deprived the Abbots of Westminster of their manor of Hyde. Henry VIII, who knew a good place as well as a pretty face when he saw one, turned the Hyde lands into his deer-park in 1536. Charles I, a century later, opened the park to the public; he also added a race-course and a carriage-drive. That early Hyde Park was not only a metropolitan Ascot and a health resort. Its visitors included duellists and a plentiful supply of robbers. But public it was in a general way and public it has remained. It is odd that when the soapbox (more exactly portable platform) orators are in full cry at Marble Arch and when a monster Hyde Park rally is organised by trade unionists or Left Wing politicians they are using ground which was first made available to all by a gift of the Stuart King who fought the Parliamentarians to the death. The Roundheads were not so generous. In Cromwell's time a charge was made for every coach and horse that entered the park.

Royalty was not always giving: in the case of Kensington Gardens it did some taking and attempted more. When Kensington Palace at the west end of the open land was acquired by William III, there were thirty acres of grounds; Queen Anne encroached on some thirty acres more, farther to the east, and Queen Caroline, the wife of George II and a lover of the royal home in Kensington but no regarder of popular rights, annexed another two hundred and fifty. She asked Sir Robert Walpole what it would cost to enclose all the royal parks. His answer was " Three crowns—those of England, Ireland, and Scotland." She wisely decided that the price was excessive.

But to Queen Caroline Londoners owe one considerable debt, the ornamental water called the Serpentine, used for boating, swimming (even in mid-winter), and for skating on the now rather rare occasions when London gets a long and severe frost. A very well-organised regatta is held there in late summer. Then oarsmen of the highest class compete in fours and eights, with sculls, and in canoes. The various events are run off in rapid succession so that the spectators, who pay nothing, have no long intervals to weary them.

The Serpentine was created in 1730 by damming the West Bourne, a stream then running down from Bayswater (hence Westbourne Grove), and from sundry ponds; there had to be much digging and the memorial to that labour is a fairly conspicuous mound at the south-east of Kensington

Palace. This might be taken to be a burial tumulus conceal-
ing the bones of Londoners killed by one of the recurrent
plagues or in a ferocious outburst of civil strife when some
Napoleon of Notting Hill marched east to conquer. But
its significance is not medical or military; it is aquatic, and
when George Lansbury, Labour's East End Minister of
Works in 1930, made the well-equipped Lido for mixed
bathing he was using in a popular way the lake dug out by
order of the Queen who would have swept the people out
of all the royal parks had not her Prime Minister told her
the likely cost. It is one of the curiosities of London
language that it seems impossible to construct a bathing
pool without recourse to Venice. It has always to be called
a Lido after the Adriatic sands of pleasure once very
fashionable. The word is pronounced Leedo or Lido
according to democratic choice.

The name of the Serpentine itself is also a queer one. It
suggests a tangle of bends, all " crinkum-crankum " as they
said of ornamental waters in the eighteenth century. A
slight curve in the centre is all its claim to snakishness.
This usually brownish mere within a green island gave
trouble in its time and there is a nasty smell about its
history. In the Age of Anyhow casual treatment of lakes
seemed natural to the careless authorities of a town ill-
governed or scarcely governed at all. A sewer from the
north was allowed to flow into the Serpentine during the
early years of Queen Victoria's reign with very dangerous
results; rowers were poisoned and fevers caused by the
emerging gases. There was a big agitation for reform, and
reform was slow in coming: but in 1860 the sewage was
diverted and the lake disinfected. Another danger lay in
the rash entrance to the waters made by incompetent swimmers, for whose safety the Royal Humane Society employed
the famous architect Decimus Burton to create a rescue and
first-aid station.

Londoners have now the freedom of some of the lawns

of Kensington Palace; so they have got back more than William III first took and have profited in the end by Queen Caroline's activities. Though grasping, both she and Queen Anne before her had the sense to employ landscape gardeners who could take an opportunity. " Beautify," said Polonius, is a vile word, but it need not be a vile thing, and nobody can sit beside the Orangery of Kensington Palace on a summer day and not think kindly of " beautification."

The limitation of the Hyde Park area is its general levelness of terrain. I cannot help wishing that one of the monarchs had insisted on the careful planning of some well-placed hillocks which, suitably timbered, might have broken the monotony. Diversity of one kind was achieved by the making of the Serpentine, but that snake which is no snake would have watered a more attractive Eden if there had been an eminence or two to mitigate the flatness and to yield what would have been a superb view for those who climbed it. There is, after all, still time to construct a midget mountain in mid-London and we have machines to do the digging and mounding now. But doubtless there would be an outcry. Londoners often tolerate the destruction of old and handsome buildings with discreditable apathy. But they would probably be shocked at an attempt to add to the natural features and amenities of their Eden. I again use the word " Eden " because the word " paradise " has come to us from the ancient Greeks, to whom it meant a park.

The history of Hyde Park is a medley of the modish, the raffish, and the rough. The fops of the Restoration used it for parade. Congreve's Millamant in *The Way of the World* spoke of a fashion for driving there in " a new chariot " on the first Sunday of the month " to provoke eyes and whispers," a practice she did not wish to share. That was a continuing panorama of elegance; the Victorians liked to be seen driving with a fine turn-out of horses, footmen, and grooms. The riding in Rotten Row, a name which sounds shabby but is probably a corruption of " Route du Roi," was increased by the doubling of the track's width in 1853.

The age of the motor-car has not diminished the popularity of riding, but the standard of equestrian elegance has been much reduced, a fact severely criticised by gentlemen of the old school. The economical jodhpurs and shoes are more on view than the perfectly cut habits, breeches, and riding-boots that gleamed aforetime. One of the strangest equestrian sports of Regency bucks was driving, or racing, with a curricle or four-in-hand along the slippery surface of the Serpentine when a hard winter had sufficiently frozen it. There were inevitable crashes. The less wealthy took their chance of a fall by dancing on the ice, while others risked their limbs and those of their horses by their glacial gallops. Millamant's use of the word " chariot " was then fully justified.

The more ferocious side of Park behaviour was represented by duelling. In 1712 both the Duke of Hamilton and Lord Mohun were killed in a duel there and two Members of Parliament fought it out less lethally in 1763 when John Wilkes was wounded. Later democracy had its day of fury in 1866 when the railings were torn up in a vast meeting organised by the Reform League; there was much use of truncheons and a company of Foot Guards intervened with fixed bayonets. Many were injured, but luckily no one was killed.

A curious but harmless combat was the sea-fight staged on the Serpentine in 1814 to celebrate the victories in the Napoleonic Wars and the visits of the Emperor of Russia and the King of Prussia. The Battle of the Nile was presented in mimic form and fireworks blazed. Waterloo gave further cause for high jinks in Hyde Park. The Great Exhibition of 1851 covered acres with its glass and the Volunteer Movement brought Victorian Londoners to their self-imposed drills, obedient to the Tennysonian appeal, " Form, riflemen, form." In 1939 the anti-aircraft balloons went up from the grass while shelters were dug into it.

Whenever the town is deeply stirred, there will be something happening in Hyde Park. It may be only an aesthetic rumpus. When the Bird Sanctuary was established in memory of that great far-ranging naturalist W. H. Hudson in 1925, and Jacob Epstein was commissioned to contribute a statue of Rima, the forest spirit of Hudson's *Green Mansions*, its modernism was found repellent by some lively and loutish folk who tarred and feathered as well as derided it. We have learned to be more tolerant of the neo-primitive style in sculpture and the works of Henry Moore and others can be exhibited in public gardens without police protection.

In Hyde Park I think of John Galsworthy's Forsytes, once clustered thickly and tenaciously around it, with " Old Jolyon " in Stanhope Gate and " Old Timothy " in Bayswater. There were ten Forsyte fortresses beside the Park and the occupants evidently found the air congenial to their spirit and vitality; statisticians of the Saga will discover that the average age at death of the older Forsyte generation was well over eighty; one scored his century. They were the " solid men " of Victorian London. Though upstarts in a way and by origin immigrants from Dorset, they resembled Dickens's Veneering in their prosperous arrival: but they were very different in taste and behaviour. They had no sympathy for the flashy: they made good investments; they collected the approved thing in furniture and the arts. They would not have cared for Rima or Mr. Moore; art was not despised, but it had to be kept on the rein. Passion was suspect; it did not fit the pattern. Their author wrote of them and of his first Forsyte book, *The Man of Property*:

" If the upper-middle-class, with other classes, is destined to move into amorphism, here, pickled in these pages, it

LANCASTER HOUSE

. . . in Green Park, a small island of fifty-six acres.

lies under glass for strollers in the wide and ill-arranged museum of letters to gaze at. Here it rests, preserved in its own juice; The Sense of Property."

The fringes of the Park are deeply tinted with that juice; some of the houses look like safes. The London Museum is now in a wing of Kensington Palace; Hyde Park is also a town museum, if you can see in fancy through the timber of its trees to the old treaders of its grass and through the stucco of its tall surrounding mansions to the figures and furnishings, both massive, of the well-to-do Victorians. The flanking terraces of the park present no beckoning look and have the withdrawn, defensive aspect of a Forsyte looking at his funds.

Hyde Park I associate with the vagaries and vicissitudes of adult London life: Kensington Gardens is, for me, a children's playground. If Shelley did indeed sail paper boats on the Round Pond, he early established the nursery nature of the avenue and lawns where a myriad nannies have gossiped while their charges slept or played. If we are to have "fey" statuary, Frampton's Peter Pan is correctly sited in the Gardens and the Albert Memorial is not.

The Green Park, running south from the west end of Piccadilly, has no particular feature to commend it except that it is, in season, green. It is a small island of fifty-six acres, once containing a large reservoir and never " beautified." In the heat of summer it is much frequented by the comatose and some of its visitors, leisured but penurious, seem to make it a dormitory for the day.

The fourth of the royal parks, St. James's, is larger and altogether more attractive. It once belonged to St. James's Palace, having been looted, like Hyde Park, from the Westminster Abbey lands. It is famous now for the variety of the wildfowl on its lake and it has had queer animal occupants as well. The King of Spain presented James I with a gift of camels, and these were set to graze in the park before they were rusticated at Theobalds, the hunting lodge in Hertfordshire. There was a royal aviary, too, which gave its name to Birdcage Walk.

St. James's Park now functions as the back garden of Whitehall and the strolling ground of civil servants. The " high-ups " step across it at lunch-time to their clubs in Pall Mall; the less exalted eat sandwiches on the benches, if the weather is encouraging, and brush up their ornithology. At one time, during and just after the First World War, the spread of official business even usurped the lake and dispossessed the ducks; hutment offices were established on its drained surface. It is never easy to evict bureaucracy from territory which it has seized, but the park became itself again. It has a character of its own, " better class," perhaps, than that of its Green neighbour. If a doze is taken there, it is done more briefly and with less abandon to the bliss of insensibility. One feels that one ought to be decently dressed on these lawns; the bright hues of the mallards on the water set a challenging standard of gloss and man must live up to the fine feathers of his guests.

Regent's Park is another piece of Londoners' luck, being a further, now public, relic of royal devotion to the chase. It had a varied history as hunting ground and meadow until the percipient Prince Regent thought that something of style could be done with it. Why not a Royal Mile leading from his Carlton House, long vanished, away up north to the green fields of Marylebone? At the far end there could be another house, even perhaps a palace, on the convenient knob that was called, for its spring flowers, Primrose Hill, and there could also be villas for his friends of both sexes. The scheme did not go so far as that, but it gave us, with John Nash in brilliant charge of its execution, the sweet curve of Regent Street and the huge pleasance of Regent's Park. This was the first of London's open spaces to be carefully planned and laid out by authority.

The Regency Terraces around it, the best of them designed by Nash and Decimus Burton, have, in general, survived attempted arson and blasting by the German bombers and some home-made proposals to pull them down and do better. The Civil Service has invaded many of the old houses, and that, while it has changed their function, has been a form of protection. Better that these handsome and not easily workable homes should become a storehouse of files than that they should be replaced by the monotonous cubes and block-building of the nineteen-fifties. An urban green island is all the better for cliff scenery, and the Nash terraces, when in full trim of new paint, are as refreshing to the eye of those using the park or the park-side Circular Road as are the white cliffs of our South Coast to the eyes of travellers returning from abroad.

Nash was a strong believer in the value of stucco for the covering of London's brick, and stucco is an expensive article in a smoky atmosphere. Leave it to get dirty and flaky and its grubby, peeling surface can be extremely depressing: keep it in creamy condition and it lifts the heart of all who lift their eyes to it. At Brighton, incidentally, the eyes can be delighted with both kinds of cliff scenery, man's painted stucco and Nature's natural chalk, of which it is possible to prefer the former when it is the covering of marine crescents and terraces in the serene classical style.

" Augustus at Rome was for building renowned,
And of marble he left what of brick he had found.
But is not our Nash too a very great master?
He finds us all brick and he leaves us all plaster."

To plaster and be plastered are not in these days complimentary words. But when the plastering takes the form of stucco that is kept in good heart, as farmers say of their land, they merit a high place in the vocabulary of praise.

Regent's Park and Primrose Hill together run to nearly 500 acres and the former's Outer Circular Road covers almost three miles as it coils round the grass, gardens, and ornamental water. The last of these, with its twists among islands, has better cause to be called a Serpentine than has its sister lake in Hyde Park: owing to a disastrous submergence of skaters on thin ice during the winter of 1866–7, when nearly forty lives were lost, its depth has been limited to four feet. This measure has also made it safe, or at least not lethal, for young or inexpert oarsmen, canoeists, and hirers of the sailing-boats whose coloured sails may be seen painting the town agreeably and peacefully red on a summer afternoon.

Regent's Park I find more varied and more attractive than Hyde Park. It has none of the man-made hillocks which I suggested would nicely diversify the excessive flatness of the latter. But on its fringe there is Primrose Hill, which rises to 200 feet. The climber of that modest mountain is as little likely now to find the primroses after which it was named as he is to find Parliament sitting on Hampstead's Parliament Hill. It is an eminence of no elegance, unbeautified and unromantic, but it has evoked one of the best of all London's poems, that by John Davidson.

> " Athwart the sky a lowly sigh
>   From west to east the sweet wind carried;
> The sun stood still on Primrose Hill;
>   His light in all the city tarried:
> The clouds on viewless columns bloomed
>   Like smouldering lilies unconsumed.

> " ' Oh sweetheart, see! how shadowy
>   Of some occult magician's rearing,
> Or swung in space of heaven's grace
>   Dissolving, dimly reappearing,
> Afloat upon ethereal tides
>   St. Paul's above the city rides! '

> " A rumour broke through the thin smoke
> Enwreathing abbey, tower, and palace,
> The parks, the squares, the thoroughfares,
> The million-peopled lanes and alleys,
> An ever-muttering prisoned storm,
> The heart of London beating warm."

From my own house in Hampstead I can appreciate, at almost twice the height and twice the distance, the accuracy as well as the admirable phrasing of Davidson's vision. St. Paul's is indeed, weather permitting, swung in space and rides like a buoy upon the airy tides above the City. Because of those lines, Primrose Hill has a place in my heart, like that of the poet's London, " beating warm." Francis Thompson, with the eye of a believer saw Jacob's ladder ascending to the sky over Nelson's Column. Davidson, who was no believer in Thompson's theology, saw clouds in flower like smouldering lilies on invisible stalks. Of church and no church, they shared a genius for discernment; held by the mystery of London's skies, they were not of the millions with

> " estranged faces
> That miss the many-splendoured thing."

I am not aware of any poem inspired by this or any other park so apt and so complimentary to the London scene as Davidson's lines.

Regent's Park has many mingled amenities. Close to one reach of its waters is Queen Mary's Garden, where it is sometimes " roses, roses all the way." Here the weather-braving playgoers pass to their sessions with Shakespeare in the Open Air Theatre; when the performances are weather-beaten, they take refuge under the adjacent, convenient, and too often necessary canvas. The grassy stage among the boscage was achieved by the late Sydney Carroll, a sturdy enthusiast and pioneer who trod difficulties down beneath his substantial weight of character and person. The venture was sustained by a now veteran Shakespearian actor and producer, Robert Atkins, in defiance of some very unkind summers, for more than twenty-five years. Given the right night—and there have been years when the right night recurred with decent frequency—the spectacle of the costumed players weaving their way among the floodlit trees and through the moonlit beauty of Shakespeare's Athenian wood can be most charming. There was an unusual chance of this enjoyment in the long fine weather of 1959.

When thus illumined the setting becomes an effective blend of the natural and the contrived. At a matinée, in broad daylight, one may sit the warmer, but players in their finery and make-up seen in a blaze of sun do not mix well with the simplicity of the grass and the green thicket behind them. It is much easier to believe that here is Rosalind's Arden or the royal park of Navarre when the light is artificial. High comedy is the height of artifice: real vegetation bears hardly on that dukedom of illusion which is Shakespeare's Illyria.

Regent's Park also contains the London Zoo, but that, of course, is private and admission has to be paid for. In holiday times it attracts enormous crowds, but in this matter of exhibiting imprisoned beasts and birds I am on the side of William Blake:

> " A Robin Redbreast in a Cage
> Puts all Heaven in a Rage."

I can only think that celestial indignation is the more provoked by the sight of an eagle in similar duress or of a lion yawning behind bars at the inescapable boredom of his lot and blinking morosely at the ceaseless press of gaping humanity. I no more wish to meet the " caged and shabby tiger " in a menagerie than any king of beasts at large and hungry in the jungle. Blake in his superb poem " Auguries of Innocence " did not go on to write:

> " A tiger moping in a cell
>   Sends his captor down to hell."

But he might have done.

If incarcerated animals must be seen they are more
happily observed in the Zoo's country quarters at Whip-
snade on the northern slopes of the Chiltern Hills; here are
space and some freedom of movement. The justification of
urban zoos has been that they are educational; but that plea
has been made completely invalid by the " documentary "
films of beasts and birds in their natural surroundings and
leading their natural lives. These are available, in some
number and of brilliant quality, not only in cinemas but
frequently on television. They conduct us all over the
world and its waters and even under the sea so that we may
watch flesh, fish, and fowl going their normal and fascinating ways. Half an hour with Peter Scott and his far-ranging
colleagues of many nations is infinitely more instructive, as
well as more humane, than half a day of tramping round
aviaries and cages.

I am not suggesting that the London Zoo is not well
administered and as kindly as may be in practice to its
compulsory guests, who live without danger and get their
meals provided on time and in sufficiency. But the principle
of penning up living exhibits seems to me wrong. That
this is a minority view I willingly acknowledge. Yet, films
apart, I would rather look at a familiar waterfowl splashing
freely in the ponds of Regent's Park than at a rarity confined in the adjacent gardens of the Royal Zoological
Society. To me there is no more satisfaction in denying
scope to creatures whose essential life is to soar, swoop,
roam, and race, than in watching the performing animals
who are dragged round the country and are cowed or
coaxed into doing idiotic tricks for the amusement of *homo*
(supposedly) *sapiens*.

The parks so far mentioned are royal parks. They came

to London by the way of the Crown and they are administered by the Government through the Ministry of Works.
London's non-royal parks are governed by the London
County Council, except in the case of small public gardens
of less than two acres: these scraps of greenery are left to
the borough councils, which are by no means contented
with the L.C.C.'s arrogation of places and powers. It cannot, however, be urged that the L.C.C. does badly as a
forester and gardener: it acts as a kind of Public Trustee
for many excellent and valuable properties, and neglect of
trust is rarely, if ever, urged. My only criticism is that it
allows its staff excessive latitude in the employment of its
time.

One winter day in the fine estate of Ken Wood, of which
I say more elsewhere, my wife and I watched the planting
of the daffodil bulbs which would so agreeably contribute
in March or April to the decoration of the bank below Ken
Wood House. This task, if taken slowly, is not, in the
opinion of self-employing and suburban gardeners, overwhelmingly laborious: but some seemed to find it so in that
pleasant spot, since it took the services of three uniformed
men. One had a handy stabbing implement with which he
made a hole to receive the tuber: having punctured the soil,
he rested while another served as officer in charge of bulbs
and brought one to the appropriate receptacle: a third man
then took over and inserted the bulbs in the holes. Close
by, three more of the staff were collecting dead leaves: one
man drove a small tractor, but never dismounted, since that,
no doubt, was forbidden by his union rules: another swept
up the leaves: a third transferred the leaves to the van
behind the tractor. So six men strove with Nature through
a pleasant afternoon and nobody fainted. I do not know
whether the Ministry of Works makes such generous alloca-
tions of labour in its manning of the royal parks. For a
youngster with a taste for open air and fine scenery and a
dislike of hustle, I should say that an L.C.C. appointment

to the staff of one of its more pleasant parks would provide
a happy, carefree life.

But let us turn to the Council's major achievements and
possessions. There is a considerable parkless area running
across North London where in the Age of Anyhow the
northern railway termini were built in the eighteen-forties
and " development " was rapid and unchecked. This
swamped the old villages and farms, the Camden Town and
Somers Town that Dickens knew as a child, and provided
both the material and the sites for the huge deposits of
rubbish described in *Our Mutual Friend* as the valuable
property of Boffin, the Golden Dustman. So apart from a
few small gardens and the small space with the attractive
title of London Fields there are no really serviceable lungs
on the line running east from Regent's Park until one
reaches Victoria Park.

The latter was laid out in 1845 over 217 acres by one of
Victorian London's great landscape gardeners, Sir James
Pennethorne, who did as well for the East End in the
planning of a pleasance as the monarchs and their servants
had done for the West End. It was on the edge of Victoria
Park that Bernard Shaw housed the Rev. James Mavor
Morell, the Christian Socialist who was the husband of a
most able and understanding wife called Candida in the
play of that name. Shaw wrote ample prefaces to his plays
and set the scene in detail. He commended the prospect,
in 1894, wherever there were trees and rising ground, and
he praised the " unfurnished forum for religious, anti-
religious, and political orators." Doubtless he had himself,
in his actively propagandist youth, wagged his then suitably
red beard in that spot as a missionary of Socialism.

He paid tribute to the floral " triumphs of the admired
cockney art of carpet-gardening " and mentioned the
" sand-pit, originally imported from the sea-side for the
delight of children, but speedily deserted on its becoming a
natural vermin preserve for all the petty fauna of Kingsland,

Hackney, and Hoxton." In the intervening decades there has been a considerable cleaning up of London and its fleas are not what they were. When I was a small boy in a respectable and quite unverminous home it was expected that one might attract a flea whenever one mingled with a crowd or patronised public transport in a poor area. But the fleabite is much less common than it was and I do not doubt that one can now spend a long happy day in Victoria Park without winning the attentions of *Pulex irritans*.

In Candida's time there was a lake for immersion. Now it is a Lido which holds more than 2,000 bathers and offers sun-bathing terraces and a café. For summer evenings there are various forms of entertainment laid on. Shaw's *Candida* is not conceived as a pastoral play: but were it staged at Victoria Park the actors would be playing, as it were, on their own ground. The park, in addition to some sculpture, has a museum exhibit in the form of two alcoves from old London Bridge. Finsbury Park, to the north-west, was a Pennethorne creation, and a fine one, of 1869: it slopes down to the New River and has space for athletics and cricket and an open-air theatre. There is another riverside lung for the East End at Hackney Marsh on the Lea, a large expanse of usable recreation land. A journey by train from Liverpool Street is unlikely to give a favourable impression of North-East London's scenery; the valley of that serviceable river the Lea has received rough treatment and one must pursue the stream northward to regard it as a limpid source of pleasure and aquatic sport.

It would be tedious to give any complete list of the L.C.C.'s green islands within the county boundaries, but I shall deal with some of them further in discussing London's hill country. One can say, however, that compared with most of the English towns that went sprawling out over miles during the nineteenth century, London has been fortunate in what it saved or acquired for grass and timber and fortunate also in the present use of its islands. The explorer of a dingy area may often be surprised by finding himself among flowers and lawns. Southwark Park, for example, to the south of the Docks, acquired in 1869, has a boating lake of two and a half acres in its sixty-three acres of open land. I remember visiting it during the last war to see a Shakespearian performance: since the war the L.C.C. has greatly multiplied its supply of drama, music, ballet, and concert parties, as well as of bands for open-air dancing, in its various demesnes. What the Council cannot do is to lay on a summer climate in which these amenities can be constantly enjoyed. Apart from the drenching evening which washes all away, there is the sudden shower, the scamper to the sheltering trees, and the return to find that what was a seat has become a saucer for the rain. None the less both the organisers and the artists plod on with the good work. On a pleasant evening the green island is as full of noises as Prospero's:

" Sometimes a thousand twangling instruments
    Will hum about mine ears: and sometimes voices."

The dance band may be calling " Squares " to Old Folk Measures or " Cats " to new contortions. Squares and Cats arrived in our slang for the solemn and the jazzy about 1957. Will they linger? Slang is a short-lived article, especially in the world of entertainment.

The voice in the park is an important outlet in a democracy. The forum where the propagandists, who are usually exhibitionists too, take the stand is free-spoken. Anybody can say anything short of the grossly indecent or the riot-provoking. I used to find the animated conflicts of the Secularists and the Christian Evidence Society excellent entertainment, but I now note, at my local " forum," that there is more of political than of religious disputation. The wrangling about evolution and revelation, about the morals of the Old Testament and the miracles in the New, has apparently become tired. There was a spice of danger in it at one time because atheists who jested might be prosecuted and imprisoned for blasphemy. There were official spies taking notes of their " cracks," and so to be facetious was " a dare," as small boys say, and " dares " have their fascination. But the new tolerance has put an end to the risk and with the passing of persecution there has vanished some of the appeal of the heretical.

It is an inescapable and unanswerable complaint against London that it has failed to use its river. There ought to be more waterside gardens. The town let Vauxhall and Cremorne go. Vauxhall Gardens, on the southern Lambeth shore, was a delight to Londoners from the seventeenth century until 1859. Oliver Goldsmith was there lifted into " an ecstacy of admiration " by the union of " rural beauty and courtly magnificence " and concluded after seeing the richness of the catering and the beauty of the ladies that " we have no need to go to heaven for Paradise." Thackeray took Becky Sharp and Jos Sedley there. They could enjoy " the hundred thousand extra lamps, which were always lighted; the fiddlers in cocked-hats, who played ravishing melodies under the gilded cockle-shell in the midst of the Gardens; the singers, both of comic and sentimental ballads, who charmed the ears there; the country dances, formed by bouncing cockneys and cockneyesses, and executed amidst jumping, thumping, and laughter; the signal which announced that Madame Saqui was about to mount skyward on a slack rope ascending to the stars."

Here too, Dickens, as Boz, saw the fireworks and the balloons go up and brave amateurs accompany the intrepid professional balloonist Mr. Green. He saw also, in London's supply of tea gardens, the Sunday outings where the refreshment began with " gin-and-water warm " and then, at a kindly uncle's command, " glasses of tea all round just to keep the night air out and do it up comfortable and riglar after sich an astonishing hot day."

Vauxhall, where port and sherry cost two shillings a

bottle, became too rowdy for genteel taste and the Albert Embankment took the place of the " Paradise " which the Victorians found vulgar.

Cremorne, on the north bank, once Chelsea Farm, flourished in social glory when Vauxhall was sinking into disrepute. Here too were balloons, fireworks, the dance and the ladies. Thomas Hardy was a Cremorne visitor and wrote with gusto of the dancing there. But it was closed in 1877 and now we have Lots Road Power Station instead.

One important and valuable acquisition to set against these losses was Battersea Park, once Battersea Fields and noted for the growing of asparagus and for other forms of market gardening. The Fields were also, like Hyde Park, a duelling ground and staged so august a conflict as that of the Duke of Wellington with the Earl of Winchelsea in 1825. After long negotiations and the absorption of tea gardens as well as market gardens the park was established in 1858, another of Pennethorne's excellent achievements in artificial landscape. With a river frontage of three-quarters of a mile it pleases all tastes; both ornithologist and horticulturist have plenty to look at besides its lawns and waters. In the eighteen-nineties it was a centre of the new sport of bicycling and the crowds watched the ladies in leg-of-mutton sleeves and voluminous skirts trundling in triumph and relishing their new form of emancipation.

When the Festival of Britain was held in 1951, forty acres of Battersea Park were, after some argument, allotted to the uses of a pleasure garden over whose architectural qualities much trouble was taken. The arrangement did well enough to justify continuance. Battersea is not the most convenient site for the Welfare State's variation on the old Vauxhall and Cremorne pattern of jollification. It has no close approach by underground railway; but it has buses and bridges and there is something in the Battersea air which is authentically Londonish. Where G. K. Chesterton once lived and wrote in his early and often his best form and where John Burns raised the working-man M.P. to Cabinet level, there is a mixture now of " modernismus " in all its forms. Henry Moore's sculpture and Battersea Power Station represent the neo-primitive in art and the neo-functional in industrial construction. The Fun Fair is also of the contemporary style. Perhaps I am too old for fun fairs; they are now such aggregations of gigantic machinery that the individual seems to be only a cog in a roar of din amid dynamic creators of accelerated nausea. Why call scenic railways those lightning switchbacks which give one not a second to look at the scenery, even if there were any?

There was a time when personality was able to enter in: I remember fairs in which all sorts of vagrant and valiant persons displayed their astonishing talents. There they were, trusting to a throw of coins for modest reward while they were breaking stones with their hands, allowing themselves to be roped up—even by sailors in the crowd who knew something about knots—and then escaping, chewing up razor blades, swallowing swords, and even displaying their elocutionary and dramatic powers with extracts from Shakespeare. I never see these solo artists nowadays: they have been overridden by the vast new mechanical contraptions, and the result is a pain in the ears and the head, quite apart from any gastric distress occasioned by a jaunt on the Giant Wobble.

Further west there are, for riparian strolling, the Embankment Gardens, sometimes with orchestra, sometimes with open-air art exhibitions, but never much more than a space for seats and for a modicum of flower-beds and statuary. There are seats too and flowers on the South Bank terraces outside the Festival Hall in the presence of which edifice I am glad to look elsewhere. Whatever its internal and acoustic merits the Hall has made a considerable blot on the newly developed shore. But it is pleasant to bask among the flower-beds, facing the river. After that one has to go a long way east to find more riverside lawns.

The King Edward VII Memorial Park on the far side of Wapping is not only serviceable to its own people: it decorates the voyage by boat to Greenwich.

In a map of the County of London's open spaces, that is to say green islands lying between Richmond in the west and Plumstead in the east and between Finsbury and Streatham to the north and south, I find some eighty open spaces marked; some are considerable heaths and commons, such as those of Richmond, Wimbledon, and Putney in Surrey and of Hampstead in Middlesex; some are minor gardens. These islands seem numerous on the chart, but they are admittedly insufficient. It is estimated by those who have studied the needs and means of public recreation that seven acres of open public land are desirable for every thousand of the population. The London County Council can hope to maintain and further obtain no more than three acres per thousand on its own territory and must look for the rest outside. The use of war-devastated areas as playgrounds has helped a little: but it will be a long time before London will be adequately parked according to the standards now set. None the less there is already much more of common property in desirable places than most of the citizens realise.

It is odd that the L.C.C. should have to propagate knowledge of its existing green islands and advocate their better and general enjoyment while it is seeking to acquire, both inside and outside its boundaries, more of those areas which are insufficiently patronised at present. The problem of supplying playing fields and pitches, where there cannot be public access, especially while games are being played, is another crux in civic administration.

Meanwhile the members of the London public can gratify their rulers by taking a proper interest in what they already own, using them to their own advantage, and helping to deter those who abuse them by careless or vandal behaviour. One has to admit that the English people have very little conscience about defiling their countryside and urban parks with litter of all kinds. They have been coaxed and cajoled for years to clear up the mess after a meal on the grass and not to regard the smashing of a milk bottle as the necessary and final pleasure of a picnic. In 1958 a new Litter Act came into force, defining offences and enabling prosecutions with moderately severe penalties to follow a conviction. But since then I have noticed no difference whatever in the condition of my local heath after a fine weekend. There were still many who thought that a suitable repository for discarded newspapers was any pleasant dell, and that there was no harm in leaving broken bottles in the grass where children and dogs run and tumble. My own idea of punishing convicted offenders would be to make them do a day or days of scavenging in special overalls marked with initials known to all, e.g. F.P. for Filthy Person. That might stop it. Further exhortation will not.

But one does not wish to finish a chapter on London's parks with only a scolding of those who misuse them. All gardens, whether public and park-size or private and midget, are man's attempt to improve on Nature, an exercise which was warmly commended by one of Oscar Wilde's characters, Vivian, in the discussion called " The Decay of Lying."

" My own experience is that the more we study Art, the less we care for Nature. What Art really reveals to us is Nature's lack of design, her curious crudities, her extraordinary monotony, her absolutely unfinished condition. Nature has good intentions, of course, but, as Aristotle once said, she cannot carry them out. When I look at a landscape I cannot help seeing all its defects. It is fortunate for us, however, that Nature is so imperfect, as otherwise we should have no art at all."

Without having Wilde's Vivian in mind, I have already suggested that the monotony of London's flat-as-a-pancake parks might be remedied by a discreet construction of hillocks. I find in a very interesting book on *London's Riverside* by Eric de la Maré an even more drastic proposal. The author is a student of ancient history and a devotee of modern architecture. Bored by lack of variety in London's skylines, he advocates resolute contemporary action to amend the scene.

" The view across the river towards Battersea Park is pleasant enough, though the long river wall is monotonous. A tall slim tower is needed in the pleasure-ground there to act as a strong vertical foil to the long, low line of the wall and the dark green range of trees behind. London needs its own Eiffel Tower just there: not the timid one-hundred-and-sixty-foot-high tower proposed by the Festival Funfair people in 1956 and eventually dropped after strong objections had been raised by Chelsea inhabitants, but a grand, uninhibited phallus at least a thousand feet high."

Mr. de la Maré then quotes a letter to *The Times* supporting the idea of a " quite useless " tower on the ground that buildings are symbols and need not always be dull utilities. We are also reminded that the Eiffel Tower is " a structure which was reviled by Paris aesthetes at the time it was built and whose threatened demolition not long ago was violently opposed by aesthetes of a later generation."

To judge by the police records as well as by ordinary observation it does not appear that London's park-users need the encouragement of the vast sexual symbol which soars in Mr. de la Maré's fancy. My inclination is not to diversify our sky-view with feats of engineering or with a pile more venereal than venerable on the lines propounded. I would only enrich our land-view with some well-calcu-lated spadework. My Hyde Park Hill would not impose something alien on the scene: it would simply conform with Wilde's view that Nature has good intentions and

fails to carry them out. Thus to diversify a park oppress-
ively flat would add to the "divertising" quality of the
green islands. The verb "divertise" was used by Pepys
after a May-time visit to Vauxhall in the passage quoted
at the beginning of this chapter.

Although a popular song has located a songful nightingale in Berkeley Square the poets' Philomel avoids
central London now and is a rarity in the leafier and more
distant suburbs. Nor do fine people walk proudly as they
did in the "Fox-hall" of Pepys's pleasuring. One cannot
now look for the old Church Parade in Hyde Park after
midday on a Sunday. Yet that promenade of elegance once
was the theme of a popular musical comedy, *The Catch of
the Season*, which I relished in my boyhood. Miss Zena
Dare was the graceful catch and the chief songster was
Seymour Hicks, who jestfully praised, with a team of
show-girls in Sabbatical finery,

> " The Church Parade, the Church Parade,
>   The Church Parade beats everything.
> A sight to see and wonder at
>   For all the wealth displayed
> Of millinery art and costumes smart,
>   In the Church Parade."

Our "lyricists" of the popular musical now compose
rather better and more ingenious words for the music, but
the weekly event of the Summer Season in town was a
turn-out which would have made glad the roving eye of
Pepys. His praise of "Fox-hall" because "it is very
pleasant and cheap going thither, for a man may spend
what he will, or nothing, all as one" is more than ever
true of London's parks. The greater the sea of brick, the
more precious are the green islands. Increasingly they
"divertise."

We are frequently reminded in church of the perishable
nature of grass. But is it justly made the symbol of

6—L

mortality? It withers, but it is renewed. There is no better instance of the annual resurrection of the body. In towns which have the sense to care for their parks it is the stone that perishes and the grass that abides. London's buildings are being speedily demolished and replaced. Certain of them, the temples of the faiths and the centres of Government, are as well assured of continuity as anything can be. But elsewhere development threatens much that we thought to be secure. The parks, however, have as good a hope of permanence as any feature of the London scene. The over-looking houses may fall and be replaced in a form less likeable, at least to conservative tastes. But the seizure of the parks as building sites is surely unthinkable; the roar of protest would be immediate and immense. The royal demesnes, which the people acquired, are likely to remain, every acre of them, public property with common land and common waters. So, while the brick around may crumble, the encircled grass endures. That is a consolation which comes happily to me when I see the old edges of the grass-parks turned into car-parks and the terraces first fretted with gaps and then filled with vast new structures. Our green islands have powerful foundations. Long may they defy the volcanic upheavals of urban " Progress "!

4

Palatial

London, thou art of townes *A per se*,
   Soveraign of cities, seemliest in sight,
Of high renoun, riches and royaltie;
   Of lordis, barons, and many a goodly knyght;
   Of most delectable lusty ladies bright;
Of famous prelatis, in habitis clericall;
   Of merchauntis full of substaunce and of myght:
London, thou art the flour of Cities all.

William Dunbar

4

PALACE is a hard-pressed word. In the snobbery of names there are two contrary trends. One is to drive at grandeur, the other at humility. The latter, the proud assumption of littleness, I have already mentioned in connection with the use of the word " village " to denote a portion of London and to give flavour to a personal address. The present cult of the village is natural and likeable where there really once was a village, but it is carrying this meekness rather far when a restaurant announces itself as being " in Wigmore Street Village." Will such august and long-established Wigmorelanders as Messrs. Debenham & Freebody and John Bell & Croyden now announce themselves as village drapers and dispensing chemists to the hamlet?

Also pursuing a modish modesty, as well as the convenience of a built-in garage, are those who bed down in the old stables of the West End. There is no more respectable address now than a perch in a mews. I use the word " perch " advisedly, since the mews began life as the premises where royalty and sporting nobility mewed up their falcons. When the hawks became useless in London, the horses moved in. So the royal mews became the royal stables; then the carriage folk followed the fashion and the stables kept the name. When the horses went and the coachmen and the grooms who had been housed above and around them became less numerous, the gentry gladly moved into those close quarters which did not need a dozen unobtainable domestic servants to cope with the many floors and the heart-breaking stairs of the big town house. Still the old fowlers' name clung on as birds, steeds, grooms, and grandees succeeded to the back-yard premises. So there is now high social status in a mews address.

Palace is at the other end of the vogue in naming. It has, for reasons supposedly glamorous, been so much over-worked as to seem merely silly now, but what a reign it has enjoyed! Hotels and theatres, music-halls and cinemas, seaside piers and restaurants, dance halls and skating rinks have all been palatially inscribed. The dance bands have used the French form and that became Pally. The gay girl of our period has been Sally of our Pally. I have not met a Fish-and-Chip Palace; but there may be one. The topsy-turvydom of titles is thus completely established in a London where milady prints " Mews " on her notepaper and the saleswoman—no shop assistants now—spends her evening at the Palais de Dance and probably " de luxe " too.

Of authentic palaces London has several species. We do not, it is true, call our grimly Victorian Law Courts Palaces of Justice in the continental manner, but our legislators meet in the Palace of Westminster, which has existed in small and large forms for nearly a thousand years. The historic Westminster Hall is part of the Palace which began to house the Mother of Parliaments in 1265. The Palace chapel was dedicated to St. Stephen and St. Stephen's has remained one title of the legislature's home. The members of both Houses still enter through Palace Yards, Old and New. Having entered they are to some extent outside the laws which they make for others. Sir Alan Herbert has been happy to point out that the licensing laws restricting the hours in which alcoholic drinks may be sold do not apply to those who put discipline on the rest of us. That is because they are meeting in a palace to which the law does not apply. All-night absorbency may be a necessary solace in the case of all-night sittings, but the mere commoners may think it odd that their representatives, known as " The Commons," should be free to order their drinks long after

" Time, gentlemen, please " has been the cry and the slamming of doors has been the obligatory practice everywhere else.

The Palace of Westminster, as seen today, is the product of Sir Charles Barry's rebuilding after the great conflagration of 1834. Though designed and carried out in a style now generally lamented, this great building has none the less been highly commended by the architectural pundits. With the addition of Pugin's work on the detail, it has been acclaimed by Dr. Pevsner as " the world's major secular building of the Gothic revival," a structure planned with imagination and executed with brilliance. Here, at least, Victorianism has not been derided.

Inside it is a maze of courtyards, rooms, and corridors. A member, if his doctor has recommended walking exercise and the weather keeps him indoors, has two miles of corridors in which to promenade. The average visitor, who has been encouraged to admire the exterior, may find the interior somewhat depressing and would be unlikely to regard two miles of ambulation as a pleasing prospect. If he claims business with a Member he is admitted to the Lobby and fills in a card. While reaching the Lobby he may decide that the place is more like a cathedral which was never handsome and has now gone to seed than an efficient workshop of the nation's business. The Chamber itself, whose proceedings he can overlook from the Strangers' Gallery, is certainly less depressing: there are green-covered benches, whose tint suggests youth and innocence, qualities not always remarkable in those who sit on them. There is also a countryside touch in the surrounding woodwork, which is of native oak from Shropshire, while the ceremonial furnishings are of various timbers given by the Dominions when the post-war reconstruction was made to repair the great devastation of May 10th, 1941.

It has been recognised, in the design of the new House of Commons, that Members have much more to do than listen to each other's speeches. In addition to committee work there is a huge correspondence to be dealt with and there are constituents to be met. The average attendance in the Chamber itself, except on important occasions, is small, but of course Members have to be on or near the spot to record their votes, usually in accordance with strict party orders, when the bell rings; but that does not involve attention to the debates preceding the divisions.

Hence it was deemed unnecessary to provide sitting space for all those who have what is commonly called " a seat in Parliament." This sounds paradoxical, but there is sense in the arrangement. If the Chamber had been built to fit everybody in it would indeed look a desert with the average attendance expected when affairs of secondary importance are being discussed. So there are seats for only 437 Members out of a total of 630. This means that, on a great occasion such as the introduction of a new financial Budget, there is a scramble for a place in which to sit. It may seem absurd that what is called " a seat " involves no squatting rights. But since the days of crowding-in are few and " thin houses " are many, it is probably better for Members' morale that the room space should be limited. A speaker addressing a handful of his fellows may already feel that he is a lonely figure and that few mark him; if the Chamber provided seats for all and so were larger by another third he might be even more dismally convinced that he is " bombinating in a vacuum."

So in this Westminster Palace of democracy the affairs of the nation are conducted, or at least the start is made with the business of ruling us by consent and by law. The legislation that is passed is often and inevitably complicated and needs elucidation and administration before it can be properly applied. That is where the civil servant takes over, and the influence of the executive is generally admitted to be very great and growing greater. The word " executive " is now absurdly abused by its application to directors of business concerns; one constantly reads about " a big executive " who makes swift and supposedly brilliant decisions.   But executive is derived from the Latin " *exsequor*," meaning " I follow out," and the civil servant, not the business tycoon, is the true executive since he follows up the work of the legislators and does not create it.   But in this execution there is also interpretation of an Act of Parliament's purpose.   So a great deal of power passes from the benches in the Palace of Westminster to the desks of the bureaucrats in Whitehall.

The ancient London palaces include two of the ecclesiastical kind.   Archiepiscopal Lambeth looks across the river to the Parliamentary Palace of Westminster, and, except from the windows of St. Thomas's Hospital, there can be no better view of Barry's neo-Gothic ideas of senatorial dignity and of his plans which were so spaciously extended as to make a panorama in themselves.   I enjoyed that prospect last on the sharply cold, brightly sunny afternoon of a golden-hazy January day; the fine proportions of the Parliamentary Houses are much better appreciated from this vantage-point than they are from close by on the river's northern shore.   I saw with a new clarity how well united was the mass with the height, while the wintry sun, with a cloudless sky, gave patina to the stone as well as a gleam to the water.   For once Westminster, usually grave, had a smile on its face.

It was necessary to view Lambeth Palace from the road. Entrance, it seems, is only for parties of visitors who have applied to the Domestic Chaplain for admission in advance. So I read about the Great Hall, the summit of whose renowned hammer-beam roof was visible over the garden wall. The gateway with Morton's solid tower was mellow in the slanting light.   But even so there was a fortress atmosphere which is much more noticeable in murky weather.   There is some reason for this air of a stronghold. Lambeth Palace has had its alarums since Wat Tyler's men

LAMBETH PALACE
. . . a fortress of the Anglican faith and home of Canterbury's
archbishop.

set the Archbishop of the day running for his life to the
City. It has been a prison to many (Wyclif was held there)
and the names of the persecuted reformers live in the
Lollards' Tower. In our own time the German bombers
of 1940 and 1941 delivered their assault equally on sacred
and profane. This area was an obvious target, with the
Houses of Parliament as the bull's-eye and the river to act
as guide to the destroyers' destination. Lambeth and
Westminster had much to endure.

The Cardinal Morton whose name lingers in the Tower
had gone as a youth from Dorset to Oxford. He was the
first Balliol man to become Archbishop of Canterbury.
(There have been three such in my lifetime, Frederick
Temple, Cosmo Lang, and William Temple: so Morton
may be said, in the common phrase, to have " started
something.") His example, however, was a poor one, since
he was the very political servant of a very tough King,
Henry VII. He also practised political economy in the form
of tax-gathering on his monarch's behalf. The schoolbook
histories have familiarised the British with Morton's Fork,
a jesting name for a neat device whereby those who lived
sumptuously were mulcted for their obvious riches while
those who lived thriftily were assumed to have hoards put
by and ordered to pay up accordingly. A friend of mine
who is violently allergic to bureaucracy has a further
grievance against this exacting divine, namely that, with
his King, he laid the foundations of our Civil Service.

Morton's memory is also held up to execration as being
Henry's chief agent in a campaign to blacken the memory
of Richard III, the Crookback whom Henry VII had over-
thrown at Bosworth Field in 1485, thus terminating the
Wars of the Roses and establishing the Tudor dynasty.
There is now a strongly pro-Richard party who claim that
he was not a deformed monster but an excellent, capable
young man, grossly libelled and falsely charged with the
murder of the Princes in the Tower of London. The

maligning of Richard, it is said, was the work of a team of propagandist writers directed by Morton. Plays and books have recently been written to clear the reputation of Richard and to put Morton in the dock instead. It makes an entertaining debate. Its subject is not irrelevant to my theme of Lambeth, since Morton's Tower is so conspicuous on the riverside and so appropriate to the Archbishop's activities with its proximity to Westminster and Whitehall, to the politicians and the civil servants, and especially to the Chancellor of the Exchequer and his ministrants at the Treasury. The Palace, with its Morton's Tower at the sturdy gateway, has every right to its air of secular power and of a domination stubbornly defended.

Fulham Palace, away to the west and with England's finest croquet lawns as a neighbour on the Middlesex bank, has been the residence of the Bishops of London for eight centuries. For most of its life the pastoral work of a spiritual kind was supervised in surroundings of agricultural pasturage. More remote and without Lambeth's aura of supreme power, it has remained the more domestic of the two. Shakespeare's phrase " the moated grange " has been happily applicable to the Fulham manor house which became a palace, for its grounds were long trenched about. As the centre of the Metropolitan See it has housed important ecclesiastical government, but it is at Lambeth that the Church dignitaries gather from all over the world for high conference.

Both palaces have commanding views of the river. Lambeth's wall-hidden garden suggests a pleasant refuge, but Fulham has the more spacious grounds and has been much beloved by horticultural divines. Its Fitzjames Quadrangle shows Tudor accommodation set modestly about it; the traditions and anecdotes are of a homely kind. They tell us that the Palace had a famous home-brewed Bishop's Ale; its flower-beds were the joy of gardening bishops: it has the ghost, proper to a moated grange, the

spectre being that of Bishop Bonner, a scourge of the
Protestant Reformers who defied Queen Elizabeth and died
in prison in 1569. The great theological library was founded
by Bishop Porteous, who is said to have won a prize in a
humorous village competition for liars; his statement that
no lie had ever passed his lips won him first place. One
cannot imagine Cardinal Morton of the Fork being happy
at Fulham. There could be several reasons for that, chiefly
its distance from the headquarters of secular dominion.

Lambeth looks directly at Westminster with Whitehall
adjacent. This fact has doubtless affected and attracted
other Archbishops of Canterbury since the time when
Morton was so helpful to the secular power and the first
of the Tudors. Fulham, on the other hand, faces Putney
Hill and the miles of heath and common behind it, a territory of refuge from the urban and industrial stress.

Mention of Whitehall brings me back to a vanished
palace of which one exceptional ornament survives. This
palace was that of Whitehall where the Tudor and the
Stuart sovereigns, with a Cromwellian interval, were chiefly
resident. The relic is the Banqueting House, now the
United Services Museum. In guide-books it is usually
called the Banqueting Hall, but the booklet by Captain
Altham which is on sale there uses the word " House."
Hall or House, it stands next to the War Office on the way
down Whitehall to Westminster. It can be visited on any
weekday; most go there to see the martial mementoes,
including graphic dioramas; these are models with troops
and landscapes in miniature made to illustrate the course
of battles long ago. But they are not all so far away, since
they range from the D-Day of Julius Caesar to that of 1944.
For a minority of those who pay the two-shilling entrance
fee the fascination lies in the beautifully proportioned and
galleried building which, while it contains the uniforms
and weapons and proclaims the achievements of the fighting services, bears witness also to a change of fashion that

was to bring new beauty to the English cities and country-side. There is some demand that the museum contents should be found another home and the house used, as of old, for the ceremonial or artistic purposes apt to its own good looks.

There had been a succession of banqueting houses on this site. The early ones were insubstantial and easy victims of weather, fire, or the royal desire to improve upon the last one. In Shakespeare's play of *Henry VIII* there is an allusion to Whitehall as a new name for a district that was becoming increasingly important.

> " You must not call it York Place, that's past:
> For since the Cardinal fell, that title's lost.
> 'Tis now the king's and called Whitehall."

(Those who care to argue over Shakespeare's texts will probably attribute these jogtrot lines to John Fletcher, the alleged collaborator in this piece: but we are discussing history, not poetic style.) Cardinal Wolsey lost much by his fall, Hampton Court as well as York Place. His King had a good eye and a prehensile hand for a good place.

In the play mentioned the Cardinal entertains at York Place; there is a masquerade with " the King and others habited as shepherds." For the dance " the King chooses Ann Boleyn," discovers her to be " a dainty one " and takes a royal kiss. The play attributes this scene to the Presence Chamber at York Place, but for a masque the Banqueting House would seem to be more likely. So we may fairly assign to this spot the wooing which led to the birth of Queen Elizabeth. That Queen ordered the construction of another Banqueting House on the site in 1581. It was, in fact, the fourth. It cost only £1,700 and was mainly of canvas " cunningly painted." The canvas roof was garnished with pendant flowers and fruits. Such a structure was unlikely to last and King James I replaced it early in his reign.

The fifth Banqueting House has its place in English history, since here Princess Elizabeth was betrothed to Frederick, Count Palatine of the Rhine, and it is through this line that the Hanoverian Succession came about on the death of Queen Anne. Our House of Windsor was thus ultimately established by a marriage pledge and subsequent revels on the site of the present museum. Both the fourth and the fifth Banqueting Houses were much associated with Shakespeare as a prominent member of the team of players who enjoyed royal patronage and were known as the King's Men. We have definite information in the account of the Office of the Revels that *The Moor of Venice* by " Shaxberd " was given there on November 1st, 1604. The term Banqueting House, not Banqueting Hall, is used in this record. Exactly seven years later, on November 1st, 1611, a play called *The Tempest* was listed in the Revels Account as being presented " att Whithall before the Kinge's Majestie." Eight of Shakespeare's plays were also staged in Whitehall during the winter of 1612 and at the wedding of Princess Elizabeth in February 1613.

But this was not yet the Banqueting House we now see. A fire raged through the Palace of Whitehall in January 1619 and James determined to rebuild on a generous scale. Unfortunately the funds were lacking for the grand design. But, fortunately, the sixth Banqueting House was completed. Fortunately also the man in charge of the royal buildings was a man of genius, Inigo Jones.

At the beginning of the century Jones had been encouraged and assisted to study the art of architecture in the cities of " ingenious Italy " by the Earl of Pembroke. The first Folio of Shakespeare's plays, issued in 1623, was dedicated to " the most noble and incomparable pair of brethren, William, third Earl of Pembroke, and Philip Earl of Montgomery." That family, said the prefatory address, had especially encouraged " the legitimate Muses of this latter age " and the use of the word " Muses " in the plural must allude to an interest in the arts extending beyond that of the theatre.

Pembroke's patronage of Inigo Jones brought incalculable benefits to English architecture. Jones was so deeply impressed during his travels by the neo-classical style of building known as Palladian that he introduced it to our country. He and his pupils replaced the Tudor style and its gables and timbering with the balanced serenity of the Greek and Roman models which the Italians had preserved and developed. It was not only in London that the result was splendidly manifest; we have further witness of that splendour in the Queen's House at Greenwich. The great country houses, built with the increasing wealth of the next two centuries, also owe their tranquil dignity to the innovation begun by Pembroke's protégé. It is one of Fortune's blessings that the Banqueting House, which we see now, an early and admirable specimen of Stuart London's new look, completed in 1621, escaped the disastrous fire which destroyed nearly all of Whitehall Palace in the reign of William III. It was lucky not to be swept away when the new Whitehall of bureaucracy was constructed in the nineteenth century and to survive the air raids of World War Two.

Before then it had been adorned as to the ceiling with the paintings done by Rubens and commissioned by King Charles I in honour of his father. Those visitors who have good vision and a certain elasticity of neck can trace the progress of James to the royal insignia with an escort of the well-fleshed cherubs so dear to that painter. Under this canopy banqueting of a lavish kind was continued without stint; there are records of the tonnage of meat and the tunnage of liquor consumed there. Of the latter there were six hundred tuns of wine and seventeen hundred tuns of beer served every year to quench the banqueters' thirsts. A tun, says the Oxford English Dictionary, was "a measure of capacity usually equivalent to two pipes or four hogsheads, containing two hundred and fifty-two old wine-gallons."

But the Banqueting House was to see King Charles in ruin as well as in revel. After his trial and condemnation at Westminster Hall he spent his last night at St. James's Palace. The execution block was set up " in the open Streets before Whitehall." He passed from the Banqueting House to the road where, in the words of Marvell, a Cromwellian,

> " He nothing common did or mean
> Upon that memorable scene,
> But with his keener eye
> The axe's edge did try;
> Nor called the gods, with vulgar spite,
> To vindicate his helpless right,
> But bowed his comely head,
> Down as upon a bed."

Beside the Banqueting House one Stuart King went thus to his death and another, his second son James II, fled into exile by way of the river at his gate. It was under this roof that a Grand Convention of the Lords and Commons offered the English crown to William and Mary, Prince and Princess of Orange.

Dutch William, however, had no liking for the place. It was too damp for his asthmatic condition. One must remember that the river was then not banked in. Old prints show that at full tide it would come right up to the Palace of Whitehall, as it did to Somerset House farther east. The banksides were broad, marshy and a source of rheums and catarrhs. So the wheezing King found life easier at Kensington: asthma is a cruel complaint and who will not sympathise with his move? After the destructive fire of 1698, in which the Banqueting House was spared, there were plans for a glorious rebuilding of the whole Palace by Wren. But nothing came of them. The regal glories of Whitehall

were over, but one jewel, which might have been the centre,
with Wren as designer, of an architectural regalia, remains
in its isolated beauty. We are still privileged, after viewing
it ourselves, to agree with Horace Walpole that the Banqueting House is " a model of most pure and beautiful
taste." We have not many links with Stuart London; this
one is therefore the more precious.

The Queen's House at Greenwich has already been
mentioned. It, too, has become a museum known as the
National Maritime and an essential house of call for any
who are interested in ships and seafaring. It is another
masterpiece by Inigo Jones. He added it to the existing
Palace at the request of King James I, who had emparked
the land on the hill behind and was eager to find a pleasant
riverside depository for his wife, Anne of Denmark. Anne
has been censured as flighty, foolish, and extravagant, but
she had much to endure and lacked good advice in a Court
of bad behaviour. She had no royal duties to execute or
powers to use; it is small wonder that she found some relief
in the miming and dancing of the costly royal masques.
Women, barred from the public stages, could appear in
these and Anne enjoyed her amateur theatricals, which were
gorgeous affairs and exhibitions of rare taste as well, since
Inigo Jones often provided the décor. The King, who had
become a sexual pervert, was happy with his male favourites
in Whitehall, or as happy as that anxious, frightened, and
tetchy man could be. So the unwanted Anne was given the
Queen's House for consolation: whether consoled or not,
she had the finest architecture of her time in which to seek it.

Given a fine summer day there is pleasant voyaging to
the three riverside palaces. The nearest are Greenwich
downstream and Richmond upstream. They are linked
geographically by the Thames and historically by Queen
Elizabeth, who was born at the former and died at the
latter. Much of the Richmond Palace was destroyed after
the death of King Charles I, but there is a substantial

remnant of Tudor brick, some of which has been sensibly adapted for private residence. It does not dominate the town or its bankside, but is somewhat hidden away between Richmond Green and the Thames. Richmond has the air of a blithe and salubrious holiday town, with its many acres of playing-fields and its pleasures of boating as well as the spacious park, with its horseback riders and its herds of deer. But I always have in mind the dying Queen and the power that she loved going from her with her dwindling heart-beats and the long silence. On March 24th, 1603, there came the end and Sir Robert Carey galloped out of the courtyard to begin his strenuous and astonishingly speedy ride to Edinburgh, which he reached late at night on the 27th, arriving " be-blooded with great falls and bruises," but with sufficient breath in him to announce to King James VI of Scotland that he was now the owner of two Crowns. In our days of instantaneous communications it is hard to think of such news being carried with swift change of horses up the dim vast of the long, empty road to the north. Richmond Palace dropped out of the royal addresses: it had its hour when the great Queen elected to make it her bier.

Greenwich is a terminal port (or rather jetty) of call for the pleasure-boats. Large vessels will take one in summer on day trips from Tower Bridge away down to the beginning of the sea at Southend and to a more authentic sea at Margate. But the quick run down from Westminster to the Queen's House, a matter of forty minutes, is a sufficiently agreeable introduction to the lifeline of London's maritime and commercial being. At Greenwich there is the park to wander in as well as the Palace to admire. The Richmond journey, on the other hand, gives views of suburban London at its mellowest, with eighteenth-century suburbs behind the occasional aits or eyots, green islands of the river, Chiswick beloved of writers, Strand-on-the-Green, as charming in its title as in its small, riparian houses, and

Kew, whose Gardens are another of the royal foundations which have become a public possession and indeed a public treasure. The two waterways from Westminster are a contrast of London's work and pleasure. Richmond, reached after Kew, is happiness itself.

And so to Hampton Court, once mainly reached by the royal or lordly barges, which offered safer transport in centuries when roads were rough and their coaches or riders exposed after nightfall to the hazards of robbery under arms. Hampton has everything for the sightseer of today. (I do not use the word in any supercilious way: sights are there to be seen.) There is as much history as the most studious can absorb and there are the grounds, gardens, and ornamental, as well as natural, waters which make it a magnet for family " outings " with no thought of history lessons, architectural research, or any other improvement of the mind. The huge estate includes the Vinery which has been yielding grapes galore since 1769: the stem of the Great Vine itself is over two yards in girth and the main branch is 100 feet long. Then there is the Maze with its clipped hedges of over six feet in height. Its green walls and meandering paths between them offer the children all the delights of bewilderment; but those who enter need not be too much bemused or too long astray.

The Palace of Hampton Court was the creation of Cardinal Wolsey, who acquired the site in 1514 and proceeded to the raising of a palace and the living of a country life as regal as the King's: this was imprudent with such a monarch as Henry VIII to watch the ambitions of his cleric and to covet his demesne. Amid the stripped poverty of his ruin, Wolsey had to lament, in Shakespeare's words,

> " No sun shall ever usher forth my honours
> Or gild again the noble troops that waited
> Upon my smiles."

Troops of guests, spongers, toadies, and servants there had

been in surfeit. Wolsey had kept 280 rooms ready for those whom he entertained and his household numbered 500. His Hampton had the air of a fortress, moated and strongly walled, while it supplied the immense festivities within. A Christian prelate? We seem to be a long way from the New Testament when we enter the Court by the Trophy Gates, pass over the moat bridge to the Western Gatehouse, and survey the medallions of two Roman Emperors, Tiberius and Nero, both infamous, on the flanking turrets. Certainly a queer choice of majesties to set over the front door of a clergyman!

The immediate impression is that of power and fear mingled. At that time the mansion of a grandee had to be his stronghold too: that none is to be trusted is the moral of the Tudor methods of home-building. But Hampton has the best of both worlds, since you soon pass to the pacific majesty of Wren's designs proper to a period in which an Englishman's home need no longer be his castle. Now, with the coming of the third William and of Queen Anne, it could be a civil-suited dwelling, grandiose in size but unmilitary in its aspect, a pacific Palace for the conduct of a secure and tranquil life. Viewing Hampton from the Pond Garden " both worlds at once we see." There is the sinister Palace of Wolsey, of King Henry VIII, and of his procession of ill-fated wives, who had their Hampton days of rise and shine, fall and vanish. The superstitious believe that Catherine Howard's ghost still walks at nights. But we can escape from Tudor turrets and spectres with ease: they pass from the mind when we survey the splendours of the classical East Front.

At Hampton one takes tea in what used to be the Tilt Yard of the galloping Tudor lords and then can move on towards the river where the Georgian parties were assembled after a voyage on barges richly bedizened to see the sun go down over a pattern of geometrically planned gardens, the illuminations on the lawn, and the fireworks sprinkling the night sky. Such company was still engaged

in the intrigues of Court life and the jostlings for place and
perquisites, but its members did not fear, unless they
indulged in Jacobite adventures, that their heads would
any day tumble in the Tower. The wits and poets joined
them, no longer the humble servants of a patron, as in
Elizabethan times, but men of position themselves, free to
plant the barbs of their wit with no apprehensions and able
to take a part in the foppery of the times. Shakespeare and
Garrick were actor-authors both, but the former had lodg-
ings in Southwark and Silver Street, while the latter was a
major householder, entertaining at his own most elegant
Hampton villa with a Temple of Shakespeare in his grounds.
At Hampton you can imagine the changing centuries more
easily and vividly than anywhere else in London; here the
moat and the castle, there the many-chambered Palace and
the tree-lined alleys where Queen Caroline of Anspach,
Consort of George II, assembled her friends for gossip,
raillery, and self-display. This Queen took a particular
interest in landscape gardening and set a noble stage for
her levées in which the play of mind was as welcome as the
show of silks.

This second Hampton had been largely the creation of
William III, a man much abused for his faults and overlooked for the good things that he created. He brought a
major genius of craftsmanship to England in the person of
Jean Tijou, a French designer of ironwork, artist of the
exquisite Tijou screen of gates originally planned for the
Great Fountain Garden and now set by the riverside. His
too is the intricate balustrade on the King's staircase in the
Palace. After the great Hampton junketings of Queen
Caroline a dullness was imposed upon a place where one
would think dullness to be impossible. Pope, nearby at
Twickenham, had written of Queen Anne's Hampton,

> " Hither the heroes and the nymphs resort
> To taste awhile the pleasures of a Court."

But that came to an end with the long reign of George III, who was no Hampton man. He would have nothing to do with the place, for which he felt a strong dislike, attributed in anecdote to a boyish incident. His grandfather, it seems, had slapped his face there.

The Palace was made public property by Queen Victoria, with reservation of certain premises as " grace and favour " homes for elderly and distinguished servants of the State or their widows. A more pleasant form of pension could hardly be imagined. But, apart from these dwellings, there is admission everywhere. In our egalitarian times there is none of the old elegance about its visitors. They are, as you may see on any weekend afternoon, the sober-suited heirs of the Victorian gift modestly strolling where the dandies once glittered like dragon-flies. Pope, in a well-known line, said that Queen Anne here took tea and counsel. Now the senior members of our Welfare State take tea and their juniors " choc-ice." Here indeed is the summer tea garden of South-West London with ample parking space where once the equestrian tilters tilted. The painted ceilings and the picture galleries are there to give a whole afternoon of exercise to those who will tread the full course, round the Audience Chambers, Presence Chambers, Royal Bed-Chambers, and the like. Outside there is a vast acreage for those who prefer resting their feet in a garden to the cultural exercise of " doing " the Palace itself.

King William III began but did not complete the new Hampton Court; he did the same thing at Kensington Palace. His dislike of the damp river air at Whitehall made him decide to buy what was then Nottingham House at what is now the west end of Kensington Gardens. The pronunciation of the time was Kinsington, which sounds genteel to us; the place could have been called genteel too, since it was a quiet spot removed from the town of those years and so agreeable to a man of solitary inclinations. The unwearying Sir Christopher Wren was once more engaged on a work of royal command and once more responded nobly with taste and judgment. While the work was in progress the King and Queen were living still farther west at Holland House whose large and well-timbered estate is now open to the public, another green island of great value to street-weary Londoners.

Separate suites were added for William and Mary in the reconstructed Nottingham House; there was a Long Gallery for each where receptions could be held or a promenade taken in bad weather; we can walk in them still. There was plenty of land to the east and the Dutch style of landscape gardening was introduced; the sunk garden with its pool and screen of hedges can be overlooked by the public who have access also to the exquisite Orangery later designed by Vanbrugh and Hawksmoor for Queen Anne. The State Apartments are open, free of charge, and so is the London Museum with its lively examples of London life and costume down the ages. The Museum is housed in part of the Palace.

Approach is made from the Broad Walk which runs across Kensington Gardens from Bayswater to Kensington; it has to be made by foot, since the Broad Walk is not a road. The only carriage road going right up to the Palace is private to the Duchess of Kent and her staff and others privileged to live there. But the walk is well worth making.

The domesticity of Kensington Palace has long been a matter for approving comment. The dark brick is serene without being too sombre and the gardens are like premises enjoyed and not lawns for show. The diarist Evelyn wrote of it as " a very sweet villa." Leigh Hunt said justly that Windsor Castle was a proper place for the reception of monarchs, Buckingham Palace for the display of fashion, and Kensington Palace for taking tea. It makes a not too formal backcloth to the great apron stage of open space which stretches in front of it as far as Park Lane. In warm weather the public part of the grounds makes a favourite strolling place for mothers with perambulators (there are few nursemaids now) while the steps and surround of the Orangery, which faces south, are a popular resort for sitters in the sun.

The Palace was much liked by Queen Anne, who extended the grounds, commissioned the Orangery, made a small deer-park, and was carried in a sedan chair, being no pedestrian, to see the tulips grow and the stags graze. This has been very much a woman's house. William III had fashioned it, but the Georges did not care much for it. It was Queen Anne and especially Caroline of Anspach, most happy at Hampton as we have seen, who delighted in their Kinsington.

" Here, while the town in damps and darkness lies,
    They breathe in sunshine and see azure skies."

Queen Caroline called the sparks and their belles to the parades in her grounds; the poets rhymed its show of fops and flower-beds:

" Each walk, with robes of various dyes bespread,
    Seems from afar a moving tulip-bed."

With her passing the glory was diminished. George III moved to Buckingham Palace. But Kensington was still a home for the royal ladies. George IV settled his separated wife, Caroline of Brunswick, there, and later on rooms were found for the Duke and Duchess of Kent on their return to England with the expectancy of an heir. An heiress it was. Queen Victoria was born there on May 24th, 1819, in a ground-floor room which is now Number Eleven of the London Museum. There was she brought up by a very watchful mother and educated by the capable, but later domineering, Baroness Lehzen. And there, in the bedroom now on view in the State Apartments, she received the news of her accession in June 1837. A few hours later she was holding in Kensington her first Council of State. But she did not stay there long. The move to Buckingham Palace was immediate.

The first Queen to live at Kensington Palace was the third William's Queen Mary. To another Queen Mary, wife and widow of King Geroge V, we owe much of the interest and the charm which the State Apartments hold for visitors. It was she who rearranged and redecorated, in Victorian style, the bedroom and nursery of the young Queen Victoria. Queen Mary's care for the place was a family as well as an artistic one. She herself was born in this bedroom in 1867. It now contains some of her own property. Most fascinating are the original pieces which Queen Victoria knew as a child. In the anteroom are her toys and a spacious dolls' house built in the Regency style.

The illustrated guide sold at Kensington Palace is so explicit about the Victorian furnishings that there is no need to mention them in detail here: one can link them in fancy with Lehzen's discipline, with the strict education of the Princess in the Scriptures, arithmetic, and languages, and with bishops attending as examiners and approving their pupil. There was not much childish capering or liberty of finding fun in the Palace then. A strong character was being formed, strong enough to dominate a dominant mother when the young Queen knew that the time had come for self-assertion. That she announced her intention to be good is common knowledge: she also proved her resolve to be good at handling people.

Buckingham Palace is never open to all and its chief days of visitation are limited to the invited relatives at an Investiture for the bestowal of honours or to the " commanded " guests of a Royal Garden Party. But it is a conspicuous spectacle on its fine site among the parks and fronting down the Mall. It is quite a youngster among the palaces, but it is now the London home of the King or Queen and on its balcony the royal appearances are made on State occasions or in times of national emergency. So it is " The

Palace " in the speech of the people or " Buck House " to use the phrase of the Guards on duty.

During the seventeenth century this piece of land was in the words of Samuel Pepys " a somewhat pretty wilderness." Birdcage Walk, beside the Palace, was named after an aviary established by King James I, who also planned a mulberry garden for the encouragement of silkworms and so of the new English silk industry, which was starting to compete with the imported Italian silks. The garden became also a public strolling-place and at night a centre of what we now call " dating." Refreshments were sold, the tarts and syllabubs served appetites and thirsts to satisfaction, and amorous encounters enlivened the summer nights.

Then the Duke of Buckingham built a mansion there; King George III bought it in 1761 for £21,000 and turned it into the Queen's Palace; one does not associate that King with letters, but he created a notable Palace library which is now the King's Library in the British Museum. Queen Charlotte, on whom it had been settled, died in 1818. When the Prince Regent succeeded to the throne in 1820, he commanded a drastic rebuilding, choosing Nash as his architect. The best feature of the reconstruction was the Garden Front, not seen from the surrounding roads.

King George IV naturally took an interest in the Palace which he was expensively reshaping, but he did not care to use it as his home. It was Queen Victoria who made it the pivot of royal domesticity as well as of hospitality and ceremonial. She made many alterations and additions and more were to come after her time. The East Front, which is what a visitor chiefly sees, was rebuilt by Sir Aston Webb in 1912. It is not greatly admired, but the London public is not made up of architectural specialists and that is " The Palace " as they know it. It is there that they assemble in thousands to cheer the Royal Family after a Coronation or the ending of a war. It is there that sightseers see the Guard changed, visiting potentates drive in or out, or statesmen come to accept or lay down office. When the pulse of London is beating fast with the stress of some great national emotion, the East Front of the Palace, beset by crowds who feel this to be the hub of mighty happenings, is the outlet for acclaims of loyalty and multitudinous rejoicings.

The Marble Arch, now at the north-east corner of Hyde Park, was designed by Nash to serve as a stately entrance, but, though a notable spectacle, it was an inconvenient gateway, being too narrow for ceremonial passage. So it was removed in 1851. Outside the Palace one sees now the Queen Victoria Memorial (Sir Aston Webb was the architect and Sir Thomas Brock the sculptor). The Queen is set within a marble-fringed pool, now centre of a traffic roundabout. She is surrounded by symbolic figures. Courage and Constancy attend her. The Fighting Services are on guard. The industries and crafts of town and country get their due. So do Motherhood, Truth and Justice. The symbolism may seem solemn and heavy, but the general effect is appropriate and pleasing. It speaks for its period. When the sun is glinting on the pool and a blue sky is over the pedimented East Front, which I find more impressive than do some of its critics, here is a good stance for contemplation of " The Palace," which has long outlived its mulberry trees and its country-house status in the Duke of Buckingham's days. It has become the headquarters of the monarchy in its diplomatic receptions and entertainment. Here official business is transacted and honours are bestowed at the investitures. Here too is the home of a family whose children play on the great lawns outside the West Front and beside the little lake in the far corner.

St. James's Palace, compact of royal history, birthplace and marriage place of many sovereigns, does not open its doors. Visitors, however, can attend services in the Chapel Royal throughout the winter months. Otherwise, it is a matter of passing through various Courts and looking at the nameplates on the doors: here the chief officials of the

Crown, secretarial and financial, have their "grace and favour" houses, which externally look rather dark and cramped, but are snugly and quietly tucked away in a central and convenient spot. Here the Earl Marshal undertakes the elaborate arrangement of a Coronation, and here the Lord Chamberlain carries out historic duties including the odd responsibility for reading and passing or occasionally censoring stage plays.

One turns a corner to Clarence House, the present London home of the Queen Mother and Princess Margaret. The mansion looking out over St. James's Park was not one of Nash's triumphs and has been much altered without much visual improvement. The Duke and Duchess of Gloucester are at York House, once the home of the Duke of Windsor, then Prince of Wales.

Medievalism lingers in the headquarters of the Honorable Corps of Gentlemen-at-Arms and of the Yeomen of the Guard, who have no connection with the "beef-eater" Yeomen Warders of the Tower. It is from the balcony overlooking Friary Court that the proclamation of a new King or Queen is made with full pomp of ancient heraldry. The heralds have their bright-coloured tabards and there is sound of trumpets in the air. This is not, one hopes, a spectacle likely to be seen for very many years to come. But there is nothing of the old chivalry to be seen on any ordinary day. The various courtyards preserve an ancient quietude of their own: the atmosphere is more domestic than royal, but peacefully so: the noise of ceaseless traffic in St. James's Street and Pall Mall seems far away.

The district of St. James's, though it has lost its old theatre, is a preserving kind of place. The name of Pall Mall is simply that of an old game, cousin to croquet, which King Charles I enjoyed as Paille Maille. (This has survived in the inn garden of the Freemasons' Arms in Downshire Hill on the fringe of Hampstead Heath, close to Keats's House.) The pedigree shops for gentlemen of taste—

one can hardly call them by so common a name as male customers—still offer the best in wines and hats and shoes among the clubs in St. James's Street. Men's fashions change and the return of the bowler-hat may be transient. But, at the time of writing, the nattiest bowlers and most tightly rolled umbrellas are to be found in this area, where, in a period of lax dressing, there is still tautness to be seen.

So, for a palatial excursion, the holiday Londoner is best served at Kensington, Hampton Court, and Greenwich. The atmosphere of the Georgian " sweet villa " and Victorian nursery is indestructible in the first of these, which is not to be thought of as a place for exploration in summer only. My last visit to it was on a dry, cold February afternoon: the air had sufficient nip in it to encourage walking. The sun was just strong enough to give the old brick a cordial glow and to put a suitable tint of orange on the Orangery. As the afternoon wore on and the mist rose the sun too became an orange, hung over Kensington like a bauble on an invisible Christmas tree. The delicate, hazy light played upon the Round Pond and kindled to a kind of life the tributary statue of Queen Victoria by her daughter Princess Louise. This is not a lively example of the sculptor's art but properly reminds one of that childhood in the eighteen-thirties. King William stood booted and sworded in the grounds of his creation. There was a mewing and swooping of seagulls over the Dutch garden and its half-frozen pool, beside which a few lonely roses were still in the pink, unbeaten by the winter and the recent frosts and fogs.

Hampton provides the greater panorama of the past while serving as a country seat for democracy in search of a quiet jaunt. Winter again may be an apt time for the taking of a riverside view; when the leaves are off, there are vistas which are closed in summer and many a fine building can be better appreciated with new standpoints for the spectator who takes trouble with his looking. Greenwich beckons one down the busy river and a February

5

Meckering

The Temple of Fame stands upon the grave; the flame that burns upon the altars is kindled from the ashes of great men.

Hazlitt

O poet, come you haunting here
Where streets have stolen up all around,
And never a nightingale pours one
Full-throated sound?

Thomas Hardy

See nations slowly wise and meanly just
To buried merit raise the tardy bust.

Dr. Johnson

5

MECCA (Umm al-qura, mother of cities, capital of the Hedjaz, and religious centre of Islam) has had its name taken somewhat in vain by the British to signify any secular place of pilgrimage. It is even a trade name of dance halls and cafés. No unbeliever may enter the real Umm al-qura, but that is not a rule that we apply to any of our Meccas. An atheist can admire the splendours of Westminster Abbey or St. Paul's and one who believes that Bacon wrote Shakespeare is not barred from the hotels and the playhouse in Stratford-upon-Avon.

That town has so often been called the Shakespearian Mecca that I was there tempted by the spectacle of the busy sightseers, as they hurried from their motor-coaches to the Birthplace, the Theatre, the Church, and Ann Hathaway's Cottage, to invent a verb, which is to mecker. In that I hope I give no offence to Mohammedans since the meckering now to be discussed is of a devout kind. If I mention the shrines of sport as well as of patriotism and of culture, I can claim that cricket has been called part of an Englishman's religion.

Meckering is an important asset to the tourist industry, and here I can cite an Islamite precedent since my encyclopaedic authority on Mecca suspects that Mohammed made a pilgrimage to the holy city compulsory for believers " to ensure to Mecca the profits of the religious-cum-trade festival and so reconcile the inhabitants to the new faith." However that may be our British meckering is a genuine source of pleasure and of happiness to be stored in the mind with the aid of mementoes. These are usually not of a kind that would pass with honours an examination by a Fine

Arts Commission and Stratford's shop windows offer some
wonderfully foolish and unsightly specimens of the reminis-
cent gewgaw. But one need not buy them and there is no
doubt that visitation of shrines and journeys to the birth-
places, workshops, and graves of the eminent provide
a blameless satisfaction. So let us mecker awhile in
London.

I suppose that most would like to salute the Cenotaph in
Whitehall before going on to the tomb of the Unknown
Warrior in Westminster Abbey. They speak for nearly a
million and a half lives lost in two gigantic wars. So
colossal a sacrifice defies any majesty of sculpture; so
rightly they are of the utmost simplicity. The inadequate
may have an eloquence of its own.

The word " Cenotaph " is a transliteration of the Greek
word for an empty tomb and a sepulchral monument raised
in honour of a person or persons whose body is elsewhere.
The Whitehall Cenotaph was designed by Sir Edwin
Lutyens as a saluting point for the Victory March of July
1919: it is an undecorated oblong, with no religious symbol,
since men of all religions were included in the death-roll,
and with no martial sculpture of the figured kind; it is a
grave-stone—nothing more. So many towns and villages
were to set up, often with feeble results, war memorials of
an ambitious kind that one could wish that the Lutyens
example had been more followed. Public opinion was
impressed: the original had been in plaster only, but it was,
with general consent, replaced in the Portland stone which
has contributed so finely to London's architectural wealth.
This stone does not soil: the winds and rains scour its
surface: it takes the sun with a particular radiance. On one
of London's better afternoons, half golden, slightly misty,
the Cenotaph stands serene, unblemished, and possibly
shining in the heart of the city's politics and administration.
The inscription had to be changed to include the Second
World War; there was a just symbolism in the decision not

8—L

to make a second Cenotaph. The two wars had been one struggle against one enemy and one thing.

It was customary at first for all passers-by to give the Cenotaph the tribute of a gesture; women lowered their heads and the men took off their hats. But time wears down custom, even the custom of a salute that was so widely and patently sincere. Most Londoners walk or are carried past the Lutyens monolith nowadays without demonstrative regard to it. Since the habit of going hatless has so much increased among men this is less noticeable. On Remembrance Sunday (the second in November) the Sovereign, members of the Royal Family, the principal statesmen, and leaders of the armed forces attend a service at the Cenotaph and there are similar salutations at memorials all over the country. The two minutes' silence is nationally observed. The Cenotaph receives its wreaths and the trumpets sound.

The grave of the Unknown Warrior, which is close to the west door of Westminster Abbey, was set there by a conception of war's holocaust in which death itself becomes anonymous. The dust of an unidentified body was laid there on the Armistice Day of 1920, and many thousands of mourners brought their flowers. Black marble from Belgium covers it: red poppies continually surround it. The word " Warrior " may sound unduly poetic and romantic but, since the man here remembered may not have been a soldier in the Army, the other Services are thus included. Again, there is total simplicity in a building where many people of small significance in history at one time were honoured with sculptured sepulchres of great size and pretensions. The Warrior, so humbly and austerely couched, is the more conspicuous.

Only a whole book could properly cope with the Abbey and a visitor will be exhausted who tries to see all. But those interested in the written word will probably do some meckering in Poet's Corner. There Britain remembers the saying related by a Scotsman, Fletcher of Saltoun, that the

ballad-makers of a nation may be more important than its
law-givers. (What a shock it would be to Elizabeth's great
and powerful Secretary Lord Burleigh if his shade were to
discover that a poet-player of fairly humble origin had won
a world-wide and enduring fame far greater than any bigwig
of his period!) None the less, even in Poet's Corner, the
minstrels do not have it all their own way. " John, the
great Duke of Argyll and Greenwich " described first
modestly as " an honest man " and then more augustly as
" never exceeded in his age as Orator and General " is not
so well known to the sightseer as the scribblers round about
him; but he has great pomp of sculpture and of place. So
has another of this breed, Sir Archibald Campbell of Inver-
neil, who was once Commander-in-Chief on the Coast of
Coromandel. It is a queer assemblage in this corner to
which the Campbells have come, including Thomas Campbell of Glasgow who wrote " Ye Mariners of England "
and won a place in the Abbey for this and other
trumpet-calls of the martial muse. The still renowned and
the now unknown are neighbours in glory. Who, for
example, was that Barbara Simpson who is remembered
with honours beside the names of Dryden, Tennyson, and
Browning?

It has been said that sacred buildings usually contain the
best architecture of a nation and the worst of its sculpture.
There is plenty in the Abbey to justify that view. Those
writers may have the seemliest tribute in Poet's Corner who
have the unillustrated and unsculpted celebration of a
gravestone on the floor or a quiet plaque on the wall. At
one time the sculptors were so much under classical influence that they wrapped their contemporaries in toga-type
garments and made noble Romans of them all. Wordsworth in stone, one feels, might have embodied a country-
man or a lakeside contemplator of the Cumbrian daffodils;
instead he seems to be an ancient Stoic moodily philoso-
phising on the vanity of human existence. Addison, too,

who wrote an admirable essay on the satisfactions to be found by tomb-gazing in the Abbey, is established as a senatorial figure, the author, possibly, of his own tragedy of *Cato* but not the coffee-house man and the creator of Sir Roger de Coverley. Here one seems to be in ancient Italy and not in England of the recent centuries.

But some come alive. John Milton, though too much skied, looks down with " Il Penseroso " in his mien. Shakespeare, too, by Peter Scheemakers, comes out better than usual; here is not " the prosperous pork-butcher " of the bust in Stratford's church or the dreary " egghead " of the Droeshout engraving but a man of thought and feeling. He holds a script of *The Tempest* with the " cloud-capped towers " passage in handwriting much better than his own. One can accept him here in the Abbey as one cannot accept many of his neighbours in their Roman attire and consular attitudes. There are curious choices. Today's critical opinion would hardly give Adam Lindsay Gordon a place in this company. That Victorian singer of the equestrian life went from England's Cheltenham and Woolwich to join Australia's Mounted Police, take part in Australian politics, and versify with spirit the racing and chasing that he loved. There is a strikingly virile head of him among the poets; he has the good looks of a film star who would have been triumphant as a tough sheriff in " Westerns." Yet he shot himself at the age of thirty-seven. He had, however, achieved two things; he had won the Melbourne Hunt Cup and Abbey status too. He looks proud of it and his face is almost leaping from its stone.

Fortunately, perhaps, for Kipling and Hardy they have their place on the ground: no faltering images betray them. Dickens and Browning are likewise grave-names, but an unbearded Tennyson looks out. James Thomson has received high sculptural honours: was it a tribute to the author of " Rule Britannia " as much as to his meteorological muse of " The Seasons "? William Blake, in bronze, is one of the most successful portraits. He has a double claim to be there, that of his genius and that of one who spent many youthful hours in the Abbey working as a copyist on his pictorial art when apprenticed to the engraver Basire. The boys from Westminster School baited him and even knocked him off a piece of scaffolding, but the Gothic majesty had shaped his imaginings and inclined him to see angels, not fairies, at the bottom of a Lambeth garden: also to see, with a searing penetration, into the mysteries of human nature.

Contingencies of the grouping have this constant oddity. Above the handsome coffer of Geoffrey Chaucer there is a large and orotund tribute to John Roberts who was the very faithful secretary of the Rt. Hon. Henry Pelham. Research into the latter's career discovers that he held among other offices that of the paymaster of the forces. Whether the forces got all that was due to them, since "his influence in the House of Commons was based on systematic corruption," is a matter for suspicion. However, his Mr. Roberts may have had clean hands to justify his substantial position above the author of *The Canterbury Tales*.

Keats and Shelley have no images, only votive tablets of modest size; perhaps their humble state is the more gracious when matched with the trappings of a grandiose memorial. There is Matthew Prior, first Whig, then Tory, and always mildly witty, but little read now. His allotment of space would be more worthy of a true master of Miltonic stature than of a capable journeyman. He wrote a poem for his own monument beseeching posterity to be kind to his fame. The Abbey, at least, has shown extreme benignance.

" Here's an acre sown indeed
With the richest, royall'st seed "

wrote Francis Beaumont on the tombs at Westminster. He was thinking of the historic chapels. Of these and especially of the superb chapel of King Henry VII so much has been written so well that I will not add smallness to greatness of appreciative prose. Having meckered among the poets in their Corner I leave them with the obvious suggestion that some at least are better remembered when their works are read than when their epitaphs and effigies are studied, guide-book in hand. Addison said that the sepulchral aspects of the Abbey " fill the mind with a kind of melancholy, or rather of thoughtfulness, that is not disagreeable." With that I would not disagree.

Charles Dickens was buried in the Abbey on June 9th, 1870. He was only fifty-eight when he died and it is astonishing proof of a darting brain and of a hand no less quick that he should have achieved so great an output in that time, considering that he was constantly travelling and was also a copious letter-writer, an editor, a speaker, and a giver of public readings of his work. He dined out much and was frequently busy with his amateur acting which he so much enjoyed. His life was a turmoil of industry, honours, and quarrels. His grave is beside those of Johnson, David Garrick, Sir Henry Irvine, R. B. Sheridan, and Handel. His fellow masters of fiction, Thomas Hardy and Rudyard Kipling, are close by to the north.

For Dickensian meckerers the place of pilgrimage is 48 Doughty Street, at the north-east corner of Bloomsbury. It is a seemly house of dark brick in the style once general in that area. There is not much of the old Bloomsbury left; London University has consumed a large section between Tottenham Court Road and Russell Square, but it has built worthily on the whole and the Senate House, by Charles Holden, with its massive tower, makes a fine centre and a notable landmark. Bombs and progress have also eaten into terraces and squares where once were private houses, much favoured by the intellectuals, convenient in their central site but now unworkable without ample domestic service. Bloomsbury was famous too for its boarding-houses where living was cheap and spirits occasionally ran

high, since medical students were often Bloomsbury's
light-hearted lodgers, fleeting the time as carelessly as did
Dickens's Bob Sawyer in Lant Street, Southwark, where the
author himself had lived as a boy. Wilfred Whitten, a
journalist devoted to London and founder of a popular
literary review, now happily restored to life, *John o'
London's Weekly*, sang of it,

> " Oh mine in snows and summer heats
> These good old Tory brick-built streets,
> My eye is pleased with all it meets,
> In Bloomsbury."

Another popular songster announced in rhyme how happy
he could be on a pound a week in Bloomsbury. Money
values have altered that vision of bliss on the handsomely
planned estate of the Duke of Bedford.

But where slices of the old Bloomsbury remain—and I
should call the area Whig rather than Tory—there is the
feeling still of a district of a London Bohemia where the
lodgers with empty pockets coaxed their landladies to let
the rent wait for another week. One can imagine the hope-
ful plea. Something would undoubtedly turn up; a short
story would certainly be placed and paid for; a part in a play
was as good as won; an overdue allowance from the parents
was bound to come along. The mellowness of the brick,
ripe as plums on a sunny autumn day, gave a consoling
warmth; it was a good place for browsing over books and
then for setting out, if one had something in hand, to drift
across the Tottenham Court Road into the taverns and
restaurants of the Fitzroy Street area, now called Fitzrovia
and still Bohemian, or farther on into the savoury smells of
cosmopolitan Soho where almost every house was com-
peting in the cheap service of the inner man. The catering
is still there: but the cheapness is not. To this old Bloomsbury Doughty Street still conforms in its looks. There for
some years James Agate, the dramatic critic, blended his

application to writing of many kinds with his readiness for conversation with all manner of strange company. It was the right street for him. Moreover, he knew his Dickens.

Dickens covered a lot of London ground in the various stages of his career, but of his many habitations there is little that remains. His boyhood was in " The Borough " (Southwark) and Camden Town. Furnival Inn, where he lived from 1835-7, became the Holborn offices of the Prudential Assurance Company. After that he was two years in Doughty Street, moving on to a large house in Devonshire Place at the corner of the Marylebone Road, lately pulled down. After twelve years there he came back to Bloomsbury and lived in Tavistock Square for nine years; on that site the British Medical Association is now housed in some splendour. The house in Doughty Street would also have gone; fortunately it was saved from demolition by the Dickens Fellowship and, having escaped the hazards of the last war, is safe and kept sound.

Dickens needed a house with more rooms to house a growing family, but during the brief period at Number 48 he finished *The Pickwick Papers* and wrote *Oliver Twist* and *Nicholas Nickleby*. So in the " second-floor back " which was his study the finest of his early work came streaming out. It is easy to say that you will still find more of Dickens in a London street than in the museum in Doughty Street: the " museum," it might be argued, suggests a repository of things that were and there is no past for an author of his stature. He is with us all the time. Moreover, Dickens had enjoined in his will that there should be no national memorial. But he did not forbid the preserving of one of his homes and the Dickens Fellowship in saving Number 48 and making it a storehouse of manuscripts, editions, pictures and other relics has not been disloyal to its hero. Instead, it has properly served his readers. One may get closer to the man as he was by a visit to Doughty Street and the fact that 7,000 people, with the number always growing, pass through the premises every year is an indication that the use of the house in this way answers a widespread need.

A donation from two Americans enabled a reproduction in the basement of " such a kitchen as that in which the Pickwickians made merry in Dingley Dell." This was a rather futile undertaking. Without the Pickwickians and their host and the Fat Boy the room bears a chilly resemblance to a bit of an antique shop: there is no suggestion of festivity. It might have been better if the artificers in wax had been summoned from Madame Tussaud's to fill it with the images at whose fashioning they are so adept. Is the idea outrageous? Well, nothing could be less Pickwickian in atmosphere than the room as it is now. But upstairs one is much more happily impressed by desks and letters and the table that Dickens used for those readings which gripped enormous audiences and which Mr. Emlyn Williams has so brilliantly brought to life again in recent years.

I have been struck there by the schoolboys' books from the house in Bowes in North Yorkshire, which is the supposed site of Dotheboys Hall. They are handsome things, with excellent lettering. The pupils were obviously not ill-taught in writing and the example of arithmetic is advanced. The letter home from Master Dobson, " well in health and very happy," and saying that he is enjoying his Christmas, may have been written " under pressure," as the reporters of horse races smoothly say when the whip is being used. But the lesson books hardly indicate the illiterate squalor that Nickleby found in the appalling classroom of Wackford Squeers. There were deaths, it is true, but we can see that the master, Mr. Shaw, paid three pounds five shillings and elevenpence for a gravestone, big money in those years, and one can hardly imagine Squeers putting his hand in his pocket to that extent. There was undoubtedly a scandal of " the Yorkshire Schools " which Dickens drove up from Doughty Street to investigate and expose. But, on the evidence of the schoolbooks, his picture of the tuition supplied was drawn fancy free. He made an immortal scoundrel in the person of Squeers and Mr. Shaw's ghost may have cause for muttering " libel " if he still haunts the Pennine hillside of Bowes. But, after all, *Nicholas Nickleby* was a novel, not a Blue book. And Bowes is not mentioned by name; nor, of course, is Shaw.

But that is a small point and no Dickens addict can visit Doughty Street without finding something that he did not appreciate before. In Southwark the meckerer can see Lant Street where Dickens lived as a boy, overshadowed by the gaunt Marshalsea Gaol, of which fragments remain. But Bloomsbury holds in its air the great creative drive of that abounding and astonishing young man who had entered the world of letters as the sketch-writer " Boz " at twenty-one and conquered it with *Pickwick* before he was twenty-five.

The Shakespeare Mecca is, of course, in his Warwickshire home town and there is plenty to see there. London, where he spent most of his adult and working life, has its plaques and statues and a memorial in Southwark Cathedral: but the tide of change has swept over his city and a visitor can only say that he is treading where Shakespeare trod, very rarely that he is seeing what Shakespeare saw. There are, however, bits of buildings which were standing in his time and several in full preservation. At Westminster there are the Cathedral and the noble Westminster Hall with its twelve-bayed hammer-beam roof admiringly accepted as a supreme example of its kind. It has been the scene of countless State trials and, " if four walls told " as the saying goes, the sentence of execution would be strong among the echoes. There is a cruel irony about the early history of the Hall. Originally built for William Rufus at the end of the eleventh century, it was much rebuilt and its principal splendour was created by Richard II. But it was in the great chamber of his own devising that this king was forced to abdicate in 1399 in favour of Bolingbroke whom he had

THE TOWER OF LONDON

A conqueror, William of Normandy, began it and many have added to
the walls that never fell. Yet some of it has now the look of a toy castle.

exiled. Shakespeare's *Richard II* has a most poignant scene in Westminster Hall where the broken and abased monarch knows that he will meet no mercy. After the surrender

> " With mine own tears I wash away my balm,
> With mine own hands I give away my crown,
> With mine own tongue deny my sacred state,
> With mine own breath release all duty's rites "

there is the piteous

> " O, that I were a mockery-king of snow,
> Standing before the sun of Bolingbroke,
> To melt myself away in water-drops! "

And so to the Tower first and then to the cell at Pomfret, where murder, and no gentle thaw, ended the decline of a once promising young King.

So Westminster Hall and the Tower abide for Shakespearians. The first was a temple of justice which was often very rough justice indeed and sometimes no more than a savage revenge. To the second went the condemned. The Tower is now a " must " for sightseers with school parties ushered round in high spirits or, in school vacations, with family groups treading the soil which has been so often soaked in blood. Queues wait to see the Crowns and Crown Jewels in the Wakefield Tower, or to brush up the uglier parts of their English history in the Bloody Tower. The whole group of buildings is something that nearly everybody sees at some time in his life. It is conveniently reached by the underground railway: it is compact and it is authentic. But for me there is a curious unreality about this never-captured fortress. (If Hitler had entered London in triumph he would doubtless have used it for its old and sanguinary purposes, but still the Tower is the unconquered thing.) A conqueror, William of Normandy, began it and many have added to the walls that never fell. I mentioned unreality because, seen from across the river or from any of

London's principal viewpoints, it has the look not of some impenetrable stronghold but of a toy castle: one might be gazing at a monster Christmas present in a big and gaily lit shop window, so neat it is and trim. Were it a ruin one could believe more easily in its grim history as a gaol and execution ground. But, with the fancy dress of its Beefeaters, with the children happily inspecting the ravens as a change from dutifully parading in the museums of armour and regalia, and with the sunny amenity of its riverside promenade, the length and the lugubrious nature of its history fade away. The blocks, the axes, and the severed heads are forgotten and the murders and incarcerations seem remote and almost incredible.

Mention the Tower and many at once think of the Princes butchered by order of Richard III. Whether or not Richard was grossly traduced by King Henry VII and those who wrote history to justify his revolt and usurpation, the accusation remains and Shakespeare, who could hardly call Queen Elizabeth's grandfather a liar, sustained it in his play of *Richard III* and put a superb wreath of poetry on the bodies of the slaughtered children:

> " Girdling one another
> Within their innocent alabaster arms;
> Their lips were four red roses on a stalk
> Which in their summer beauty kissed each other."

Few people well acquainted with Shakespeare can visit the Tower without quotations springing to their lips. (He accepted the legend that Julius Caesar had begun this mass with a " flint bosom.") His chronicle plays take one insistently to the Traitors' Gate where the barges brought the condemned, many capriciously or foully victimised, on a water journey as grim as the cart-ride on land to Tyburn which was the last look of London afforded to less exalted prisoners. To be beheaded at the Tower was at least an honour.

W. S. Gilbert was not much given to unhappy endings in the composition of his stories for the Gilbert and Sullivan light operas. But, when the Tower was his scene in *The Yeoman of the Guard*, that building seemed to defy the usual felicity and to insist upon a dying fall. If one quotes Shakespeare instinctively amid the grey pile, Gilbert springs to mind no less. The Merriman of *The Yeoman* is " moping mum,"

> " Heighdy, heighdy,
> Misery me, lackadaydee."

So the curtain falls on Jack Point, the jester, fallen. The Tower must have its way. But not for the crowds who come bustling in past the restaurant and across the moat. The youngsters are having a day off, " choc-ice " in hand and fizzy lemonade bubbling inside them. The historic Tower awaits them; but the fullness of its history is a long way off. Perhaps it is as well.

Across the river and upstream is the South Bank which is the true Shakespeare country and more than that since Chaucer's Canterbury Pilgrims assembled there and Dickens found Sam Weller at work among the boots. But naturally little of Chaucer's London remains except by name: the east ambulatory of Southwark Cathedral is thirteenth-century Norman and the south transept is fourteenth-century. Some of its tower is fourteenth-century also. A good deal of the Cathedral, then the Church of St. Mary, was known to Shakespeare, but except for some brickwork once belonging to the palace of the Bishop of Winchester the South Bank of his time has been overrun by brewery, markets, gaunt riverside warehouses, and the massive electricity power station which is our latest addition to that now legendary shore. Of Dickens's Southwark there is Lant Street and Guy's Hospital, which was founded in 1721 by Thomas Guy, who had emerged successfully from the wild gambling in South Sea stock and devoted some of his luck to the service of medicine.

There is also the George Inn, rebuilt after a fire in 1676 and retaining the old coachyard with galleries. It is the best thing of its kind in London and yet there is only half of it to see, since a railway company wickedly swept away the north wing in 1889. It is now the property of the National Trust and therefore well looked after; it has a dining-room with the old-fashioned benches and a good meal can be obtained there. But it is prudent to make feeding arrangements in advance, since the businessmen of the adjacent Hop Market and the doctors and students from Guy's Hospital assure steady patronage. In Shakespeare's time, as we know from the writings of John Taylor, the waterman rhymer and recorder, it was a lodging-place of the carriers who brought the produce of the nearby countryside for sale in London. There is nothing bogus about the George: what remains is nearly 300 years old and can be fairly said to have the bouquet of its years.

Farther up Southwark High Street is St. George's Church, a Georgian building on the site of a very old foundation. To Dickensians it is associated with *Little Dorrit* and the readers of that book will meet the Southwark of the early nineteenth century in all its sinister atmosphere of frowsy, fly-blown prison life. In a curious way those who had nothing managed to drink plentifully on occasion, and some jocularity was achieved among the decaying lives of the debtors languishing within it. Because this early suburb lay at the southern approach to what was for centuries the only Thames bridge Southwark abounded in taverns. London Bridge was closed at night for security reasons and the late-comer went to an inn of necessity. Probably, too, he could lodge more economically than by pressing on into the City.

Had some provident authority made Southwark into a preserved precinct we should have had a wonderful array of the old hostelries. The disastrous fire of 1676 which destroyed much of the Southwark then existing could not be extinguished by edict. No careful guardianship by civic ordinance could have kept us the Tabard as it was (" In Southwark at the Tabard as I lay " is the twentieth line of the Prologue to *The Canterbury Tales*,) but like the George and the White Hart, where Mr. Pickwick found his man-servant and so put a warm gusher of Cockney wit into *The Pickwick Papers*, there was immediate rebuilding. It was Victorian vandalism that wiped out the seventeenth-century Tabard and White Hart in 1875 and 1889. If an Early Victorian local authority had had the sense and the power to look after its antiquities and had kept the seventeenth-century inns, Southwark would now be a centre of mecker-ing very profitable to its inhabitants. But nobody cared. Yet Southwark is a good place in which to nose about. History still hangs about it, if only as a thin, faint presence, and in the Cathedral there is a far more abiding substance of the Borough's fascinating past.

First it was the Church of St. Mary Overie. That last word is presumed to be an abbreviation of " over the river " or " of the ferry." In an amalgamation of parishes in 1540 it became St. Saviour's, but the older name lived on and has continued in the title of the Overian Players who pay dramatic tributes to Shakespeare and Dickens in the district. In 1905 the church became a cathedral owing to the division of the see of Rochester. In Shakespeare's time it was St. Saviour's and the parish church of the Bank-side, that pleasure ground made glorious by the poets and playwrights of the time and much frequented for its baiting of bulls and bears in Paris Gardens, a form of entertainment which seems as revolting to us as the spectacle, dear to the Elizabethan mobs, of public floggings and executions. Shakespeare expressed his compassion for the " head-lugged " bear which had to stand its course and for the mastiffs mutilated by the bulls, but there was no general

disgust occasioned by these profitable and royally patronised shows. In his Southwark beauty and bestiality rubbed
shoulders.

The actual site of the Globe Theatre, in which Shakespeare was author, actor, and shareholder, has been much
argued about: there is a commemorating tablet on the wall
of Barclay's Brewery in Park Street. That was roughly the
position of the playhouse which was built in 1599, burned
down in 1613 owing to the careless discharge of cannon
into a thatched roof during a performance of *Henry VIII*,
quickly rebuilt, closed by the Puritans in 1642, and pulled
down a year or two later. Owing to Shakespeare's emergence as the supreme English poet and dramatist (I say
" emergence " because, though well praised and financially
successful, he was not deemed to be completely pre-eminent
in his own time) the Globe has brought especial honour to
Southwark.

The Bankside has had a long life as an aviary of the
Muses. First of England's singers was John Gower, whose
tomb is conspicuous in the Cathedral and rightly so, since
he spent his later years in the priory of St. Mary Overie.
He appears as Chorus in the Shakespearian (or semi-
Shakespearian) play of *Pericles*, presumably because he was
a great collector of romantic stories: these he adapted in
30,000 rhymed eight-syllabled lines in his *Confessio Amantis.*
He is made to speak in that metre in *Pericles*. Gower was
liberal in his views and sympathised with the Peasants'
Revolt of 1381. Chaucer concluded his epic of *Troilus and
Criseyde* with a dedication

> " O moral Gower, this book I directe
>   To thee."

The effigy on the tomb shows the poet's head pillowed on
the books of his composition. He has been regarded as a
heavy-handed composer of verse that plods. Chaucer came

9—L

in with a brisker motion and made story-telling dance light-foot in his poetry.

Here was naturally the church of the region's writing men. The names of several are engraved on the floor. John Fletcher, a busy script-writer, as we might say, and partner of Francis Beaumont, died here in 1625. Beaumont, who predeceased him by nine years, was honoured with a place in Westminster Abbey; this was presumably due more to social reasons than to literary merit. He was the son of a knight who had a high legal position. Fletcher was Shakespeare's successor as the chief playwright to the company known as the King's Men. Philip Massinger was buried in the Cathedral in 1640. He had created one character who outlived the centuries, the grasping Sir Giles Overreach of *A New Way to Pay Old Debts*. This ogre's adventures in avarice for long provided a part dear to actors strong in the presentation of a frenzy. Bringing us very close to William Shakespeare himself is the Southwark gravestone cut for his brother Edmund. We know little of Edmund except that he was the youngest of a large family, came to London to follow in William's footsteps, fathered and lost a bastard son who was buried in St. Giles's, Cripplegate, died at the age of twenty-seven, and was buried in the church " with a forenoone knell of the great Bell." The sexton's record names him as a player and says nothing of attempted authorship.

The funeral was on December 31st, 1607, and the death of the young man may have been assisted by the extremely cold weather of that winter. The Thames was so firmly frozen over in January 1608 that there were sports held and all manner of salesmanship was brisk on the ice. Scotsmen will learn with pleasure that along with beer and wine there was " usquebaugh " (whisky) served at the mid-river stalls. The frozen surface was strong enough to permit braziers with pans of coals to be erected on it. Wrestling, football, and running of races, as well as usquebaugh, helped to keep the youth of Southwark warm in this tremendous freeze-up. The players could hardly perform through such a winter in the unroofed theatres of the Bankside and this may have stimulated Shakespeare and the King's Men to acquire a small covered theatre to the north of the river. This was " The Blackfriars," where they had their second and very popular base of operations from 1608 onwards.

In view of the comparatively mild winters of London's recent years the idea of crowds revelling on an icebound Thames seems fantastic. The great frost of 1607–8 can hardly have affected the race of waters through the narrow arches of old London Bridge, a race so rapid that navigation of a passage under the bridge was notoriously dangerous. But elsewhere the river moved more slowly than it does now, since there were no great embankments to contain and narrow it: the water could spread out to marshy shores where it would freeze quickly. There was the flow of the tides to counteract that and the cold must certainly have been far more severe than any we are used to undergoing now. The people of the time wore thicker clothes than we do and would oppose a well-padded figure to the fangs of an east wind. But the larger houses with their great halls must have been bitterly cold without any central heating. " Roaring log fires " have a romantic sound, but much of that heat goes up the chimney and the rest of it warms chiefly the nearby portions of the room. One cannot envy the Londoner, even if he could take ample tots of imported usquebaugh, as he coped with that winter in which Shakespeare saw his young brother interred in the church beside the Thames.

The Shakespeare Memorial in the Cathedral was the work of Henry McCarthy and was unveiled in 1912. It presents the busy actor-manager and poet resting from labours and lying on his side; behind him is the Southwark in which he worked, with its episcopal palace (the Bishop of Winchester's), its share of London Bridge, and its theatres.

Here is by no means a major tribute to far the most renowned of the Borough's eminent men. American visitors
will be gratified and possibly surprised to find the founder
of Harvard University honoured with a chapel. This was
dedicated for the good reason that John Harvard was born
and baptised in Southwark in 1607 and was a tough enough
baby to survive that terrible winter.

It is strange that Harvard should be linked with both the
great Shakespearian Meccas, Stratford-upon-Avon as well as
Southwark. John's father, Robert, had married Katherine
Rogers, daughter of Alderman Thomas Rogers of Stratford,
in April 1605. The Alderman was a prosperous butcher
and maltster and rendered great service to the Borough
Council. The link became a double one since the Alderman's younger daughter, Frances, married William Harvard,
brother of Robert. One is left wondering why Southwark's
two Harvards went a-wooing in Warwickshire. Did Shakespeare suggest a country holiday one summer and take
Robert for a ride which was to end in a marriage so fertile
to the scholarship of the United States? I can find no
evidence for such an excursion, but it seems to me a
reasonable guess.

The Harvard Chapel was instituted by Harvard men in
the early part of this century and the Harvard window
above it was dedicated in 1905 by the American Ambassador, Mr. Choate, himself a Harvard man. He expressed the
hope " that all Harvard men will come to the rock from
which they were hewn and to the hole of the pit from which
they were digged." It might have been more gracefully
put, but the sentiment is sound. John Harvard went to
Emmanuel College, Cambridge, at twenty, which was late
for those times, and stayed there for some years. He took
holy orders, emigrated, and was soon prominent in his new
home, being made a freeman of the colony of Massachusetts
in 1637. He died a year later, at the age of thirty-one. But
his bequest of money and books to a college being built at

New Town, near Boston, was to bear fruit a thousand times over. New Town changed its name to Cambridge and the new college took the name of Harvard, and as that has won its world reputation. Thus Harvard men and many Americans with New England interests and associations should follow Mr. Choate's advice and visit Southwark as a rock from which the life-giving waters flowed west.

At Stratford they can also visit Harvard House, the well-preserved home of the Rogers family, which was bought, at the persuasion of the novelist Marie Corelli, by Edward Morris of Chicago, and given to Harvard University. It is a notably fine example of domestic architecture in Shakespeare's time, having been built in 1596, when the future Mrs. John Harvard was a child. Its timbering and wood carving are especially remarkable. It is indeed a pity that Southwark's homes of that period all went up in smoke or down before the axes of demolition.

There are many more literary shrines in London, of which Dr. Johnson's house in Gough Square, off Fleet Street, is well worth a call. The Doctor had been taking the country and hillside air of Hampstead for the sake of his wife's health, but in 1748 he moved to a William and Mary house in this square " well inhabited by persons of fashion." There he wrote his tragedy *Irene*, his Rambler Essays, *Rasselas*, and the famous Dictionary. He left Gough Square in 1759. The top floor became known as Dictionary Garret, but the house was to have a dismal history, with threats of destruction. Cecil Harmsworth fortunately bought and restored it just before the First World War and it is now a memorial and a museum.

The ancient and adjacent tavern called the Cheshire Cheese, many years famous for its pie of assorted meats and its veteran parrot, has a Johnson Corner with a copy of the Reynolds portrait. Johnson was a great tea-drinker. " I suppose no person ever enjoyed with more relish the infusion of that fragrant leaf than Johnson," wrote Boswell.

" The quantities which he drank of it at all hours were so great that his nerves must have been uncommonly strong not to have been extremely relaxed by such an intemperate use of it." We think of tea as stimulating rather than relaxing, but to Boswell it was evidently what is now called " a tranquilliser." Johnson, however, gave high praise to taverns as well as to teapots. " There is nothing which has yet been contrived by man by which so much happiness has been produced as by a good tavern." Other bliss-conferring taverns of the Fleet Street neighbourhood have had mention and praise from famous authors. Pepys ate lobster, sang, and was " mighty merry " at the Cock, and Tennyson, a port-drinker, has given some immortality to " the plump head-waiter at the Cock " and to the five o'clock pint of that wine which was customary with its fanciers.

Hereafter I shall deal with the literary associations of Highgate, where more of such history is in the air than in the remaining brick and stone. Keats House in Hampstead is the authentic habitation and workshop of the genius whom Hampstead air could not save from his tuberculosis. Nowadays treatment in a sanatorium would almost certainly have saved him, as modern medicine, with its antibiotics, could have prolonged the life of many a gifted person who died young. The House lies on the south-eastern edge of the Heath and the nightingale, which moved Keats to write his famous ode, has no descendants to sing there now. But it remains a semi-rural villa, well preserved, first with handsome American aid, by the Hampstead Borough Council. It shows the usual type of relic, letters, pictures, first editions and writing-desk. It is not a dusty museum of letters, but a living centre of readership, since there is a branch of the borough's public library next to the Keatsian portion.

The house was originally a part of Wentworth Place and as such it was the home of Charles Brown, friend and host

of the poet from 1818 to 1820. In the other portion lived
Fanny Brawne, whom Keats loved. Keats had previously
lodged higher up the hill in Well Walk, where John Con-
stable, the painter, was to settle in 1826 and to give enduring
beauty to the Heath as then it was: except on its built-up
fringes it is not very different today. Thomas Hardy in his
lines on " A House in Hampstead, Sometime the Dwelling
of John Keats " wrote sadly of the changes wrought " on
the misty slope one time your home," a spot " where
streets have stolen up all around " and never a nightingale
is heard. But he ended with some consolation and justly so.
He found more of the essential Keats in those Hampstead
gardens where that poet heard the bird-song and made it his
own than at the sepulchre in Rome where, in Hardy's
words, he " tuneless, cold, passed to the dim." I suppose
that many believers in life everlasting would not like the
afterworld to be called " the dim," but is there not something frightening in that promise of Eternal Light that goes
with some funeral valedictions? Always to have the light
kept on is one of the tortures favoured by the confession-
extractors in police states. Is there no sleep in heaven?

However that may be, there is nothing dim about a spring
or summer descent by Downshire Hill to Keats House in
what was John Street and is now Keats Grove. One passes
the little church of St. John, defined as " a proprietary
chapel," tiny, classical, and stuccoed. It had been built in
the year when Keats came to live beside it. Its worshippers
are Evangelicals who like no pomp of ritual and certainly
are unlikely to favour the Keatsian view that

> " Beauty is truth, truth beauty: that is all
> Ye know on earth and all ye need to know."

None the less, this chapel is " rich in the simple worship of
a day." Before writing this I had just strolled down the
slope to Keats House on a morning when March was
obediently performing its proverbial job of going out like a

lamb. Light clouds gambolled in a fleecy sky: the east wind that had plagued us with frore skies had yielded to the zephyr. The almond trees were in their sudden flush of pink which yearly takes us with its sweet surprise. The bell-cote —it is no spire—of St. John's has its pastoral look as though it were indeed summoning a flock. New painted, it shone against a backcloth of the heights beyond the Heath. The noise of the now ceaseless traffic that grinds up Rosslyn Hill to Hampstead High Street was decently remote. If any piece of inner London (and Keats Grove is only just over four miles from Charing Cross) can claim to be, in the memorable words written by Keats upon another matter, a " still unravished bride of quietness," and a " foster-child of silence and slow time," it is here upon such a day as that of my approach to Keats House. And there are many days as tranquil: this I can affirm as a neighbour.

Oddly this is a haunt for Communist meckerers too. On the far side of the Heath they can pay their respects in Highgate Cemetery to the newfangled tomb of Karl Marx which has replaced the humble old one which long sufficed as a modest receptacle for the red flowers left by the faithful. But by the Hampstead Ponds, opposite Keats House, they can meditate on the hoped-for liquidation of all capitalist society and the disappearance of the bourgeoisie in the surging flood of class warfare. The ponds themselves, with their ducks and gulls and patient fishermen, do not suggest anything of romance, riot, or revolution, but hither came Marx and his family, tramping it from their home in Soho in an hour and a quarter, to have Sunday picnics and to lark about. His friend Wilhelm Liebknecht has left a curious portrait of Marx as a lover of holiday outings, a Hampstead " regular," a ready drinker, and a man gladly forgetting to plod on with another chapter of *Das Kapital*. After six days of coping with capitalism in the Library of the British Museum, Karl, it seems, relished his domestic junketing on the seventh day among the beer barrels, winkle stalls and shrimp barrows of the Heath, as it then was. He mingled malt with the muses and spouted Dante and Shakespeare with gusto and a prodigious memory.

The shellfish are now on sale chiefly on Bank Holidays when the Fair is raucously providing its swings and rounda-bouts. These are times well avoided by the poet's devotees. Keats Grove does lie back a little from the invasion and the din, but the " unravished bride of quietness " is then in some danger of losing its peculiar virtue. Here too came the fictional Mr. Pickwick, shortly after the death of Keats, to examine and report upon the tittle-bats and other ex-amples of pond life. Must one call Pickwick only a figment of a novelist's fancy? He has, for me, as much actuality as any of the others whenever I pass this way and see small boys spooning about for whatever the water's edge may yield to their biological scrutiny. Keats, Pickwick, Marx—here, in one corner, is united the strangest of all spectral company.

Those who arrive in Hampstead by tube have an easy walk down to Keats Grove or a short stroll up Holly Hill to find a meckerer's paradise. Here the plaques of remem-brance, once sombrely brown and now more cheerfully blue, are frequent on old walls. On the left, as you breast the slope, is the home of George Romney whose vision of Nelson's Lady Hamilton has a conspicuous place in the orangery of Kenwood across the heath. The house has a rustic and a timbered look and is apt to the arboreal road and names around about, Holly Hill, Elm Row, and the Grove. Opposite to him in a tall brick house there dwelled for many years a lady from Lanarkshire, Joanna Baillie; she paid a compliment to the Hampstead climate by sur-viving for more than ninety years while she composed Scottish ballads and " Plays of the Passions." She was both a contemporary and a neighbour of Sarah Siddons, who applied her tremendous powers to a part in one of the Baillie passion-dramas. But she did not remain a neighbour for long. Mrs. Siddons lived in a charming little house at the extreme brow of the Hampstead summit, but she was only there for a while in 1805: after that she moved to the then more approachable rusticity of Westbourne Farm, Paddington. Her Hampstead home has no plaque, but the letter " S " over the door.

On the way up the hill there is the rather formidable, almost fortressy Old Grove House in which George du Maurier spent twenty years drawing for Punch and contributing to fiction and theatre, with *Peter Ibbetson* and the more remembered *Trilby*; his son, Sir Gerald, lived across Heath Street in the finely placed and finely surrounded Cannon Hall whose ample garden is spread like a green apron down the hill-side. The Hall has no plaque; but none who saw Sir Gerald in his mastery of the natural school of acting will forget him. His daughter, Daphne, like her grandfather a novelist of high quality as well as of great popularity and a playwright too, spent her youth at Cannon Hall. Hard by and nicely sheltered from the traffic of the hill is Grove Lodge where John Galsworthy spent his later London years and carried the Forsytes on their well-liked way.

For the bookish browser Old Hampstead is an agreeable strolling-ground with an aroma of great names and recollections; for those who want a seat on a day when the weather is suitable to such a session, there is the old, large, and seemly garden of Fenton House. It costs a shilling to go in and, in such surroundings, can yield a good shillings-worth of quiet thought on the books and plays and paintings that were made upon this piece of London's roof, a pent-house of the Muses.

6

Hills to the North

A steeple issuing from a leafy rise,
  With farmy fields in front and sloping green,
  Dear Hampstead, is thy southern face serene,
Silently smiling on approaching eyes,
Within, thine ever-shifting looks surprise,
  Streets, hills and dells, trees overhead now seen,
  Now down below, with smoking roofs between,—
A village, revelling in varieties.
Then northward what a range—with heath and pond!
  Nature's own ground; woods that let mansions through
And cottaged vales with billowy fields beyond,
  And clump of darkening pines, and prospects blue,
And that clear path through all, where daily meet
Cool cheeks, and brilliant eyes, and morn-elastic feet!

                                              Leigh Hunt

6

BEING by nature fond of hills and mountains, I am inevitably bored at times by the comparative flatness of the London area. I snatch at what petty heights there are and have long lived on one. I even dream of escape into some upstart rolling country in the middle of the level urban sprawl. Oddly, those dreams have come more than once and were identical. They have not visited me lately; but, although I rarely remember what I dream, these rustic mirages of the night do not wholly fade away.

In one I find myself turning north out of Fleet Street, my life's workshop, and instead of going up Fetter Lane to Holborn—what a grimly symbolic name is that Fetter Lane! —I immediately begin to climb. Soon I reach a rocky plateau which stretches away up to Islington. Among the rocks there are fields and from this island, green and grey, I look down on the city. The fields are open grassland, not cultivated. There is nobody about nor any animal either, but some cry and flutter of birds. I wander about for a while and then find myself off that strange shelf again and coming down into something like Aldwych.

The other escape-dream happens in a different region and not one where I have ever worked or felt the fetters. It begins in St. James's Park or thereabouts. I turn west. Instead of Belgravia there is a large lake and at the end of the water the ground begins to rise, not sharply towards rocks as it does in Fetter Lane, but gently towards downs. It is as though I were walking straight into Berkshire or Wiltshire and was at large among the undulating solitudes of the grasslands and the ancient ridge-ways which are intermittently humped with the barrows of neolithic man.

Villages lie below, but my journey is along the tops and it is easy going with the turf elastic and the air keen. In this case I do not recollect returning. I wake up while I am still beside a beech clump on a knoll or among the great sarsen-stones which are scattered between Marlborough and the megalithic majesty of Avebury.

The psycho-analysts can get on with that. What they discover may be fashionably sordid and sinister: this seems to my inexpert, but I hope common-sensible, self no more than a stirring of subconscious resistance to a life in which an altitude of 400 feet is the top of one's daily experience. In any case I am not continually indulging in the self-pity of a prisoner " barricadoed ever more, within the walls of cities," to lift a phrase from William Wordsworth. Like all Londoners I have my modest ration of hill country and I am grateful for that minim of a mountain liberty. The fantasy and fiction melt: the facts of London geography remain. They have their consolation.

London may be described as a clay saucer with nicely decorated rims. These timbered or downland margins are close to the centre on the north and farther removed to the south and west. Their height is inconsiderable, if one thinks in terms of genuine hill country. But the eminence of a ridge must be judged, at least in part, by the kind of terrain from which it rises and from which it must be seen. The values of a " townscape," even more than those of a landscape, are relative.

If you are travelling north-west on the top of a bus along Tottenham Court Road, or even if you are only walking in that street in a Johnny-head-in-air manner, you will notice on a clear day a wooded range away over Camden Town. It is only four miles away, but it has a look not only of distance but of substantial elevation. Should you surmount those slopes, again with the provision of good visibility, the view over London to the south and east presents what a geographical realist would dismiss as mere hummocks but which to a city-bound person are sizeable and comforting horizons. So, when the estate agents advertise a desirable residence on the Northern Heights or even in the Surrey Highlands, they are not talking complete nonsense. There are summits about. G. K. Chesterton said that " Over the hills and far away " is one of the finest lines of poetry in the English language, and it is easy to agree with him. But it is one of the great pleasures of living in London that it is not a case of Shakespeare's " far-off mountains turnèd into clouds." Chesterton can be rewritten, with loss of beauty but with accuracy, " into the hills and close beside."

This raised perimeter of the clay saucer is made of more clay, some sand, and a greater quantity of chalk, especially on the southern side. However trifling the measurements may seem to a mountain-lover, there is a heartening spectacle. A Londoner can raise his eyes unto the hills and be delighted: he can also raise his limbs unto them with encouraging speed and ease, especially if he dips underground to reach his upper-ground. Once seated in a Tube train he is carried from Leicester Square to Hampstead Station in less than fifteen minutes and, when he has been shot up in the new-model lifts that make London's longest lift-journey go in a flash, he is within five minutes' walk of the roof of London at the Whitestone Pond and the tavern of Jack Straw's Castle.

The altitude of this ancient tavern is 440 feet, but the view is spacious and superb. The south-easterly prospect across the town to the Kentish hills has one feature that always strikes me as strange. " St. Paul's above the city rides." Certainly, but its " aboveness " looks trifling to one standing on a spot of which Macaulay wrote, " High on bleak Hampstead's swarthy moor." Yet the height of St. Paul's Cathedral, from the floor to the top of the cross, is 365 feet. (Did Wren calculate one foot for every day of

the year?) Thus St. Paul's is only seventy-five feet below
one's stance as one takes a drink in the garden of the inn:
yet it looks a mere pimple and not the mighty masterpiece
that it is.

There is no castle: it is odd that the hills round London
were not castled for protection. When the Romans came,
and probably before that, it was deemed sufficient to
fortify, with what became the Tower, the centre of Lud's
town of Londinium. Hampstead and Highgate seem
obvious sites for baronial keeps, but the Norman kings
took a wider view and defended the capital with castles at
some distance, of which Windsor is the most notable
example.

Jack Straw was one of Wat Tyler's men in the Peasants'
Revolt of 1381, when hard times and the iniquity of a poll
tax which was to be levied at the same rate on rich and poor
created an insurrection in South-East England and East
Anglia. The size of the revolt was not small, but atrocities
were few. With no general killing the rebels seemed to have
London at their mercy, but they listened to the appeal of
the young King Richard II, who was only fifteen, and
believed in his boyishly proclaimed regard for justice and
reform. They were foully cheated by the nobles round the
King rather than by Richard himself, and with the loss of
their leader Tyler, who was stabbed by the Lord Mayor of
London, they lost also their determination and their
chance to create a democracy of emancipated serfs. Such a
democracy might not have survived long; but, with the
King's promises broken and the nobles, who had suffered
an early panic, recovering their nerves, the upsurge was
bloodily destroyed before its leaders had an opportunity to
show that they could organise a new order as well as menace
an old one.

Jack Straw is now more remembered than Wat Tyler
and that because of a tavern on a hill-top. His radical ghost
can welcome at any rate the open-air forum for public

speakers on the other side of the Whitestone Pond where the small boys of today launch their diesel-engined and radio-controlled new-model vessels or, with less funds and more conservatism, set a mere sailing-boat to cross the small and safely shallow pool. On Sunday mornings the voices of Communism and several other -isms are freely raucous beside Jack Straw's. The audiences, however, are now small and apathetic, drawn more by a tepid curiosity than by a keen intellectual thirst. Thirst of the material kind is amply satisfied at the inn which has had a colourful history as a resort of literary men and as a training centre for prize boxers. Half of it was blown away in the " blitz " of the Second World War, and it is now a mended but smaller establishment, which serves no meals. As an undergraduate I used to dine there well enough for half a crown in a room whose windows surveyed the contours of the " swarthy moor " and the smoky bowl of London below.

A short ridge-road leads across the Heath to Highgate. Just where the Borough of Hampstead ends and the administrative area of Finchley begins, there is another tavern of long renown. This is The Spaniard's, probably named after a servant of a Spanish ambassador who went into business as an innkeeper in the seventeenth century. It was a fine position, but there was some gallantry in its occupation, since the district was renowned for its highwaymen. " That wicked and fatal profession of Padding the Road " earned both those adjectives, since the local malefactors not only robbed the travellers but were caught and hanged there. In the seventeenth and eighteenth centuries the traveller was in peril, but sometimes he had the grisly and possibly satisfying spectacle of seeing " a felon, long since put to death, hang crackling in the sun." Macaulay made Hampstead one of the beacon sites in his lay of the Armada victory and it still collects a rowdy element to watch bonfires and to discharge fireworks on November 5th, a date on which it is well to avoid Jack Straw's and The

VIADUCT AT HAMPSTEAD
The Red Arches pond on Hampstead Heath

Spaniard's if one does not care to have crackers flung at one's face or into one's ear by some rollicking lout. At other times a visit can be recommended: the latter house has a charming little garden in which to enjoy a session with a pint on a warm summer evening.

Charles Dickens was a frequenter of Jack Straw's Castle and he knew The Spaniard's too. For thither he sent Mrs. Bardell with her friends to take tea and bread-and-butter and also to absorb something stronger, just before her removal, for a matter of legal costs, to the Fleet Prison. It was here, reached by the Hampstead stage-coach, that Mr. Raddle reflected in Mrs. Bardell's company on the natural consolations of Hampstead Heath which was then " truly rural." " For lone people as have got nobody to care for them or take care of them or have been hurt in the mind or that kind of thing, the country is all very well. The country for a wounded spirit, they say." At this observation Mrs. Bardell, who would nowadays be called the victim of a traumatic neurosis, burst into tears. But there must have been many wounded spirits since then who have found on the hills of London the remedy for lacerated sensibilities and afflictions of the soul.

A. E. Housman has stated that he found that an afternoon walk, following a pint of beer, was a likely prelude to the composition of poetry. As he lived in Highgate when he wrote *The Shropshire Lad* and since an obvious stroll was along the ridge to Hampstead, it is at least possible that the scene of Mrs. Bardell's sobs and of Mr. Raddle's remarks on " wounded spirits " may have been the source of those lyrics in which world hatred so often finds the metre and the melody more appropriate to happier things.

> " Be still, be still, my soul: it is but for a season,
> Let us endure an hour and see injustice done."

Jack Straw and his doomed comrades of a revolt that fought injustice in vain would have known the sting of that.

Another popular surge which swept over Hampstead occurred in 1780, when the " No Popery " riots associated with the name of Lord George Gordon carried an angry mob to the recently built mansion of Caen Wood, or Ken Wood as it is spelt now. They were seeking vengeance on the hated William Murray, Earl of Mansfield, Lord Chief Justice. The rioters are said to have been stayed by the landlord of The Spaniard's, who saved the person and property of the Earl, a self-made Scot, by ladling out liquor so freely that the alcohol overcame their indignation and kept them happily besotted until troops arrived. The Tea-Garden, as Dickens described the inn, was not in his day, as it is now, a pleasant halt for the public on their way to the entrance of Ken Wood. That superb estate and house designed by Robert Adam remained private property until the generosity of the Earl of Iveagh presented both mansion and gardens to the nation in 1926. The Iveagh fortune was based on the admirable brew of Dublin stout: so Guinness has not only been, as the advertisements claim, good for us, but good to us as well.

What Mansfield, as a Scot, would have called his " policies," i.e. his grounds, were laid out with a masterly sense of landscape gardening. The view across the lawns over the lake to the beech-covered knoll is as fine as anything I know among London's green hills and islands. Since it was two Scots, Adam and Murray, who created Ken Wood and an Irishman who passed it on to the public, London should here, as for many other things, be thankful to its immigrants. The Iveagh gift, it must be remembered, was made before the incidence of soaring costs and crushing taxation in recent years made the ownership of fine houses a punishment instead of a pleasure, so that to be rid of them is to be much relieved.

The woody part of Ken Wood is said to be a remnant of the old Forest of Middlesex: it is certainly a splendour to the eye both in the flush of May and in the gold and bronze

of its October tints. The autumn glory is a particular
pleasure of mine; even in summer there is rarely a crowd;
later in the year there are only a few old folks about: sometimes nobody. So one can wander in solitude when the
south-wester is making its assault on all the foliage that an
early frost has left.

> " With the great gale we journey
>   That breathes from gardens thinned,
> Born in the drift of blossoms
>   Whose petals throng the wind;
> Buoyed on the heaven-heard whisper
>   Of dancing leaflets whirled
> From all the woods that autumn
>   Bereaves in all the world."

Buoyed is indeed the right word for the lift of spirit which
the little journey brings. Those last two lines have as much
of airy October in them as has any other couplet in the
English language and I cannot walk at that season amid
London's northern copses without them coming to my lips.
Housman, their author, did not, I suppose, have the entry
to the privacy of Ken Wood when he was a Highgatian of
the eighteen-nineties; but the words may have bubbled up
as he walked out from his lodging to the neighbouring
hills. And, when October has passed, there is still abounding beauty in the fragments of the Middlesex Forest. Surveying the skeleton trees one can cite Swinburne instead of
Housman then:

> " Thou art noble and nude and antique."

The nakedness of branch tracery against a December sky
has a breath-taking and most delicate filigree. The colour
of the woods in winter, with a mist from the lake wreathing
up into the umbered trunks, is as agreeable to the senses as
any of the emerald enamelling that early summer brings.
Naturalists, with the keenness of eye proper to their kind,

have reported a richly varied population of birds in these parts. My own sight is not so keen nor has my luck been so good; I have never seen the blue coruscation of a king-fisher on any of the adjacent Highgate ponds. But there is plenty to see without that piece of avian radiance. In the way of fauna, there is an old tradition of foxes and badgers here within five miles of Oxford Street. A friend who was looking recently at an empty house on the verge of Hamp-stead Heath heard a curious noise under the floorboards: he raised a loose slat and found a badger with four cubs. Highgate people tell of foxes crossing the road at night. So we of the northern hills have still the country quality at our doors where Mr. Raddle discussed the balm of sore minds.

History without tears is easily studied hereabouts. The mansion of Ken Wood, with its collection of old furniture and Old Masters, is open to all as an example of the taste, as well as the opulence, of an eighteenth-century milord. I am not compiling a museum guide and shall leave the visitor to walk for himself amid the native portraiture and the foreign purchases. There are problems of domesticity to ponder as one surveys the vast and far-separated kitchens. How did the gentry contrive to get their meals served reasonably hot?

Passing out through the eastern gates of Ken Wood one finds a string of ponds, two supposed to be secluded but not sufficiently railed off to prevent the raids of birds'-nesting boys, and others used for sailing of toy boats or bathing. There is high diving of the highest class at one of these meres and a boy champion who won imperial honours in 1958 learned his plummeting here. The ponds are the legacy of another Scot, William Paterson: they were made early in the eighteenth century by damming the rivulets coming down from Ken Wood and were intended to give North London a regular water supply when people were depending on the chancy product of local wells. But

the New River, of which more will be said later, was bringing a sufficient supply from Hertfordshire and Paterson's
provision was not much employed. But this chain of
waters, with no utilitarian function now, remains as a piece
of suburban jewellery on a sunny day, when their otherwise
sombre surface is lit up.

Probably to many people the name of Dick Whittington
is that most easily evoked by mention of the word
"Highgate." Whittington was a boy from Gloucestershire
who became a London mercer, wealthy, esteemed, and a
Lord Mayor. He held the office four times between 1397
and 1419. He was naturally popular at Court since he lent
money to three kings, Richard II, Henry IV, and Henry V.
He was buried in the City, at St. Michael's Paternoster in
College Hill, to the rebuilding of which he had contributed
lavishly. An inscription on his tomb said that "As a
fragrant odour was the fame of this Richard Whittington,
the flower of merchants, the founder of a College of Priests,
and also of an almshouse for the poor." St. Michael's, as
Wren had rebuilt it, was shattered by a flying bomb in 1944.
Any remnants of Sir Richard's body must have been
cremated as well as interred long before that since the early
church was burnt down in the Great Fire of 1666. But his
name goes marching on thanks to an eighteenth century
legend about his young life and hard times, and thanks,
also, to the British institution of pantomime which keeps
the Whittington story, as well as many fairy tales, alive
every Christmas, to the popular satisfaction.

The pantomimes show young Dick entered as a shop
assistant to a draper called Fitzwarren. The historic Whittington was apprenticed, about 1371, to a Sir John Fitzwarren, a merchant adventurer and a member of the
Mercers' Company. Portraits of Whittington in stained
glass—there was one in the City's Guildhall—introduced
a cat and, when some reconstruction of St. Michael's was
going on after the havoc wrought in the Second World

War, the skeleton of a cat was found immured. Presumably a stray cat had died, perhaps of hunger, in some cranny and had been walled in. Whatever the origin of the bones, the name of Dick Whittington is ghosted by a cat and the ghost takes lively form in the pantomime, which would be unthinkable without the antics of a skilled animal impersonator, when Puss follows Dick to Highgate Hill, after his dismissal by Fitzwarren on a false accusation of theft.

Highgate came into the Whittington story in the eighteenth-century version. On those slopes he heard Bow Bells and turned again to win, with the aid of his good mouser, a fortune and a mayoralty. (Bow Bells, incidentally, have nothing to do with Bow in the East End or its parish church of St. Mary Stratford Bow. They belong to the campanile of St. Mary-le-Bow, which John Betjeman describes in the *Collins Guide to English Parish Churches* as " the most elaborate and famous Wren Steeple." Those are true Cockneys who are born within the sound of these bells, the distance now to be measured presumably at night-time when the din of city traffic is hushed. The old name of Bow was derived from arches either on the old pre-Wren steeple or in the foundations.)

But we are straying from Highgate, whose Whittington Stone, erected in Sir Richard's memory in 1821, is not far up the hill which leads from Holloway to Highgate Village. This was chosen as the site of Dick's pause for rest and for his hearing of the peal which suggested his turning round and later on led to his upward progress in finance. According to this siting of the stone he had not sunk weary on the summit: there was some way still to climb. His name has been more familiar than that of any City magnate and may remain thus; so strong is legend. The story plainly has some basis of truth since it is linked with an actual Fitzwarren, and I have no sympathy with the dry-as-dust historians who must always probe a legend to find a myth and then explain the myth in terms of money as do those who turn the

Trojan War into a fight not for a fair Helen but for eastern trade.

Why should we doubt that Sir Richard had a fancy for cats and later made a prosperous voyage to Morocco? And why not also accept the boy's northward exit from the City after some row with his master, a journey which would naturally take him to Highgate? In any case, there every Christmas he reposes for many an English audience, impersonated by a lady of good looks, displaying a well-shaped leg in tights and thigh-boots, and wearing a pheasant feather in her (or his) jaunty medieval cap. There is a new tendency to drive out feminine beauties from this traditional role of Principal Boy and substitute burly male baritones in their place. This bit of realism is odious to many who cling to the routine of a century. If Sir Richard's ghost has any sense of humour or of looks in a lady he must much prefer to be perpetuated by a " smashing " soprano.

To move up Highgate Hill past the Whittington Stone is to walk, in imagination at least, into the seventeenth century. For Highgate was early favoured as a site for country residence. It was a great advantage to be on the main northward road when all roads were rough and many impassable in bad weather, and when, too, highway robbery was more likely to be encountered on a side road than on a main one. It was more prudent to follow in Dick Whittington's legendary track than to take less-frequented routes and risk the passage, say, of Hampstead Heath. (On the day of writing this, in 1959, the police are hunting gunmen there!) Hence there was a fair sprinkling of the big houses and the " noblemen's seats " on the Highgate section of the northern London rim.

It is true that Oliver Cromwell never lived in Cromwell House on the right, a mansion of Cromwellian date and famous for a magnificent oak staircase of the period. But the Ireton family was at Ireton House, and, since General

Ireton was Cromwell's son-in-law, there is a likelihood that the Protector came on family visits and left his visiting card in the naming of Cromwell House.

On the left side, as one mounts the slope, there remains a portion of Lauderdale House, a grandee's mansion, on which time has inflicted the usual alterations and restorations. This habitation of that crafty Scottish Earl, later Duke of Maitland, has been put to democratic uses, and now serves light refreshments to those who stroll or bask in Waterlow Park, which, with its ponds and ducks, its aviary and little waterfall, makes a charming pleasance on the site of Lauderdale's grounds. This park of twenty-six acres was given to the public in 1889 by Sir Sydney Waterlow. I wrote of people basking, but the sculptor of Waterlow's memorial statue remembered the English climate and provided Sir Sydney with an umbrella. It is said that Nell Gwynne lived there with Lauderdale at one time. When she had finished with the oranges at Drury Lane she picked her friends, from the King downwards, with a nice sense of where and how to abide in elegance. You may not now absorb strong liquors in the cafeteria of Lauderdale House, but you can rely upon a tot of orange juice with which to sip the immortal memory of Nell.

In July of 1666 Pepys drove in Lord Bruncker's coach-and-six to visit Lauderdale, who was Scottish Secretary of State. They had royal business to discuss and the buying of prize goods for the King. There Pepys met " Scotch people, pretty odd company." There were Scottish airs played on a violin. His lordship supplied music, but did not relish it. He said that " he had rather hear a cat mew than the best music in the world and the better the music the more sick it makes him; and that of all instruments he hated the lute most and, next to that, the bagpipe." As an early member of the London Scottish Lauderdale was not a creditable specimen; Pepys must have been disgusted by this dismissal of the musician's art that he loved, but Lord

Bruncker assured him that the Earl was a man " of mighty good reason and judgment."

What did the Philistine Earl make of his neighbour, Andrew Marvell, one of the most delicate and discerning poets of that century and indeed of all our centuries? In the London County Council's volume on Highgate in its *Survey of London* it is stated that " no documentary evidence has been found to justify the firmly held tradition that Marvell lived there." But the absence of a document does not disprove a " firmly held " belief. The tradition has been so well established that a memorial tablet has been set in the roadside wall. Here there was a house in the Elizabethan style until it was wickedly pulled down in 1868, when respect for famous and historic buildings was rare.

Marvell was a Cromwellian and assistant to John Milton in the Latin Secretaryship. He survived the upheaval of the Restoration and became a Member of Parliament for Hull. In 1663 he travelled from London to Moscow as secretary of a trade delegation which, in a manner familiar to such bodies, wasted months of time and did no trade. The Russians talked and banqueted; there was a supper which lasted nine hours and involved the service of 500 dishes. Marvell, said Aubrey, was no hard drinker in company, but liked a rummer of good Rhenish to refresh his spirits as he wrote. Moscow's cups can hardly have been to his taste. He returned by way of Stockholm and Copenhagen: he had been away a year and a half on his public duties. He must have welcomed the privacy of Highgate, since he was especially the singer of " Fair Quiet " and expressed his preference for " delicious solitude " to " busy companies of men." He saw vanity in seeking to win the palms of public life by incessant labours. These sentiments are not common in Members of Parliament.

Marvell should in fancy be appointed the Honorary Laureate of all M.P.s past and present. His mind wove its way gently into any scene, from that of " Mexique Bay " to a Yorkshire garden, and discovered eternity in the fading flower as much as in the quickening spring.

> " Casting the body's vest aside
> My soul into the boughs does glide;
> There like a bird it sits and sings,
> Then whets and combs its silver wings."

These are lines for remembrance if one loiters among bird-song in Waterlow Park. Here, too, when the papers record another international crisis or some further idiocy of mur-derous rioting, we can see, for contrast, the peaceful parade of the flowers.

> " Each regiment in order grows
> That of the tulip, pink, and rose."

It is easy to share Marvell's pacific dream " After the Civil Wars":

> " Unhappy, shall we never more
> That sweet militia restore,
> When gardens only had their towers
> And all the garrisons were flowers,
> When roses only arms might bear
> And men did rosy garlands wear? "

Sir Sydney Waterlow did well to give the Londoners a garden-park where the House of Commons poet lived next door to the able but insensitive Scottish Earl.

More than fifty years before Marvell died in 1678, Francis Bacon, then Lord Verulam, a man who had fallen in disgrace from the post of Lord Chancellor but remained free in his county seat at St. Albans and untiring in author-ship, philosophy, and enquiry of all kinds, came to a curious end on Highgate Hill. The village cannot claim him as its citizen, but it might somewhere have a tablet to the man who died there for the sake of further knowledge. The end came at what was then Arundel House and is now the site occupied mainly by St. Michael's Church. On a snowy day early in 1626, when he was at the age of sixty-five, he was moved to reflect on the preservative powers of refrigeration, a subject now familiar to all. Reflection was not enough; he wanted experiment. So he purchased a Highgate pullet, had it cleaned, and stuffed it with snow in order to test the results. In the process he caught a severe chill. If Lauderdale later felt like vomiting in Highgate at the sound of music, Bacon had the same distress in the same place for a better cause. He was taken to Arundel House and put to bed. According to Aubrey the house-servants were negligent, for he attributed the following disaster to damp sheets. But Bacon before his death wrote a letter of thanks to Lord Arundel. He said nothing of neglect, but spoke of good care in " a happy house." Here is his own description of the incident.

" My very good Lord,—I was likely to have had the fortune of Caius Plinius the elder, who lost his life by trying an experiment or two touching the conservation and induration of bodies. As for the experiment itself, it succeeded excellently well; but in the journey between London and Highgate, I was taken with such a fit of casting as I know not whether it were the Stone, or some surfeit or cold, or indeed a touch of them all three. But when I came to your Lordship's House, I was not able to go back, and therefore was forced to take up my lodging here, where your housekeeper is very careful and diligent about me, which I assure myself your Lordship will not only pardon towards him, but think the better of him for it. For indeed your Lordship's House was happy to me, and I kiss your noble hands for the welcome which I am sure you give me to it. I know how unfit it is for me to write with any other hand than mine own, but by my troth my fingers are so disjointed with sickness that I cannot steadily hold a pen."

So, at his end, wrote (or dictated) a great master of
English prose. He died in the arms of one called Sir Julius
Caesar, a name which has for us a Shakespearian as well as
a Roman ring. Those who believe, as I do not, that Bacon
also wrote the works of Shakespeare in his spare time must
attribute to Highgate Hill, if Bacon were also the master
poet, the death of the greatest and most versatile author
who ever lived.

Poetry again haunts the hill-top. Samuel Coleridge was
long a Highgatian at Number 3 The Grove, where he died
in 1834. This is the most handsome end of a notably
attractive terrace; the gardens of the houses still provide a
scarcely broken rural view across Hampstead Heath to
Jack Straw's Castle. A house in the Grove has long been
one of the most coveted of London's hill-top niches. It has
been a homing-ground for talent as well as for wealth.
Among those authors whom I have visited there were
John Drinkwater and J. B. Priestley, the latter in the house
where Coleridge lived. A. E. Housman, as I have said, was
a Highgate man for nearly twenty years, lodging round the
corner from the Grove at 17 North Road. It is unlikely
that he had many visitors; he was not comfortable company.
A Highgate loyalist can fairly claim that the slopes and
summit of his hill, a tiny area, have given as much to
English literature as any other part of London.

Turning east one drops down Southwood Lane to Highgate Woods and Queen's Wood which the L.C.C. in its
brochure called *Open Air London* claims to be " one of the
loveliest wooded areas of its size in London." With this I
find it difficult to agree; to me there is an air of melancholy
and of shades too sombre. But the coppices contribute
substantially to the great circlet of hills and greenery on
London's northern brim. In April to this woodland you
may go " to see the cherry hung with snow." Housman,
who got more of his inspiration from London than from

Shropshire, took an interest in Highgate Woods and complained about the thinning of them which opened up less
attractive vistas, including lines of washing hung out to dry.
It is a fair guess that he wrote after a walk in Highgate
Woods his blossomy, cherry-white Easter verses, which are
perhaps more familiar to a wide public than any others of
his except the lines evoked by the bells heard on Bredon
Hill. For here the wild cherry proclaims the spring before
the tardy oaks come into leaf.

Thence it is a short ascent to the top of Muswell Hill,
named after the ancient Moss Well, whose waters were
deemed a sovereign cure for scrofula in the Middle Ages.
Owing to scarcity of vegetables and to absence of imported
fruit, on which we rely so much to our health's advantage,
affections of the skin were extremely common at that time
and the Moss Well was much visited by those afflicted with
what we now call " Vitamin C deficiency." Pilgrimage was
made to a shrine of Our Lady of Muswell. The east side of
the hill has an almost precipitous descent; standing on the
crest one surveys a vast London panorama across a valley,
one of whose rivulets was called after the Moss Well. In
old maps it appears as Moselle; but do not look for vines.
The lower ground is occupied by the inhabitants of Hornsey
and Crouch End, who are not, in the main, cultivators of
the soil.

There is a knoll above Harringay and Hornsey, on which
is perched a monstrous edifice. Edifice is a word derided
by stylists, but it is surely permissible for such a structure
as the Alexandra Palace. It was opened in 1873 as what
Coleridge would have called, had he been living at the time,
a " stately pleasure-dome." It was almost immediately
burned out, but soon was restored and reopened, offering
the public spacious grounds, a theatre, a racecourse, and
many other holiday amenities. During the 1914–18 war it
was made a home for Belgian refugees and then an intern-
ment centre for German and Austrian civilians. The officer-

in-charge was a well-known gourmet who happily included among his compulsory guests some of London's leading chefs.

In the nineteen-thirties and -forties the British Broadcasting Corporation made this useful eminence the home of its television service and a towering mast announces that fact. News bulletins are still issued from there. Part of the gigantic building, popularly known as Ally Pally, is also employed as a rink for roller-skating; this fast and furious exercise was much favoured fifty years ago and here it survives despite the greater vogue of ice rinks. The television workers established in the palace have lived in one of London's major minarets, with a townscape of vast extent. When shafts of sunlight are driving down upon the urban haze Blake's vision of London " builded over with pillars of gold " is radiantly realised. I remember a Priestley essay about wandering in the huge nave and aisles of a then desolate Ally Pally. " Bare ruined bars where once the sweet port flowed," he suggested. It is not an easy place in which to sniff the scent of old revels; but on the right kind of day it is a wonderful place from which to admire the paint-box of the London sky.

At this point the hills fade away and there is no more conspicuous height to the east until the valley of the Lea has been crossed and the Epping ridge has been mounted. That, it is true, is no mountain, being rather less exalted than Hampstead and Highgate. But the Epping Forest is something of a miracle in the way of rural preservation on the fringe of the great urban mass. On the north-west there are remnants, handsome indeed but fragmentary, of the old Forest of Middlesex; here is an abiding as well as an ancient forest, impressive in bulk as in beauty. Harold Clunn in *The Face of London* calls it " one of the finest recreation grounds in Europe and perhaps the largest and most beautiful domestic park owned by any city in the world. It is almost incredible that within a dozen miles of the Bank

of England there should exist a tract of country so sequestered." The woodland lies mainly on a ridge twelve miles
long and from one to two miles wide and covers 5,600
acres.

To visitors coming from countries much greater in size
than ours this may seem little enough, but in England we
have to reckon in acres where others count in square miles.
The timber includes thick copses of hornbeam and beech
with grassy intersections; the Forest has its lakes and ponds
and meets the needs of fishermen as well as of boaters and
bathers in the summer. It has a varied animal life and is a
deer park as well as a refuge of foxes and badgers. It is
easily traversed by car along the central ridge-road to the
town of Epping itself, with deviations to such viewpoints
as High Beech, but, once off the few roads, the walker can
find genuine solitudes. The town keeps its rural look
despite its growth in size. One might be in any market
place of rural England.

It could all have been lost in mid-Victorian times and
some of what the public now own had to be rescued at great
cost of agitation and expenditure. Between 1850 and 1870
illegal enclosure was being briskly carried on, but there
were powerful champions of popular rights and the menace
was checked. The Epping Forest Fund Committee and the
Corporation of the City of London put up a splendid fight
in the Law Courts to stop further annexation and in the
raising of purchase money to recover land that was lost.
Finally, when Queen Victoria came in the month of May in
1882 to dedicate Epping Forest to the public use, the
amount of common land then handed over was nearly
twice as big as it had been twenty years before. The City
Corporation has since proved an admirable guardian of this
great estate.

At the time of Queen Victoria's inaugural visit there was
none of the convenience of transport existing today. Clunn
recounts that the Queen travelled by special train from

Windsor, " changing at Acton to the Kew and Hampstead Junction line, thence by the North London Railway to Victoria Park, and by the Great Eastern Railway to Chingford." Now it is possible to reach the Forest direct from Oxford Street by the extended Central London Tube railway, which surfaces after burrowing beneath the city. Approach by car is easy by the North Circular Road which links Ealing with the outskirts of Hampstead and Highgate and swings east through Tottenham. Yet, owing to the vastness of London and the separation of West from East, few West Londoners ever think of going to Epping. Middlesex and Essex are neighbouring counties, but they do not intermingle in their social pursuits. This is as well for the isolation and loneliness of the Forest; the Middlesex folk have ample green islands of their own and do not need Epping's wilderness; but they are missing much if they never make a single visit there. Eastward again there is Hainault, another piece of forest open to all, which has had its poet in Ruth Pitter who

" Threading the silent, mist-bedewed
        And darkening thicks of Hainault Wood "

found the region " dear beyond all telling." The Essex place-names thereabout make poetry in themselves; like Kipling's English flowers " almost singing themselves they run," Hainault, Pyrgo, Havering Bower, Foxburrows Farm, and Lambourne End.

The men of Kent and Surrey may be surprised and vexed to find that my London " hillmanship " has been so much confined to the north. They can reasonably claim that their own Downs have ampler spaces and greater altitudes than the mere knobs of Middlesex and Essex. My reply to that is to emphasise the nearness of the knobs, if Hampstead, Highgate, and Epping must be so described, to the centre of things. That to a Londoner is a matter of great value. The domestic and parkland splendour of Ken Wood is

close at hand. The even greater splendours of Knole near
Sevenoaks are not.

The North Downs seem to me better classed as " Home
County " than as metropolitan. I gladly admit that on the
summit of Leith Hill, which just fails to make the thousand-
foot grade of height, you occupy a more exalted gazebo
than you do at Jack Straw's Castle and that you have
Kipling's dim, blue goodness of the Sussex Weald to add
to the London landscape. But the citizens of Dorking and
Reigate do not, I think, want to be called Londoners,
whereas the people of the northern hill-suburbs most
certainly are Londoners. Nor does Epsom seem to me as
Londonish as Epping. For adjacent hill-country in Kent
there are the slopes above Greenwich and the spur of
Shooter's Hill where there is a woodland belt of a mile and
a half long. Shooter's Hill itself gave the old travellers by
the Dover Road their first view of London: it equals
Highgate in height. The amount of open land in this area
is remarkable; there are no single units as large as Hampstead Heath, but there is a rich diversity of copse and
common. But between the two main rims of the London
bowl there is a difference. The northern hills are in the
town; the southern are in the counties. Since the inhabitants of both would probably have it so, why grumble?

7

Going to the Play

Here one acts a tyrant, on the morrow an exile: a parasite this man to night, to morrow a precisian, and so of divers others. I observe, of all men living, a worthy actor in one kinde is the strongest motive of affection that can be: for when he dyes, we cannot be perswaded any man can doe his parts like him.

Sir Thomas Overbury

James: How shall we spend the day, Sam?
Samuel: Let's home to our studies and put cases.
James: Hang cases and books that are spoiled with them. Give me Jonson and Shakespeare: there's learning for a gentleman. I tell thee, Sam, were it not for the dancing-school and play-houses, I would not stay at the Inns of Court for the hope of a Chief Justice-ship.

Thomas Nabbes in his " Comedy of
Tottenham Court," 1633

7

THERE are some forty theatres which can be described as " West End." The old Outer Circle of suburban houses has been cut down to two large establishments in Streatham and Golders Green. There is also, as I write, a theatre at Stratford in the East End tenanted by a " progressive " company called Theatre Workshop, some of whose productions have recently been promoted to the West End. Its patrons arrive from assorted areas, mainly westerly; that is because the theatre in Britain is a Class Institution. Class Institutions, such as certain schools and social clubs, are run by those who like their own kind in breed, tradition, habits, and income and want to keep other types outside. The British theatre is a Class Institution for an exactly opposite reason. The outsider will not come in. Naturally artists want as many patrons as possible: naturally people selling entertainment want as many customers as possible. But the millions vaguely and foolishly known as Working Class—the numbers of non-working Londoners of working age are now negligible—have long preferred the films or "the wireless." In the nineteen-fifties they began to like the films rather less and television much more. Now millions of Londoners have the theatre out of mind, except for an occasional coach-party trip to a popular musical or to the panto-mime after Christmas.

In Victorian and Edwardian times the working class had its melodramas. It had them locally and, for especial treats, it would flock up to occupy the cheaper seats at the Lyceum to see lurid pieces in which villainy was flashing its teeth and its jewels and penurious virtue was at last rewarded with a wedding that could fairly be called golden. At Drury Lane there was a pulsating panorama of this kind every autumn and it was equipped with abundant spectacular effects then deemed to be miracles of contrivance. A horse race would be run on a revolving stage. An earthquake would shatter a city and so the heroine, escaping from an awkward evening in menacing company, lost her home instead of her virtue. The stage engineers contrived a perilous pageantry of shipwrecks and railway accidents from which the righteous were promptly and properly rescued.

When the films started to present crime and catastrophe on a far more lavish scale, the snarls and tears of melodrama disappeared and the massed chorus of a mammoth musical took their place. The millions soon found cinemas handy in every suburb, with seats at bargain prices. So the Outer Circle theatres turned their stages into screens and became cinemas too; the houses where I went as a boy to see Fred Terry as the Scarlet Pimpernel, Julia Neilson as Nell Gwynne, the Benson Shakespearian Company, touring teams in West End musical successes, and so forth, were either showing " the pictures " or used for the preparation and distribution of broadcast concerts and television shows.

Yet, with all this decline and fall of the Drama in Greater (and rapidly ever-greater) London, the West End theatre has astonishingly held its own. Within a square mile there are usually forty playhouses showing either " straight " plays or musicals and very often there are more managements seeking tenancies, while grumbling at what they denounce as extortionate rents, than there are premises to accept them.

In the great cities outside London playhouses perished rapidly during the nineteen-fifties. If the competition of the films had not emptied them already, the pressure of television did so then. Yet the Central London theatres flourished. It was astonishing evidence of the magnetism of the capital, since large numbers of the playgoers were visitors to the city. They would not attend their theatres at home even with " London attractions," brought to them with excellent casts, usually in the course of pre-production tours. Here would be the London article, but few would bother with it at the local Grand or Royal. The desired thing is to go up to Town. There is that business trip, with expenses paid by the firm, and the wife comes too. There are all sorts of excuses, in addition to ordinary holiday travel, for " going to Town." There are, for example, the great trade exhibitions, especially the Motor Show; during the week of the latter business at London box-offices is notably brisk.

Of late years there have been the coach parties. Making a journey has a vast appeal in our time; people who would not look at a play cheaply in their own neighbourhood will drive or be driven many miles to see it more expensively " Up West." The seats, it is true, are likely to be cheaper than they would be if bought singly at the box-office, because the coach party can make block bookings at reduced rates and is strong enough to drive a good bargain while it drives up for its jaunt amid the lights of London. So valuable are the coach parties that one of the principal London managements keeps a special department at work solely on arranging these mass visitations. The journeys are made not only from the outer suburbs but from all the Home Counties towns and even much farther. Not to get home until the small hours is no bar to the coach-party member: it is even part of the fun.

I have been told by a manager who has watched the playgoing business through a long life that nowadays, after three months have elapsed since the West End opening, the bulk of the audience will be non-Londoners. In summer there are many visitors from abroad: during the rest of the year there are the thousands who find an evening in an hotel lounge to be insufferable—and that aversion is easily understood. Above all, as I have said, there are the parties. The baritones in the pierrot and pierhead shows I used to attend as a boy during my summer holidays had a favourite " number " about the Jolly Old Coaching Days. They roared it out with plenty of heigh-ho, gallop-along and tootle-of-horn sentiment. The vanished four-in-hand, so dear to these vocalists, has been replaced by the forty-in-a bus. And the new coaching days are very jolly for those who live by the theatrical industry of the capital.

The " class " aspect of the theatre, to which I have alluded, is maintained in the rank and quality of the patrons. They are overwhelmingly middle class, and that class has widened its ranks in London and around. It has not increased its income to the same extent as the so-called working class, but somehow it manages to see the plays or shows it wants: probably the chief decline has been in the number of well-to-do women who had time and means for stalls at a matinée.

The practice of going to a West End theatre in evening dress after a good dinner has almost entirely disappeared. There are as a rule a few theatres which present their pieces at eight or even eight-thirty; those are smart comedies or revues. In the majority of cases the opening is at half-past seven, which means either a high tea or a drink and a sandwich before the play and a snack on getting home. Some people dislike this; I do myself, but I live within five miles of the West End and can manage later hours. Many other playgoers, as well as the coach parties, have come from much farther off and want to start on the way home by ten o'clock or shortly after.

Theatre prices, private boxes excluded, run, as a rule, from one guinea on the ground floor to three and sixpence near the roof. Seats bought through an agency (the word " Library " for agency hangs on with no reason for its survival) will naturally carry an extra charge, just as the block-booking seats will be cheaper. The theatre managers like to claim that the rising cost of seats has kept well behind the rising cost of living and they can point to the fact that the half-guinea stall was introduced to the West End in the eighteen-sixties when that sum was indeed a large matter and certainly the equivalent in purchasing power of two pounds today. But they do not mention the very sharp increase in the price of the less expensive seats.

I myself became a playgoer in London as a frequenter of the pit; this was the area now called " back stalls," with seats sold at twelve and sixpence or ten and sixpence. It is true that the pit was not bookable: one took a chance of getting in or, if the play was a success and the theatre likely to be full, one joined a queue outside and waited for the doors to open half an hour before the curtain rose. This was a waste of time and a strain on the legs and the patience, (we did not hire stools in those days.) But one was entertained while in the queue by the " buskers " who performed various antics, sang, or cracked jokes, subsequently passing a dirty-looking cap whose contents were usually coppers or the smallest of small silver. Furthermore, youth did not mind standing with a book or paper in hand and the " buskers " for diversion. The reward was a first-rate place for half a crown, which encouraged my playgoing and that of many others who could not possibly consider paying more.

The seat gained was no " fauteuil " but a place on a fairly comfortable bench, with the risk of occasional commands, if the house filled up, to move along, sit closer, and make room for more. This behest was resented. Why should some late-comer who hadn't queued be shoved into a good place? There was cheapness too in the price of programmes, which were twopence in the pit and sixpence in the stalls. This meant that " the student class " was not kept out of the theatre altogether or driven up to the shilling gallery for which one also might have to queue and in which one suffered posterior aches and pains, since the seats were as a rule damnably hard.

So the half-crown pit was a real bargain for those who could tolerate minor discomfort with the prospect of a really good place for seeing and hearing. We pittites used to allege that the front row of the pit was the best place in the house, and that was a reasonable claim since the half-guineas did not as a rule reach far back and the front of the pit was conveniently close to the stage. Furthermore the barrier between the pit and the stalls was a fixed bit of fencing and the management, if it had a success, could not push the stalls back and reduce the pit to a meagre row or two. The pit was indeed our stronghold and a great asset to the future of the theatre, since those who were attracted by its relatively cheap position and the others who could only afford the much cheaper but more remote as well as stuffy gallery, were likely to become playgoers for life and, with rising prosperity, to be stallites later on. " Catching them young " was prudent. The student class of our time gets no such encouragement since back stalls will cost its members half a guinea, a charge prohibitive to them. The prices do vary a little from theatre to theatre, but it is true in general that any but a very lofty place will now cost anything from ten to fifteen shillings. Few students can manage that.

As to the theatres themselves, they possess amenities mostly unknown in New York where the value of land in the central areas is so enormous that there is no room for spacious approaches or foyers. It must astonish Americans to enter Drury Lane Theatre with its grand entrance and capacious halls, corridors, and bars. The most attractive of the London playhouses, however, is the Haymarket, which is not so lush or lavish in its accommodation as Drury Lane but has a beautifully urbane and reassuring air. It is a pleasure to take one's seat there; one feels that so agreeable a house must surely yield agreeable entertainment.

All sorts of drama has been staged there at one time or another; but it is primarily the home of good comedy, not " sexy " and brash stuff, but plays informed with a civilised wit and a style that suits its mannerly habitation. For the dramatist and players it is a rewarding niche, since it rarely has a failure and a piece produced there is likely to do better business than it would elsewhere.

The history of the Haymarket is a long one. All old London theatres have been rebuilt at one time or another; when lighting by lamps and candles was the only form of illumination and there were no efficient fire brigades there were constant and disastrous blazes: also the type of building and accommodation inevitably went out of date and new forms of staging and seating were necessary. The first theatre on the Haymarket site was built in 1720 by a carpenter called Potter who managed to contrive a modest building where once had been an inn; his total expenditure, including fittings, scenery, and wardrobe, was only £1,500. The present Haymarket Theatre dates mainly from 1905, but it retains the fine classical portico with six columns and rounded windows above them which John Nash, supreme among late Georgian architects, erected over his new Haymarket in 1820. There is a most fascinating view of the theatre's frontage obtained by those who approach it from the west, coming out of St. James's Square along Charles Street. The Nash portico stands cool, serene, and gleaming; there could be no better invitation to step inside.

Drury Lane is half a century older, if one considers site rather than structure. In the rebirth of the theatre after the restoration of the monarchy it was built for Thomas Killigrew and his King's Company in 1664. Nell Gwynne is said to have sold oranges in the pit before she sold her charms to the King. She was early an actress, but never as successful on the stage as she was in male company off it. But she became an apt speaker of the Prologues and Epilogues then in vogue and fascinated Charles II by her

THEATRE ROYAL, HAYMARKET

. . . the Nash portico stands cool, serene, and gleaming; there could
be no better invitation to step inside.

contribution of this kind to a play called, rather aptly, *Tyrannic Love* in 1669. Brief life was her portion; she died at thirty-seven. It is now denied that Chelsea Hospital, Wren's noble building for aged and infirm pensioners of the Army, was built by order of Charles II after a suggestion from " pretty, witty Nell." But these picturesque legends do not easily die. It may be true that the idea was taken from the Parisian Hôtel des Invalides, but it is hard to see how any strict historian can prove that Miss Gwynne never whispered the notion of such a charity in the King's ear. He might certainly have listened if she did.

The history of " the Lane " has been written in flames. Killigrew's house was badly burned in a widespread con- flagration in 1672 and that brought in Wren to design its successor. This theatre had quite a long life; it suffered dam- age during a riot in David Garrick's time and was restored. It was rebuilt on a vast scale in the seventeen-nineties by Henry Holland for Sheridan; the new house held 3,600 people. There was a disastrous fire in 1809. The new Drury Lane, whose architect was Wyatt, has survived in most of its exterior, but the auditorium was reconstructed in 1922. But the splendid vestibule, rotunda, and staircase of Wyatt's design remain; these are the only interior parts of a Georgian theatre still remaining in London. So the play- goer at Drury Lane IV is being received in the august halls and amid the grandeur of Drury Lane III. There are statues, plaques and medallions to remind him of the mighty past and its masters of comedy and tragedy. To pass within these doors is at least to feel that the age of the grandees has not altogether passed.

There are many who testify to the existence of a ghost in this house. The spectre is unlikely to have been disturbed by the German bombs which crashed into and failed to smash effectively the hive of industry which Drury Lane became in 1939 as the headquarters of ENSA, the organisa- tion which supplied entertainment to all the many fields of war. The sardonic remarked that if an ENSA show did not scare a spook to death, no high explosive had a chance of firing it out. As a matter of fact ENSA was able to employ, along with some concert parties that were not of unchallengeable merit, most of the leading players of the time and some who were in the direct succession of Old Drury's theatrical sovereigns. It was not all "corn and capers."

The chronicles of the house, or of the various houses on the same spot, have been properly illustrious, with inevitable intervals of mediocrity. People now prefer for serious or classic drama a smaller and more intimate playhouse; but Shakespeare did get back to the stamping-ground of Garrick and Kean in the mid-winter season of 1957 when Stratford-upon-Avon's production of *The Tempest* was brought up from Warwickshire and Prospero appeared in a strikingly novel presentation of the part by Sir John Gielgud. He gave us an angry middle-aged man deprived of his rights, a rendering far removed from the usual episcopal and bumbling bore.

> " Though with their high wrongs I am struck to the quick,
>   Yet, with my nobler reason, 'gainst my fury
>   Do I take part; the rarer action is
>   In virtue than in vengeance."

A suitable message for Christmas, and, when Christmas came, Shakespeare, with Stratford's aid, completely contradicted the view that in the West End Shakespeare is " murder at the box-office."

Christmas was essentially the Drury Lane season fifty years ago. The annual pantomime ran all round the clock and well into March. The daily matinée began at one-thirty and lasted till nearly six: the evening performance began very soon after and was no less lengthy. So the drolls had to be at it from midday to midnight with one brief interval, while the management annually " surpassed itself," as the notices said, by laying on ever more bounteous, more breath-taking spectacles. Breath-taking to the critics, as they averred, it well may have been, but not to me as a small boy who found his lungs completely unaffected by the panoramic flood of wonders. In particular I could not abide the long, gaudy ballet in which, if the subject were floral or jewelled, a battalion of ladies of all ages paraded. (There was no need for skilled dancing in those times.) They ambled about with astonishing flower-pots on their heads or gems the size of eggs all over their persons. This was for most of the children a prolonged tedium; but children in the theatre will politely endure what is obviously wearisome. The adult is politely assured of absolute bliss. After all, the comics will return. There will be the crash of crockery in the Baron's kitchen, the riot in the Dame's schoolroom, and the papering of the parlour with abundance of slap-dab and collapse in a sea of paste, the authentic Christmas joy.

But I was unfortunate with my Drury Lane Saturnalia. I missed the zenith of the zanies' fun. I never saw Dan Leno, who became a legend. The clowns who followed him were of moderate merit, creatures of the knockabout routine. The pantomime programmes then divided the cast into Mortals and Immortals. Fairy Godmothers and Demon Rats were of superhuman status. Dan Leno was naturally listed, in his comedy parts, among the earthbound. But to his generation he was as magically immortal as Grimaldi had been to the lovers of harlequinade a century before, and too early a death did not part him from countless memories.

Pantomime wilts when the daffodils rise. Spectacular melodrama then took its place, and the melodrama, like the pantomime, inevitably had to surpass itself. This meant bigger and better earthquakes, shipwrecks, and calamities on road and rail. When the films made small beer of such theatrical spectacle, Drury Lane turned to the big musical and it has been mainly living on that ever since. With a capacity of 3,000 it is madly dangerous to risk a modern " straight " play of any realistic and unspectacular quality. There must be the mass appeal. With a half-empty house the great open spaces in the auditorium have a disastrous effect; the actors are inevitably defeated. They might be addressing the occupants of isolated benches in a chilly park. I attended one of the few musicals which had failed to attract and sat in a solitude which made play-acting a penance for the mimes and playgoing a dismal incarceration for the audience. After the triumphant incursion of the American *Oklahoma!* on April 30th, 1947, there was a sequence of transatlantic " wows " with occasional inter-lopers not so victorious. Then Shaw-plus-Broadway came galumphing home during the autumn of 1958 with *My Fair Lady* and Drury Lane's box-office was busy as never before. The problem of finding a suitable tenant for a house holding 3,000 at a sitting had been solved for years to come.

A house of ripe age and atmosphere was lost when the St. James's Theatre was pulled down in 1958 to make way for the inevitable block of offices. There was a lively campaign to save it; but profit was stronger than protest. Theatres are inevitably menaced when site values soar; they are used only at nights on six days of the week with one or two matinée performances which is not as rewarding as property used commercially. Also, should a play wilt or die quickly, they can be a great source of loss. The positions which they occupy are precious and can yield far greater income for each square foot of ground space if a lofty block of business premises takes their place. It is, however, part of the London County Council's town-planning policy to refuse permission for the destruction of theatres unless some very good reason can be shown. But there was a mistake made in the matter of the St. James's: it was said to " slip through the net."

There was a case against the St. James's Theatre. It had its ancient history, dating from 1835. But it was not regarded by the architectural specialists as owning great architectural value. Its seating was far from ideal: at the end of the sides of the auditorium the sight-lines were very bad. It had the old-fashioned, view-obstructing pillars in some parts. It needed a drastic reconstruction, which would have demanded a big capital investment. Its position, slightly out of the Shaftesbury Avenue theatre-nucleus, was not helpful since it was unlikely to attract the chance patronage of passers-by or the overflow from a house with a big success.

But it had about it the memories of an old pleasure-seeking elegance.

> " The ladies of St. James's
> 　Go swinging to the play.
> Their footmen run before them,
> 　With a ' Stand by! Clear the way! ' "

Few living people can remember the kind of seigneurial patronage which Austin Dobson, that neat contriver of nostalgic rhyming, had in mind. But the St. James's was the frame for Sir George Alexander, who was an able performer in Pinero's dramas about the moral problems of the upper classes. He was one of the matinée idols of Edwardian London. To have been his tailor must have been, in Savile Row, almost the equivalent of a royal command. His admirers were of a loftier social rank than the devotees of Lewis Waller, the accepted master of costume-play gallantry and period heroics. The latter's gallery public formed a K.O.W.—Keen Order of Wallerites. There would never have been anything so common as a Keen Order of Alexandrians. The photographs of Alexander stood in silver frames on desks and tables in drawing-rooms. I remember one such possessed by my stepmother. I remember, also, going to the pit

" To see that entertaining play
' The Second Mrs. Tanqueray '."

This was at a revival. I was not a playgoer in 1893, the date
of Paula Tanqueray's arrival at the St. James's. As a boy I
rarely missed queueing for my pit seat for the latest production in this house. So I had more reason than many to feel
the gap and resent the replacement in King Street, St.
James's.

During the Second World War the destruction of buildings in the capital, especially in central areas, was so severe
that the London theatre could almost be described as
fortunate in not suffering even more casualties than it did.
It did lose totally the Shaftesbury and the Queen's in
Shaftesbury Avenue, but the latter has at last been rebuilt.
Two smaller theatres, both of distinctive character, were
also lost. The Kingsway, just off the west side of the
thoroughfare, was reduced to a shell. The Little, in the
Adelphi, vanished altogether. There were plans to recon-
struct the former in 1956 in order to house the experimental
work of the English Stage Company which subsequently
settled at the Royal Court Theatre in Sloane Square. I
remember the Kingsway as a home of what is now called
" social realism." It was there that I saw Granville Barker's
pungent picture of a respectable home and a seemingly
respectable lawyer's practice, *The Voysey Inheritance*, and
several productions by Lena Ashwell of pieces which would
today be thought tamely conventional but were then what
is now called " off-beat."

The Little was an enchanting midget, architecturally a
hall rather than a theatre yet possessing the right playhouse
warmth. It was perfectly accommodated to the old, classical
good looks of the eighteenth-century Adelphi, to which the
brothers Adam gave their serene urbanity of style and to
which the home of the Royal Society of Arts bears testi-
mony still. Great figures of the theatre had lived almost

12—L

next door, Garrick, Shaw, and Barrie among them. The Little Theatre was for a while the home of what was then called the New Drama. This was presented in many forms, Ibsenite, Shavian, and Galsworthian. After the First World War there were seasons of "horror drama," an English version of the French Grand Guignol. Here was a tiny temple of the Muses, but not always austerely so. It could be happily used for intimate gaieties. The Little Revues were "known to their own" in the nineteen-thirties and afforded the salty pleasure of Herbert Farjeon's sharp, satirical sketches and neatly phrased lyrics. The destruction of the Little Theatre makes a small gap in space, a large one in affection.

In any case so diminutive a house would have been uneconomic today when all costs of producing and running a play have increased so heavily. Little theatres are financially out of date. There must be an auditorium which can, with a success, reap the full benefit of a success. But, if the dwarfs are now financially impossible, the giants can also be difficult. The vast Stoll Theatre in Kingsway, which cannot really be in a bad position since the successful Strand and Aldwych Theatres are close by, succumbed in 1958 to the housebreakers after a chequered career as opera house, theatre, cinema, and home of ice shows. Its end had a curious distinction. It was packed not only by Shakespeare but by Shakespeare at his earliest and worst. In 1956, at Stratford-upon-Avon, Sir Laurence Olivier and Vivien Leigh had volunteered to appear in the shambles of *Titus Andronicus*, a play so drenched in the gore of outrageously melodramatic horrors that it is very rarely acted at all. Peter Brook's production was a most ingenious concealment of the crude atrocities, while Sir Laurence, as Titus, brought out all the latent merits of a tragic role in which there are embryonic hints of King Lear. It was midsummer and the town, full of foreign visitors, was much intrigued by the presence of a masterly production and performance of a long-spurned play which could be described as a reject on the fringe of the Shakespearian canon. So the doomed Stoll faced disaster with a curious triumph. A newspaper headline might have said, " Bad Play Makes Good."

It is a condition of the proposed edifice on this site that it shall contain a theatre, somewhere in the bowels of the new and more profitable pile which is to arise. It seems likely that in urban centres, where land values become continually more costly and building development must soar high in order to guarantee greatly increased rental value, the theatres of the future may have to be incorporated in huge business premises. The London County Council is always strict about fire precautions and plentiful exits and those difficulties will have to be met. But a theatre needs no day-light and can be reasonably embedded in another structure with modern methods of ventilation. After all, there is nothing particularly new in this. The Criterion Theatre, a popular centre of light comedy, has been living below ground since 1874, without losing the sanction of the L.C.C., presumably because it has exits at the back as well as on the Piccadilly Circus front.

A stranger in London who is eager to do some playgoing cannot rely, as a rule, on finding continuous policy at many London theatres. Changing tenants arrive with their private fancies and cater for different tastes. But some guidance can be given. We still have no National Theatre, but a site on the South Bank has been allocated and awaits the pleasure of the Chancellor of the Exchequer to guarantee the bill. This, for suitable building and endowment, will now run to two million pounds; at one time the job could have been decently done for a quarter of a million. What money as well as time we have wasted by delay, even after the foundation stone had been royally laid in 1951! Charles Dickens was campaigning for a National Theatre more than a century ago.

Meanwhile there is the " Old Vic," also south of the river, but easily reached over Waterloo Bridge, and with more parking space for cars near by than is usual in any London place of entertainment. The " Vic's " astonishing history has been an epitome of London life. First as the Royal Coburg it housed, in late Georgian times, Shakespeare and spectacle; it declined into a rough and rowdy music-hall of the Victorian poor and was rescued for the cause of temperance with concerts and with opera that was genuinely popular and hardly grand because it had to be so cheap; then Shakespeare was brought in humbly and stayed to conquer, with sometimes lustrous casts. In the nineteen-fifties the thirty-six plays in the First Folio of Shakespeare's works were given in their entirety. When that work of devotion was completed the programme was broadened to include modern and foreign classics. Whatever is on view there is likely to be a play of historic interest and dramatic quality, sometimes including star players of the highest rank. This is made possible by the readiness of such players to go there at much less than normal salaries and secondly by a substantial subsidy from the Arts Council. The reputation of the " Vic " stands high in Europe and America and its foreign tours have been rewarding in money as well as in repute.

Opera dwells at Covent Garden, struggling financially owing to the enormous cost that opera always entails, but well supported. There may be ballet there instead and the prestige of British ballet, which rose with exhilarating speed in the decade after 1945, has been well sustained both there and at Sadler's Wells, a house set on the first slopes of the hill to the north of Central London. The future of Sadler's Wells has been in question. But there is enough determination among the local authorities to sustain its life. Something of theatrical value will be found on the road to Islington where for nearly two centuries Londoners have absorbed the hygienic waters of the well and the stronger liquors usually preferred by lovers of a show.

There are other theatres where the kind of fare provided is

predictable. The Coliseum, being properly colossal, despite the curious spelling of its name, will have a large musical; so probably will the Palace, which is too palatial, as a rule, for the straight play, though unlikely visitors of distinction have called there, including the German Company of Brecht.

The Palladium has nothing to do with the goddess Pallas on the safety of whose image the security of ancient Troy was supposed to depend. That image became a symbol of defiance. " The Palladium of our liberties " was the kind of phrase that the eighteenth century liked to roll out. Pallas Athene was also the Grecian goddess of wisdom, but London's Palladium is not a fountain of philosophic drama. It is a gigantic music-hall where there is usually " a show " with a star comedian, since the old music-hall of separate individual turns has been largely replaced by a mixture of song, dance, and comedy with some such title as *Light Up The Town* to cover the whole. It is a warm-hearted house where everyone arrives expecting a good time. All are ready to laugh before the curtain goes up and to " roll in the aisles " when there is the slightest cause for such demonstrations of delight. Another big house far better suited to musicals than " straight " plays is the Saville, close to the Palace. It has its own brand of elegance and a particularly spacious underground foyer where one feels that one ought to be in evening dress. But few are, and there is no need to be.

Passing from the immense to the intimate, one must mention the Westminster, close to Buckingham Palace and fairly to be described as the Queen's Local. It was once a chapel, but became a small, cultured, and comfortable theatre in 1931. Its handicap is to be rather off the theatre map; but its life under various managements has been extremely distinguished and I should say that its record for plays of quality has been as high as that of any of the London playhouses. It has frequently lost money for its tenants, but it has never lost quality. Farther out is the

Lyric Theatre of Hammersmith, remote, but atmospheric, scarcely famous for comfort, but with a place in the affections of many. Its main success has been with small musicals, either in revivals, like that of *The Beggar's Opera* which ran for over 1,400 performances under the direction of Sir Nigel Playfair, or modern like the operettas of Sir Alan Herbert or, now, of Sandy Wilson and others who bring wit and melody up to date. At the many central theatres not mentioned there is much less predictable fare. Their plays vary with the taste and fortunes of those who rent them. In this class the Globe is most likely to have a successful modern play.

That actor of wide experience as well as of superb voice and presence, Henry Ainley, once said to me, " We players must remember that the theatre changes every five years." He may have overstated the rapidity of alteration, but there are considerable shifts of style within a decade, and in the years just past, with the purchasing power of money much reduced, economic necessities brought other adjustments. For example, there was a time when the audience at a comedy of manners expected three changes of scene in a three-act play. There would be an agreeable start in Lady Swithering's country house with a view of the grounds through the french windows; then a move, perhaps to a villa by the very blue Mediterranean; and last a return to the panelled library of the Switherings' house in London. These would be attractively presented at reasonable cost. Even the versions of Shakepeare staged by Sir Herbert Beerbohm Tree at Her Majesty's Theatre with a full spread of canvas and " supers " galore for the crowd scenes and the pageantry were able, up to 1914, to pay off their production expenses in three months. That sort of splendour is impossible now, and the modern comedy is nearly always confined to a single set. For some kinds of plays it is a modern practice to have one composite scene: the stage is divided into sections, showing the edge of the garden, a

room in the house, and possibly another room beside it.
There may also be a glimpse of a room upstairs. This is
fairly costly to build, but, once built, it is static and there is
no need to have scene shifters kept expensively at work.
But the result has a messy look and important episodes may
have to be acted in one of the side sections, which is a
handicap to the players and may give some of the audience
an awkward and even a limited view of the proceedings.
The absence of the three different scenes for a three-act play
is something of a loss; but it is inevitable.

The West End audience has abandoned any standards of
" dressiness " and, while the seats grow more expensive,
those who occupy the most costly may arrive in sweaters
and slacks. That playgoing may be freed from any obliga-
tions of " full fig " has its advantages: it makes the theatre
part of ordinary life and not the venue of a social occasion.
Since, during the nineteen-fifties, there was a vogue for
plays with sordid surroundings, squalid characters, and
ugly goings-on, it would have been absurd to expect that
their audiences should dress up for themes and spectacles
so drab. The titled were out of the cast and the tramps were
in. Why wear a dinner jacket to see a play called *Live Like
Pigs*, which was in fact as grubby in its characters and events
as was its title? Why wait for Godot in fine linen, since
this much discussed drama was all talk in tatters? The
flood of American plays and films into the West End provided London with plenty of low and violent living in the
Deep South and a clammy mixture of blood and sweat and
sex. There was abundance, too, of the argot and the antics
of New York gangsters and their molls, much too of the
vocabulary of American service-men, a lingo both limited
and lurid. When I was attending this Dustbin Drama, with
its slum scenery and sleazy circumstance, I thought that it
might well be attended by people dressed to suit the subject,
in their oldest and worst, or even in overalls.

On the credit side of the London theatre today must be

put its greater liberty of subject and courage in acceptance of themes from which our parents would have turned away in timid disgust. The old idea was that we went to the theatre to be taken out of ourselves; the members of a new public were eager to be taken into themselves, however ugly or dismal might be the spectacle of that interior. The escapism of the smart and trivial three-act comedy in which the players had to be well tailored or sumptuously gowned members of the idle-rich class narrowed the field of available subjects and made the theatre something of a toy. Now it is much more a workshop and the almost total surrender of his powers of censorship by the Lord Chamberlain has enabled the students of sexual licence or perversion to pursue their studies on the stage as well as in the bookshop. The charge of being non-adult no longer applies.

Since the theatre changes radically, if not in five years, at least in twenty, there is almost certain to be a reaction before very long against the view that nothing is real unless it is repulsive; that opinion was strongly held in the nineteen-fifties by playgoers who liked to think themselves " progressive." There is no likelihood of economic conditions permitting the old kind of variety and amenity in the scenery employed, but I should not be surprised if the present licence in the use of what used to be called filthy talk were to be less employed. It may be that " plays for Puritans," to use a Shavian title, will become fashionable, if not for reasons of austere morality, at least because audiences have been forced to realise that the bawdy can be boring and that it is possible to be intelligent without rolling continually in the muddier deposits of psychology.

One thing seems to be certain. The London theatre has weathered the successive storms of competition by silent film, talking film, sound radio, and television. It was always said, as each of these rivals arrived, that this would be the end of the costly, inconvenient Living Theatre. But the collapse has not come. There is evidently something magnetic and indestructible in the appeal of the actor in person. The more that invention could do to mechanise our recreations, the more that could be gained from the press-button or knob-switching appliances of the stay-at-home and television age, the more likely, even the more certain, seemed the eventual closing of the West End theatres. But it has not happened. The foreign tourist wants to see our theatre and not our television; so does the native who has come up to London on holiday or on business with holiday pleasures attached. So do the coach parties. The Londoner himself, though, as has been said, he is not the determining factor in the very long run of a play, is still a considerable playgoer, even at midsummer when to be immured in an auditorium has least attraction. Then the playhouses may be as well attended as in the darker, shorter days.

To me the call seems strongest in those autumn evenings when there is a flicker of red sunset to be seen as you look west down Piccadilly—there are some exquisite mixtures of pink and violet and grey to be caught by such a glance—and when the lights come up like a skyful of stars in the windows of the tall office buildings. There is a huge emptying of humanity into streets and stations at that time and myriads are bent only on the quickest possible escape to the suburb. But the West End has a beckoning finger and there is an invitation to remain which a minority will happily accept. A town lit up is a town at its best, as anybody can discover by taking a turn on the Thames Embankment on a clear night. London has greatly improved the decorative side of its illumination, especially along the river. There is a liveliness in that air which quickens the appetite for illumination of another kind, the spark of personality at large upon a stage. There is something unnatural about going to the play in daylight. It is the autumn and the winter blaze of theatre fronts that best calls one to the age-old and enduring make-believe within.

Make-believe is the kind of phrase that infuriates some earnest playgoers; and rightly so, if make-believe be all. The down-to-earth (and even down-to-the-drains) Social Realists have had a good innings at the Royal Court Theatre in Sloane Square: and not recently only. For thither I went in my boyhood to attend the Socialist and Radical realists of the Edwardian epoch, Shaw, Granville-Barker, Galsworthy, hard-reasoning middle-aged men rather than explosive young ones. They wrote with their reformist brains as well as their rebellious feelings and wrote far better than the much-discussed Angry Young Men of the late nineteen-fifties. But these have given satisfaction to their own side and their work made the necessary contrast with the theatre of illusion and escape.

The theatre as refuge from reality, not its mirror or its platform, will probably continue to be the prevailing choice of the up-in-town London visitors who are the props of theatrical finance. The younger writers practise a drama of make-revolt instead of a pastime of make-believe. There is nothing new in that. It has been going on since Euripides and Aristophanes, one with poignant tragedy and the other with uproarious comedy, attacked the war-mongers of ancient Greece. London cannot claim to be an Athens, but in its theatres there is still the voice of the heretic as well as of the entertainer. To each playgoer his own. Theatre Street should have its many mansions.

8

Thoughts by the River

One may not doubt that, somehow, good
Shall come of water and of mud:
And sure the reverent eye must see
A purpose in liquidity.

Rupert Brooke

He had to restrain himself from accosting some passer-by with
the question, " Say, but is this little wet ditch here the Historical
River Thames? "

H. G. Wells, " Mr. Britling Sees It Through "

I love any discourse of rivers.

Isaac Walton

8

LONDONERS are not alone in taking much for granted: but, because of their vast numbers massed in a petty space, they have more reason than most to be agreeably surprised when certain things which would be easily done in a small community are successfully contrived for the benefit of millions. Chief among these is the emergence of unlimited water at any hour when they turn a tap; they do not, and could not, get it for nothing, but the fact that nearly seven million people living in an area of 576 square miles with a few little hills and no rain-gathering mountains can use a daily average of 330 million gallons of water—and have used as many as 468 million gallons on a hot summer day—should make them aware that a remarkable service is being rendered.

The providing body for the region is the Metropolitan Water Board. But the M.W.B. can only supply what Nature provides; the storage, piping, and cleansing is theirs. The raw material is laid on, as to five-sixths of this gigantic flow, by London's two rivers, the Thames and the Lea, neither of which is large by Continental standards; the Lea, indeed, is quite a minor stream. The proportions of the supply are two-thirds from the Thames, one-sixth from the Lea, and one-sixth from wells; these are mostly in the chalk and greensand of Kent and the south-east stretches of the London rim of hills.

The Thames as it meanders down from its pleasant Gloucestershire springs through the still lonely water-meadows west of Oxford and then into the suave, well-timbered reaches of Berks and Bucks is, for most, no more than a pleasant spectacle; one thinks of racing oarsmen in their slender craft and of dallying baskers in their solid punts and dinghies. A pleasure steamer chugs by: fishermen sit pensively vigilant. London is reached and the Thames becomes tidal and commercial, yet gracious here and there until it is completely urbanised. Then, too, it becomes exciting with its prospect of towers and spires on land and of its life-giving traffic on the water. There is great delight of the eye: there is also essential service of the body, millions and millions of bodies. If anything went wrong with the Thames, London would first pant and then perish, since water is the prime necessity of a great city. One must remember also that in times of drought the Thames is itself a tap turned off; the M.W.B. cannot draw on the river at all if the flow over Teddington Weir, close to which are the most important intakes of London's water, falls below the stipulated level of 170 million gallons a day. This fall has occurred in dry summers, but not, strangely, in 1959.

After heavy rains and with some melting snow the wintry scene will strike the viewer as watery enough. Miles of Thames Valley meadows may be flooded and the river instead of gliding starts to gallop. A water shortage then seems a ludicrous thought. But the floods, impressively shown on the screens of film and television and seeming to make compendious oceans, can vanish in a day or two. The English climate is incalculable. An old tradition calls February the fill-dyke month: then the skies should be teeming and all the ditches should be brimming. But I am writing this at the end of February and London has had only one sprinkle of light rain during the last four weeks. During that time, in the M.W.B. area, we have been served with nearly 10,000 million gallons of water, two-thirds of it coming out of the Thames. For the London conurbation there are other water-supplying bodies coping with the needs of the fringe. But the M.W.B. has to keep the taps running from Ware in the north to Sevenoaks in the south and from Sunbury in the west to Southfleet in the east.

Since the Thames and, to a much less extent, the Lea can surprisingly do the job, if they are helped by well-planned storage, the problem has been the provision of gigantic reservoirs. Motorists as they drive in or out of London through Staines, on the chief south-westerly approach by road, curse the place. They may be held up a long time before they can cross the bridge over the river and I would not care to be a resident of the main street of Staines where the cars are lined up for exasperating waits with brief, jerky moves forward while frustrated drivers mutter and moan. But the levels round the town are the cistern of London and without Staines London would be parched and very soon plague-stricken.

One does not see these lakes so essential to London: they are hidden behind protective banks and this makes Londoners still less aware of the service they render. That a new Staines reservoir with a capacity of four and a half million gallons was completed in 1947 is the kind of news item that gets a line in the papers. But its importance is as great as that of miles of warehousing for the storage of food. From the huge unroofed reservoirs near the river the water is passed on for a double process of filtering, chiefly through gravel and sand, and then for chlorination. Thus disinfected, it is pumped onward into London where it mainly passes through small covered reservoirs set, if possible, on high ground. The Thames, having large towns like Oxford and Reading on its banks, is by no means a limpid, lucent, unpolluted river and it is always a marvel to me that this murky source of supply can both meet so much demand and serve health so efficiently. Chlorinated water has not the same fresh flavour as natural spring water; but the chemists have got rid of any strong taste of chlorine and London must be prepared to lose a little in savour to gain so much in freedom from bacilli. In other parts of the world one may be naturally nervous of sipping a glass of water: in London there is maximum security.

LONDON'S RIVER

. . . with Cleopatra's Needle.

The value of wells is bound to diminish as building of suburbs eats up ever more miles of agricultural land. For development of this kind replaces with streets and drains the spongy ground whose absorbency carried the rain down to the subterranean deposits on which the water-gatherers used to draw. The more we build, the more water do we need for the new houses and the less water do we get from under the soil, since the rainfall is increasingly swept away unused into the sewers instead of finding its way into Nature's cisterns. Moreover, the higher our standard of living, the more taps are turned, the more plugs are pulled, the more baths are filled, and the more motor-cars are washed. At present Londoners are using more than fifty gallons a day per person of all ages and that figure is far more likely to rise than to sink—not that anyone would want a decrease of washing or of the industries that are great consumers of water. Though a Londoner looking at the river in the centre of the town may contentedly decide, even when the tide is low, that there is still plenty of Thames left, that stream has got its work cut out and more work coming to it. The reason why the river in London is not so broad as it was in earlier centuries is not only the building of embankments: we have already deprived it of more than 300 million gallons every day before it reaches the town, whereas our ancestors " milked " it only with a few small water-mills.

The Lea, or Lee, as the Water Board prefers to spell it, seems almost a midget set to cope with the giant problem of meeting the demands of East London and its expansion into Essex. Rising near Luton, its course, running east and then south, is only fifty miles long. Until it is over-whelmed by London, it has the appearance of a modest country stream. It suffices to stock a series of big reservoirs, but it is having to be helped out from the west. Across and under London there is now being laid a new pipeline which will convey eastwards millions of gallons from the Thames basin. The Wandle running into the Thames from the south and giving its name to the Wandsworth area survives as a minor river and may be seen from the railway after leaving Waterloo. But it is not a source of water supply.

I used the word " survive " in this case because so many London streams have perished by submergence and have dwindled to the dismal status of a drain. As a result London is full of watery names with no water to show for them. Westbourne and Bayswater to the north of Hyde Park are memorials to the West Bourne which descended from Hampstead Heath by the way of Kilburn, where it was the Kil Bourne. It was known farther on as Baynard's Water; hence our Bayswater. Crossing Hyde Park it was the raw material of the Serpentine and on its way to the Thames it flowed through what is now Sloane Square; there its remnants are still present in a conduit to be seen above one's head when one is waiting for an underground train in Sloane Square Station. The Tybourne had a similar course from the Hampstead watershed, coming down to Hyde Park, where it named Tyburn, the famous place of execution, and then going east into what is now Stratford Place (the Street Ford) and south to the Green Park. It was then the source of an old reservoir known as " The Bason."

Further east was the Fleet, which can be seen at its source on Hampstead Heath. It trickles out of the Vale of Health pond, just below the summit where is Jack Straw's Castle, and works through the other Hampstead ponds. After that, in these times, it goes underground as a drain. Its old meanderings took it towards King's Cross, where people crossed it at Battle Bridge, and so on to join the Hol Bourne at what is now the big east-west thoroughfare of Holborn. Then, broad and navigable in its old state, it passed through the defile which became Farringdon Road, on to Ludgate Circus, where it gave a name to Fleet Street, and so, by way of New Bridge Street, into the Thames.

The creek which carried the Fleet into the Thames was

13—L

once a much-used harbour. A petition of the fourteenth century, concerning the working of a tide-mill, said that a dozen ships with merchandise were wont to sail up to " Holebourne." But the waterway was continually being choked with rubbish and filth. Now it is one of London's more valuable sewers and is, of course, invisible as well as sanitary: but for many centuries it was an open drain, and as such, being so conspicuous and central, it constantly reappeared in English literature. Our modern phrase " the name stinks " was certainly applicable to this receptacle for

> " hair of measled hogs,
> The heads, houghs, entrails and the hides of dogs."

To that observation of Ben Jonson's must be added Alexander Pope's reference to the dead dogs carried along on the " disemboguing streams " of the Fleet Ditch,

> " than whom no sluice of mud
> With deeper sable blots the silver flood."

We may note that early in the eighteenth century Pope could still call the Thames silver. Disembogue is an impressive word for the debouching of a river into larger waters and need not imply filth: but there is something in the look of it which suits the history of the Fleet, so innocent a rivulet on Hampstead Heath and so repellent a culvert by the time medieval London had done its worst with it. In its early life Fleet Bridges took people from the City to the Strand and drinkable water also; one of them carried wooden pipes of which there is a picture in the Soane Museum in Lincoln's Inn Fields.

The City has still its Walbrook, a short street between the Mansion House and Cannon Street Station. But the waters of that brook, once navigable, were roofed over during the fifteenth century. In South London the Effra came down from Norwood to Dulwich, where it is still visible for a short stretch. The lost rivers of hereabouts have a musical

echo in their names. The Falcon Brook rose near Nightingale Lane in Balham, the Neckinger contributed to Ber-
mondsey's marshes and passed a spot called St. Thomas-a-
Watering, and the Tygris, with its Mesopotamian echo,
was a rivulet—or some think a canal—in the Elephant and
Castle district. Even when London seems most drab to the
eye, there is, thanks to its place-names, music in the air. As
far as nominal values can enhance the urban scene, there is
something of Chaucer's London left in Southwark where
the Canterbury Pilgrims gathered and in the surrounding
region where nightingales still sing at least in the map and
Elephant, Castle, and Tigers are the relics of romance.

The most conspicuous of London's old rivers is that
called the New River, which earned its title as an original
creation in the reign of King James I. It can be followed
on its way from the springs of Amwell and Chadwell in
Hertfordshire to Islington and Clerkenwell, where now,
close to the historic Sadler's Wells and the new theatre and
opera house referred to in the previous chapter, are the
headquarters of the Metropolitan Water Board. The district
of Canonbury, close to Islington, has recently become
fashionable with writers and artists: the eighteenth-century
houses and Canonbury Tower, a genuine antique, give it
distinction. The Tower was the home of Sir Francis Bacon
for nine years and of Oliver Goldsmith in the following
century: its panelled rooms are of great beauty and our own
time has added a small theatre where one of the best of
London's amateur companies, the Tavistock Players, keep
up a steady flow of production; this must seem pleasantly
appropriate to those who believe that Sir Francis found
time to be Shakespeare's hand as well as his own learned
brain and busy lawyer-self. At Canonbury there is also a
pleasant public garden where one may sit by the waters of
the New River, the work on which was completed during
the nearby residence of Bacon at the Tower.

The river itself was a blessed innovation for Londoners:

it was the first fully planned and properly executed effort to give them a clean and regular water supply. Hitherto they had depended on small streams and wells; that there were plenty of them is shown by the number of London place-names ending in -well. But wells may dry up and in a town without proper drainage they may be fouled. Water was also drawn from the Thames. As early as 1580 one Peter Morris had leased an arch of old London Bridge, through which, owing to the narrowness of the arches, the river ran with a speed dangerous to boatmen. To tap this power Morris erected a waterwheel with pumps attached, an ingenious arrangement for its time, and this was able to guarantee a certain flow to the neighbouring parts of the town. But how much the craft of filtering was understood by Morris we do not know. It is hard for us to understand why the Londoners of that period and earlier were not poisoned by the water they drank. People develop immunities from diseases in time, but the path to such safety is sacrificial.

The methods of water supply elsewhere in the town were elementary. Water, most of it from the Thames, was brought in wooden pipes to conduits. These were cisterns, sometimes decorated and good-looking affairs, whence the citizens could serve themselves by personal cartage or by the employment of professional water-porters. These men had a patron, St. Christopher: their guild or trade union, which for a while resented the incursion of the New River as being damaging to their livelihood, was called the Brotherhood of St. Christopher. They had a renowned thirst for other liquors, stronger tipple than that which they carried and distributed. One of them, called Cob, is to be met in Ben Jonson's comedy *Every Man in his Humour*. He carried water for a merchant called Kiteley and refreshed himself at the sign of " The Green Lattice." Conduit is a word which survives in Conduit Street, between Regent Street and Hanover Square, and was several times used by

Shakespeare in his liquid similes and metaphors for blood and tears. Juliet, when weeping, is scolded by her father with an allusion to the cisterns of the town.

" How now! A conduit, girl? What, still in tears,
Ever more showering? "

There is " a conduit with three issuing spouts " cited to describe the bloody mutilation of Lavinia in *Titus Andronicus*.

The vessels used by Cob and his kind were called tankards; they resembled those with which we carry fuel to our domestic stoves. A contemporary picture of the Little Conduit in Cheapside in 1583 shows the pipes linked with the cisterns and a number of huge tankards waiting to be filled. The bearer, having drawn his load, then went on his rounds like a milkman in our time. As supplies were improved, by pumping from the Thames and later by the arrival of the New River, people of sufficient means could contract for a private service by pipe. An agreement of this kind made in 1616 arranges for a citizen and his wife to have " a pipe or quill of half an inch bore to the service of their yard and kitchen by means of two swan-necked cocks for twenty-eight shillings and sixpence a year." That was a considerable sum of money then, probably equal to a water rate of £20 today.

During the early years of King James I there were long negotiations for a new, properly piped water supply by means of an artificial river drawing on the valuable springs in Hertfordshire. The arrangements dragged on. The country landlords were, as happened again during the coming of the railways, resentful of invasion and innovations. A few progressives readily gave permission for the river to pass through their land; others had to be coaxed and compensated. The driving force behind the New River plan was a man from Wales, Hugh Myddelton. He was a worthy representative of the new capitalists who

were known as Adventurers or Projectors. They realised
that investment at home might be just as serviceable and
possibly in the end just as rewarding as was the fashionable
purchase of shares in the piratical maritime ventures raiding
the Spanish galleons and islands in the West Indies. We
get much of our information about the social scene of the
time from the comedies written for the stage: in these it was
the habit to satirise the new rich and make great game of
their acquisitive operations. Naturally the writers seized
on and caricatured the extreme types of greed; but there
were examples of the new wealth very different from
Jonson's Sir Epicure Mammon. The latter was a grossly
sensual consumer of luxuries, probably ill-got. Men like
Myddelton had vision, energy, and served London to its
great benefit at more risk than profit to themselves.

Myddelton was also a mining engineer, working on
deposits of silver as well as of gold in Wales. In North
London he and his associates created the New River which
had been dug over a course of thirty miles, ending at what
is still New River Head on the slopes above Clerkenwell.
The Round Pond into which it flowed no longer holds
water, but the bowl is there and beside it in the land surrounding the headquarters of the Metropolitan Water
Board is the stump of an old windmill used for hauling up
the water: since dependence on wind is so hazardous, this
was replaced by horse-power and later on by steam. But
the base of the windmill is still prominent. The pioneer
Myddelton is rightly honoured with a statue in Islington
Green and by the naming after him of a large square close
to the New River Head. He was made a baronet by King
James, who had shown good sense in taking up shares in
the New River Company and so helping the work to proceed when the City financiers were growing nervous. There
were no quick returns, but prosperity came in the end.
Incidentally it is still possible to buy shares in the New
River Company, but they will not be an investment in water

nowadays. The M.W.B. took over the water and the company now owns land and houses, some of which have a distinctive decoration of chocolate paint on the ground floor and cream above it.

King James had good reason to curse his investment on a winter day in 1622. He was riding to his favourite sport of hunting at Theobalds in Hertfordshire when his horse stumbled and threw him into the icy water of the stream he had helped to create: however, he suffered no more than acute discomfort and he drew his dividends at last. His son, King Charles I, exchanged his inherited shares in the New River Company, called the Royal Moiety, for a perpetual yearly payment of £500. This was called the King's Clog and it is still paid to the Crown by the Water Board as a successor to the New River Company.

The new buildings of the Board incorporate a particularly fine room which has the panelling, plasterwork and decorated roof brought from the old Water House of 1693. King William III looks down from a painted ceiling; one feels that King James I or, better still, his able and persevering projector and adventurer, Sir Hugh, might have that place of honour. It is of him I think when I see his waterway threading North London (it is still used as a channel for distributing water from the Lea) and adding to this service by its tranquil decoration of the urban view. It is a great thing to have been the founder of a city: it is no small thing to have invented a complete new river which was to yield, along with minor and belated profits, a major gain in public health and convenience.

With water thus handy the seventeenth-century spa of Sadler's Wells was able to do more than serve salubrious drinks. It became a water-garden and a popular resort. First there was " Miles's Music Room." In the following century a theatre was added by its proprietor Rosoman— still remembered in the naming of Rosoman Street—and the water was used for grandiose aquatic spectacles. The district became an important suburb of the entertainment industry and among its famous names was that of Grimaldi, London's beloved clown of the early nineteenth century, whose appearance in the pantomimes and harlequinades of the time drew the city to the Wells.

Later Edmund Phelps made it a Shakespearian shrine; in his eighteen years of tenancy (1844–62) he produced thirty of Shakespeare's thirty-six plays and, what is more, he ended the long-established practice of hacking the texts about, rewriting them, and adding happy endings to the tragedies. After Phelps had let London " see Shakespeare plain " there was a change to popular drama whose old-style actors of the grand manner were immortalised in Pinero's ever-popular comedy, *Trelawny of the Wells*. " The Wells " was reopened as " a temple of the Bard " and northern sister-house of the " Old Vic " in 1931: but it was discovered that North London was not as eager for the classical drama as was the South Bank. So Sadler's Wells began, with much better support, to specialise in opera and ballet, and that continues. But " straight " theatre was restored for some weeks in the summer of 1958 when the visit of the Moscow Art Theatre crowded the house at prices well beyond the ordinary and drew enthusiastic tributes as well as packed audiences. The acting was in Russian, but as three of the plays were by Chekhov, whose work has been so much produced and also read in Great Britain, that was no hindrance to appreciation.

The visitor to Sadler's Wells Theatre will be met by a vast cubic block of flats on the other side of the road. This may please some tastes in architecture, but it seems out of place to me. Surely this piece of land should have remained a piece of history too. A local tavern with the name of Shakespeare over its doors does something to make this old fountain of health, pleasure, and the arts, as well as of water, aware of its old and colourful existence. The Water Board maintains its old " New River House " address as well as its fine chamber of 1693: there is here a nice stretch of open space and room to breathe. The theatre preserves its service of eye and ear with opera and ballet at the highest level. The names of a square and streets near by are loyal to Myddelton and the rural springs of Amwell and Chadwell on which he drew. But the building of flats of today is a stark assertion of another age. It is natural to wonder what the nineteen-seventies and -eighties will say about the vogue in construction favoured by the nineteen-forties and -fifties.

I have wandered far north of the Thames, to which a return is due. It is an undeniable fact that Central London has missed in the past great opportunities to make fine use of its river, especially on the South Bank. The Thames should supply views as well as feeding reservoirs and providing the raw material of harbourage and wharves. In 1951 the Festival of Great Britain made an exhibition area of the reach round the Charing Cross railway bridge, but most of the structures were temporary. The Royal Festival Hall remains, admirable in its acoustics and scope of accommodation. The main concert hall holds 3,400 people and its stage will take a choir of 250: its restaurant and amenities take the eye. Its exterior is not so much admired. If this is to be an Arts Centre, with a National Theatre adjacent, the Festival Hall will not be easy to fit into a unified design.

Where this piece of public land ends at the side of Waterloo Bridge we have a National Film Theatre which caters for the minority who want pictures of special quality or rarity and, because it is quite small, the house is usually well filled by " the passionate few." The title " National " may give a wrong impression, especially as so many of the films shown are foreign ones. But it is an excellent thing to have that kind of specialised cinema where exhibitions of the world's best film work are constantly on view. Close to it is a pleasant café-restaurant and the garden beside it is a useful spot for midday rest and refreshment, with benches amid well-kept flower-beds and a fine reach of the river in front of one.

A little farther east, on the north bank of Blackfriars, there has recently arisen a riverside theatre within the precincts of the City, that old enemy of the players and now their helpful ally. The address, Puddle Dock, is realistic; the name of the playhouse, the Mermaid, is romantic. It was created by the single-minded energy and devotion of Bernard Miles, an actor with a wide range of successful activities in everything from Shakespeare to music-hall. He had previously had a little private theatre of his own in the garden of a house in St. John's Wood, but the possibility of something more public and especially of something on a spot so rich in Tudor theatrical history drew him to the Thames and to the area of Blackfriars where Shakespeare and his colleagues acquired a sister-house to the Globe Theatre across the River. He and his wife, known as Josephine Wilson on the stage, devoted themselves to untiring labours of persuasion and organisation. The City granted a niche on the riverside; many City and other firms were coaxed into helping with funds; " the profession," as well as the public, came in with their own subscriptions and with the advantage of their names in raising subscriptions from others. The building once begun was pushed forward during the winter of 1958–9 and by May the house was ready for action.

It was always part of the policy that it should serve City workers, so early evening performances were planned to suit their convenience and to provide an interlude between leaving the office and catching the homeward train. Provision of a meal, as well as a seat, at moderate prices was also deemed essential to the creation of a playhouse with its own atmosphere, amenities, and social attractions. So the playgoers could sup where they had been spectators and enjoy the panorama of London's river as well as of English drama in all its aspects. Bernard Miles planned according to his belief that the English are far too much divided in their entertainment. He hated the separation of the cultural from the common and of the highbrows (now called egg-heads) from those of shallower skulls. His programmes were to be such as all could appreciate. So there it is. Miles went to work like one of the Jacobean Adventurers and Projectors. As Myddelton, with his obstinate refusal to be daunted, gave London its New River, so Miles gave the old river its new theatre and was immediately successful.

The view from his theatre-restaurant, set immediately above the water, as from any other perch by the Thames, was bound to include at low tide an expanse of mud. Some believe strongly that a tidal river is a curse to a city because the shores must be exposed in an unsightly way. That is one of the arguments which have been put forward for a Thames barrage. For more than a century there have been suggestions and lately there have been detailed plans for keeping the tides out of Central London. One scheme was for a bridge with sluices to be built just above the entrance to the main group of docks; there would be locks and canals for bringing in the smaller vessels which wanted to come upstream. The Thames above the barrage would thus be tideless and slow-running and the mud-banks would not be exposed.

It may happen. Meanwhile " mud in your eye " is part of the scenery. Personally I do not find it so offensive. To see the run of the tides is a reminder that London is a sea-port. If so much of its wealth has come that way, we must take the rough with the smooth. There are some who welcome the low-tide beaches, even if mud and not sand makes up most of them, because they can delve there for the astonishing variety of articles that get stuck in the silt. When the river has receded they go scouring for these bits and pieces and some valuable stuff has been found, including relics of past ages which contribute to our knowledge of social history.

In one way, and that a very important one, we have vastly improved the riverside scene. That is in the lighting of it at night. The Thames is now ribboned with silver after dark and the view up and down stream from any of the central bridges is a superb one. The ugly, squalid patches are obscured and the great floodlit buildings stand out with seeming splendour even though they be those which the critics of architecture deem second-rate. There are two ways in which to see London's river at its best: one is from the south on a day of sunshine when the Portland stone of the Wren spires in the City stands out with the radiance of jewellery. The old churches have been given many complimentary names; W. E. Henley's description of Fleet Street's St. Bride's as a " madrigal in stone " is probably the most often quoted. Whether you think of them as music or as gems, their beauty, in the right light, is a thing to lift the heart.

The other way is to come out from a concert in the Festival Hall or from a play of Shakespeare's at the " Old Vic " and see the illumined river-line while the music of instruments or of poetry is still sounding in one's ears. This is to see London as a Cinderella who has been released from her kitchen rags and has been sumptuously dressed for the Prince's ball. A town lit up is a town set free. The age of electricity has had its architectural as well as its illuminating value. The huge Battersea Power Station is truly functional: it proclaims power and so does the much later pile on the Southwark shore. There is no nonsense about these massive lighters of our lamps and the nocturnal kindling to which they contribute is a decoration as well as a utility. In the fairy tale a magic lamp gave power to Aladdin and now power gives lamps that work their magic on the riverside night.

9

Games in Season

The brazen throat of war had ceased to roar;
All now was turned to jollity and game.

John Milton

What works, my countrymen, in hand? Where go you with bats
and clubs?

W. Shakespeare

A time there is for all, my mother often sayes,
When she with skirts tuckt very hie, with gyrles at stool-ball
* playes.*

Sir Philip Sidney
(Stool-ball was an early form of cricket)

9

For the lovers of games there are Meccas in plenty. For cricketers, and students of cricket, Lord's is the premier place of resort. This is indeed a lordly spot, but the name is derived from a man and not from a class, a clique, or a nobility of aspect. Mr. Thomas Lord prepared his first site for the game, which had much advanced in favour during the latter half of the eighteenth century, in 1787. That was on land which is now Dorset Square, lying between the Baker Street and Marylebone railway stations; he moved his property farther out into St. John's Wood twenty-five years later and the first game was played there in 1814. Great martial events were happening in Europe, but wars then were not of the " total " kind that we know. For England, behind its " moat defensive " of the seas, military campaigns were more like matches played away by touring teams. So Miss Austen could write her novels of a countryside for whom Napoleon was only distant news, and not discussed at genteel soirées, while Mr. Lord could proceed with his cricket pitches and the players could go into action on a tented field of a peaceful kind. Lord's was just coming into its own when the Battle of Waterloo was being fought.

It became the headquarters of the M.C.C. (Marylebone Cricket Club), which was established as the ruling body of the game. Thus its imposing building where the members gather is not only a grandstand: it is a Parliament as well as a Pavilion, with its own sessions of the Cricket Cabinet by whom the laws of cricket have been made and may be altered; here the senators of the sport sit in conference and here national teams are chosen. It is the kind of place in which pious offerings to the heroes of the past are naturally made. First among these and most eminent of the Victorian players was Dr. W. G. Grace, who began as a Boy Wonder and ended as the Grand Old Man (or Mogul) of the game. In 1864, at the age of fifteen, he played for the All England Eleven. When he was sixteen he had played twice for the Gentlemen against Players and for England against Surrey. So one may rightly bow one's head at the Grace Memorial Gates to the terrible child—terrible at least to bowlers— who was to continue for some forty years, magnificently bearded and as formidable in mien and conduct as in batsmanship, to be the Ancient of Cricketing Days. His doctorship was of medicine and not of laws or divinity and he is said to have interpreted the laws of cricket with an occasional eye to his own advantage. One may wonder what became of his patients in the summertime? Well, what became of Dr. Watson's patients when he was out and about with Sherlock Holmes? They had to wait on more important business.

When I first went to Lord's from Hampstead, I paid a penny fare on my Green Atlas horse-bus from Swiss Cottage; I paid another sixpence to go in. So, with the existing prices of ginger beer and buns, I could have a long day of delight for about fifteen pence. The entry now is half a crown (with a reduction for the non-adult) and the charge is raised for Test (International) matches. Quite high prices are charged for seats in the various stands. At an important match there is always a good attendance and for a Test match a " capacity " gate, which is now well over 30,000. That does not compare with the 60,000 at a big association football match or with 100,000 for the Cup Final to be seen early in May at the vast Wembley Stadium. But it is significant of an astonishing fact. To Europeans, except the Danes, cricket is slow; to Americans, except in one academic niche in Pennsylvania, it is an unbearable dawdling. By the English it is constantly said that first-class cricket has become, owing to defensive and safety-first methods of play, deplorably dreary and a mockery of its old gay self. Yet, while we grumble, we go. Many county teams have suffered from the poorness of the spectacle which the all too cautious batsmen provide; but any big contest at Lord's or even a county game with leading teams involved draws a big crowd. The lure is still there; we mutter, but are magnetised.

No doubt it is the circumstances as much as the cricket which draw people to Lord's. Given a fine day, there is a splendour now rare in the drabness of most urban goings-on. The trees of the surrounding gardens remind us that St. John's Wood is here a district still timbered. There are coloured flags in the air; the great Pavilion, with its fine collection of old cricket paintings, has more than the size and something of the atmosphere of a major country house. (Entry to it is only obtainable by accompanying a member of the M.C.C. during Test matches or of the Middlesex County Club during county games.) The grandstands, which have had to be steadily increased in recent years, live up to their name and are duly grand. But nowadays, if the seats are crowded, the public can settle on the grass round the rim of the arena, just as on a village green.

There are village greens handy for those who like the sport in its simplicity. " Go down to Kew in lilac-time, it isn't far from London," was a famous line of a poet who went out of fashion, Alfred Noyes. Kew Gardens are a flower-lover's Mecca and a tree-lover's too; they are one of the fine legacies of royal expenditure which have passed into public hands; those who obey the beckoning rhyme will pass by Kew Green with its church and exquisite surrounding of period houses. There, at a summer week-end, the game goes on as Gerald Bullett, a less-known but fine poet, sang of it.

" Patient, dramatic, serious, genial,
    From over to over the game goes on,
    Weaving a pattern of hardy perennial
    Civilisation under the sun."

At Richmond, farther on, there will be the weekend cricket played by amateur clubs of high standing. And there will be seen, as in a village meadow, a more spirited type of batting than one may encounter at Lord's.

There is no longer the old elegance of costume, which once made a dress parade or a top-hat muster at the fashionable matches. But there is a sense of being in the world centre of a game that maintains its fascination over the English-speaking world from the West Indies to New Zealand. Perhaps the batsmen, penned down by the new kind of leg-side bowling and by the fielders close around them, seem unable to attack and to send the ball skimming to the boundary as of old. Where is Mr. Jingle's Dickensian gusto for the game, " Warm—red-hot—scorching—glowing "? Ply your questions and you get the answer from the clicking of the turnstiles.

Cricket seems to be indestructible—at least here. The days of high dignity, when Old Jolyon Forsyte of John Galsworthy's family saga took his place on the Pavilion benches, may have gone. To laugh or be noisy then would have been like brawling in church. Now, when there is a West Indian team visiting, their coloured supporters arrive in clamorous and rip-roaring spirits: they cry aloud, they scream with mirth, and they actually behave as though enjoyment were not a shameful thing and better concealed. The great Doctor would have sadly wagged his beard at such levity; he might perhaps have demanded discipline, like a judge ordering the court to be cleared. Laughter at Lord's! The cricketing ritualists may frown: but I have found it an agreeable change.

Across the river, in Kennington, early home of Charlie

Chaplin, is the accurately entitled Oval ground, the egg-shaped headquarters of the Surrey county eleven. That team has been frequently victorious during recent years and had a succession of wins in the County Championship. If cricket's House of Lords is in St. John's Wood, at the Oval we have its House of Commons. The proletarian atmosphere is perhaps less conspicuous now: the levelling-up process of the Welfare State has mitigated class distinctions and has made Londoners " much of a muchness." So the Oval is not quite the popular playground that it used to be, with clamorous and free-spoken commentary provided from the ringside seats. When I first went as a boy to the Oval there was plenty of audible praise and censure of the players: it could be acid in content but it was jovial in manner. The bars were well patronised and some of the absorbers would come back to their benches with their tongues loosened and their sense of humour overflowing, like the froth of beer on their lips.

There was then a resident poet called Craig who had his lively cricket verses printed and was allowed to go round the ground selling them for a penny or so for a sheet. That sort of thing could not have happened at Lord's. Now Lord's has lost some of its old decorum. Not only West Indians take liberties once unimaginable. I have even seen a spectator, a youngster with a vast beard, stripped to the waist on a warm day and sun-bathing in this semi-nudity: he was, I suppose, an undergraduate since he divided his attention between the game and a learned textbook. The sight would have horrified the old brigade of St. John's Wood patrons, especially as this happened at the Oxford and Cambridge match which used to be very " dressy." Meanwhile the Oval has gained in the propriety of demeanour which has diminished at Lord's.

In any series of Test matches the final and possibly decisive game is played at the Oval in mid-August. It was once the belief that nobody of any social importance stayed

ST. JOHN'S WOOD

. . . once a grove of the goddess Aphrodite as well as a meadow for
the cricketers.

in London after the beginning of that month. There was a thing called the Season, and that was over when Goodwood Races came at the end of July. Were there not yachts to be sailed at Cowes and shooting-parties on the northern moors? But the departure is not so complete now. The " somebodies " go to work like the " nobodies " and may be kept in Town, even in August. Also this is the high season of holiday tourism. There are few big cricket matches at Lord's after July, while the Oval with its busy August programme will be well attended.

Its scenery is far from sylvan. The great squat cylinder of the gasworks beside the ground reminds the Oval spectator that a city must live by its fuel. It is true that the frequenters of Lord's are aware of electricity in the making, but the provision of that utility does not so closely dominate the setting of the stage. The new grandstands at Lord's have increasingly concealed the foliage of the pleasant and very costly St. John's Wood houses which have gardens adjoining the ground. There are huge cubes of flats continually replacing the single homes, but " The Wood " is still, in patches, an arboreal suburb.

In the early part of the nineteenth century there was a tradition that the villas then built there were used for the maintenance of pretty ladies by gentlemen of wealth who had their major establishments and their possibly less attractive wives elsewhere. From the centre of the town it was a short, convenient drive in a " chariot " or later in one of Mr. Hansom's new two-seater cabs. Thus " The Wood " became a grove of the goddess Aphrodite as well as a meadow of the cricketers. The altered housing of today has not turned the district into a dull one. But if the pursuit of raffish hours is conducted in flats instead of in the old Georgian villas the new pleasures have lost the old atmosphere. Chambering in Number 100 of something-or-other Court has less romance than the aforetime love in a cottage with a curtain of lilac and laburnum between the stucco and the street. If St. John's Wood is no longer Joy's garden suburb, it remains the Mecca of the cricketers with no danger of an overthrow. Any effort to build on that turf would be regarded as an insufferable crime. There will always be a green islet where the shades of Mr. Lord and the Regency bucks, who had a fancy for batting as well as for boxing, can flicker to and fro, like those Lancashire stalwarts so hauntingly remembered in verse by Francis Thompson.

Lord's is also a resort of the tennis players. By that I mean the fanciers of the venerable indoor game, with its almost heraldic vocabulary, which has come down to us from the Middle Ages. The number of courts with the right architecture are few throughout the country and, therefore, the players are few too and the game is not " news " to the general public. Its successor lawn tennis, regarded by the mid-Victorians as a suitably gentle and lazy-paced exercise for country clergymen and long-skirted young ladies, has made a triumphant progress in public favour. It has also become so strenuous an exercise that only a thoroughly trained and superbly fit performer can win the highest prizes. It is a solecism to call this widely popular game tennis in the presence of an enthusiast for the royal and ancient indoor diversion. He insists that it is lawn tennis and may curl his lip a trifle as he mentions this upstart. But a huge public is now interested. The court provides an arena of limited size so that the viewers on the spot cannot compare in numbers with the spectators at cricket or football matches. But television has brought the lawn tennis champions to the eyes and even into the hearts of millions.

These " aces " remain nominally amateurs, but their dedication to the game throughout the year, either on grass and hard courts out of doors or on wooden-surfaced courts indoors, has to be so intense that they could not possibly reach the summits unless they either had large private means or were sustained by liberal expense allowances. It is generally agreed that, with lawn tennis a full-time occupation, the situation has become ridiculous. Here are performers who can draw paying spectators on a considerable scale. Why should they not be properly paid? Professional players are few and there is no such interest in professional matches as there is in professional golf competitions. The expense allowances have been carried so far that " amateur status " has become a piece of nonsense in many cases. I was recently informed by one of the " high-ups " of the game's administration that, when he sympathised with a player who had been put out of action for some months by an accident, the latter replied that he was well insured against loss of income. This from an unpaid amateur was charming.

The leading male players often become professionals when they are established as champions, but they have to earn their very high salaries mostly in America, where a touring " circus " of those experts can draw tremendous gate-money. The best entry to this golden but inevitably rather brief life of glory is by way of London's Wimbledon, headquarters of the All England Lawn Tennis Club, which used to include croquet in its attractions. The Championships, held there towards the end of June, bring the finest players from all over the world. It is rare for an English competitor to win. The Americans, and now the Australians, have, with occasional exceptions, been dominant for many years. The rewards of victory may be glory only: or they may include an invitation to " go pro " and join one of those money-spinning " circuses."

The Central Court at Wimbledon is as capacious as may be and terrific contests are assured. A " men's singles " match, running perhaps to five sets, can be a greater test of physical and nervous endurance, as well as of accuracy and brilliance in stroke play, than is provided by any other game. It offers a superb spectacle. But there are difficulties in the way of seeing it. Seats for the Centre Court are very hard to obtain. Also, since the Championships occur at the time of year when London may be having one of its infrequent spells of blazing weather, the close-packed arena, with the sun beating on it and any breeze unlikely to penetrate, can be indeed a hot spot. At Lord's there is a big open space where the air may enter. I would rather be there in a heat-wave, even if the cricket be slow and dull, than at Wimbledon where the game is certain to be extremely fast with the excitement continuous instead of sporadic or absent altogether. I must confess myself a TV Wimbledonian.

London has no golf course deemed worthy of a major championship. That is inevitable because of its abundance of clay soil. Golf was born on the sand dunes where rain soon disappears, the turf is springy, and the ball, instead of being cupped in mud, sits up invitingly. Clay is either baked too hard in a heat-wave or sodden and " stolchy " after rain. London's nearest thing to a championship course is at Walton Heath, high on the North Downs, heathery, handsome, and quite difficult enough for most. It is hardly, however, a London course. Much closer in there is Royal Wimbledon which has its soggy patches on the low ground after rain, but is remarkably rural, and even heathery, considering its nearness to the centre of things. The Royal Mid-Surrey course at Richmond is agreeably level for those whose advancing years make a mixture of climbing with club haulage burdensome. It has a good deal of gravel as well as clay: it is extremely convenient to reach, either by train or road: and it provides a spacious prospect of Thames Valley parkland with the fine trees of Kew Gardens and the Thames to mark its borders with beauty.

Those who are more concerned with easy-going and scenic amenity than with the vast length and difficulties of a championship course are well suited there. The view from the far side of the course across the river and the water-meadows to Syon House, the historic home of the Dukes of Northumberland, can be a comfort even to those whose hearts have been broken by their own inadequate performance as golfers. This is *rus in urbe*, only a dozen miles from the centre of the conurbation, with hardly a house in sight, and when in sight, as at Georgian Isleworth, gracious. The birds of the countryside have made it their London address. Partridges breed there, pheasants drop in from Kew Gardens, herons rise from the river banks and go on their stately way to Richmond Park, swans may be in flight, and kestrels hovering overhead. To a golfing bird-watcher this must be a course on which to lift the head is all too easy. Mid-Surrey is strangely named since it could not be nearer the London edge of that county: but at least it can claim to be a surprising piece of countryside considering its position.

Within twenty or twenty-five miles of the West End there is an abundance of attractive and renowned golf courses: they lie mainly to the south and west, in the sandy stretches of Surrey, where the pine-woods give plenty of opportunities for pullers and slicers of the ball to rub up their forestry. Worplesden, Woking, Sunningdale, Wentworth—to a golfer's ear these names are sweet and musical invitations. Important competitions are held on them, as also at Walton Heath, already mentioned, and at Moor Park and Sandy Lodge to the north-west. The Ryder Cup, contested by the leading professionals of the U.S.A. and Great Britain, has been fought for at Wentworth, whose beauty takes the eye while its length may afflict the limbs of all but the " young tiger " class of player. But the rulers of the game are conservative and abide by the old belief that golf and the seaside are inseparable partners. So the Open Championship always compels a trip to the beaches in Scotland, in the North of England, or on the Kentish coast. But London golfers have no cause for grumbling: they have their chances of pleasant park golf very handy and of a more exciting round among the heather-edged fairways not too far away amid the conifer copses of the Home Counties.

For Rugby football the venue is Twickenham. Sport-reporting journalists have long been addicted to a venue, a word restricted to Fleet Street and to fields of play. We do not have a shopping venue in Oxford Street or a cultural venue in Chelsea. But let us keep it for Twickenham, whose river banks have much to commend it as a summer suburb but whose nearness to water and water-meadows is no blessing later on. On a misty day of December or January the visibility at the headquarters of the English Rugby Football Union may become very poor during the dull droop of a short mid-winter afternoon. Twickenham's playing turf, however, is well drained and trimly kept. The enormous stands inevitably darken the ground when the sun is low and therefore there is better entertainment assured when England is playing Scotland in the brighter, longer light of March than when Wales is visiting in January. The worst match for a clear view, but also one of the best for a rousing game, is the meeting of Oxford and Cambridge in mid-December. There is room for 50,000 spectators on the terraces and in the stands and on the big occasions a full house is certain.

It is commonly complained that Rugby football is not providing as lively a spectacle as it used to do. It is sadly obvious that here, as in the case of cricket, the powers and skills of defensive play have overcome the capacity of the attackers to open up the game and score in the old way. It would have seemed both incredible and deplorable to players of previous years that the English fifteen in the winter of 1958–9 was never able to score a single try and yet had the comparatively good record of two drawn games, one victory, and one defeat simply through the scoring of penalty goals. Rugger, as it was earlier designed and achieved, used to offer a breath-taking spectacle of players ribboning out across the field and passing the ball to the speedy runners on the wings: now defensive measures manage to strangle this form of attack before the sprinters get a chance to show their paces. Many a wing three-quarter may spend a whole game with only the barest chance to get off the mark and go flashing for the opponents' line. But, as in the case of first-class cricket, while the crowds natter about a game that has gone wrong, they roll up as of old for the major matches. They grumble, but they go.

The largest sports arena in London is the Stadium at Wembley, between London and Harrow. The Romans would have called it a Colosseum, but it is innocent of killings. Built for the lavishly organised Empire Exhibition of 1924, it became the venue of the association football Cup Finals thereafter. The Cup Final is now so vast an attraction that it has to be played for early in May after the football season is over, since there would be disastrously small " gates " for other matches on that afternoon. This event is televised with the result that millions of " the fancy " stay at home to see it.

My impression is that the home-viewers have a better idea of the proceedings than some of those who are on the spot. This is because the Stadium is so vast that a seat at the top of one of the stands inevitably provides a distant bird's-eye view, and not all of us are as long-sighted as hawks. I have watched a Cup Final from one of these lofty perches and I felt, as I felt many years ago when watching all sorts of armies and personalities in an Empire Pageant there, that the performers were tiny articles, not human beings. Or was I surveying diminutive leaves in the wind? The Stadium is also used for the Rugby League Final (a professional game, distinct from the Rugby Union games at Twickenham, which are strictly amateur) and at various times it has housed torchlight tattoos and an American-style rodeo, as well as international association football matches.

But the Wembley day of days is that of the Cup Final, when the vast arena could be filled twice over, despite the temptation to see the affair for nothing and with no discomfort of a crowded journey by taking up an arm-chair seat beside " the telly " at home. The Cup Final is the climax of a knock-out competition for which amateur teams can enter as well as all the leading professional sides. The preliminary rounds provide feverish excitement, especially as sides of small reputation are sometimes able to be Davids and overthrow the Goliaths of great strength and fame. But these gallant giant-killers usually fade out before the Final, for which, as a rule, two First League teams arrive with a tumultuous following from their own towns. The bedizened supporters splash a paint-box on the London streets with the mufflers, rosettes and comic hats displaying the colours of their teams. The winning eleven go back in glory with a whole city cheering their advent with the treasured Cup. The British are supposed to be stolid folk, but football rouses them to frenzy and " Cup fever " is an annual and astonishing malady. " Like the hectic in the blood it rages."

To a detached observer the fuss about the Cup seems out of proportion. In any knock-out competition there is a large amount of luck. Injured players cannot be replaced by substitutes and so a side suffering by an accident which puts one of its members out of action, as frequently occurs and sometimes quite early in the game, has to struggle on with ten men against eleven, a handicap likely to be as fatal as it is unfair. There is more real merit in being top of the First League than in winning the Cup, since the supremacy in the various Leagues is decided by points accumulated in a series of forty-two matches played between the end of August and the end of April. Thus to have plodded on and maintained a steady level of success is a better test of excellence than is a journey through the rounds of the Cup matches in which a fluked goal or a physical mishap may determine the issue. To be top of the League is much: but in public opinion winning the Cup is more. Football crowds are not composed of logicians.

Wembley also houses in a great hall many other athletic events, including ice hockey, which is the fastest and toughest of spectacles, boxing, which is the bloodiest, and indoor ice-panoramas, which contain the most exquisite examples of grace, speed, and poise combined. In the Wembley Pool there are swimming contests. Ice hockey is not a native game of the English, and Canadians are often dominant in teams with English names. It is played at such a pace that one's eyes dazzle at the furious charges, tackles, and counter-thrusts. The fact that players offending against the rules are put publicly on a kind of stool of repentance until released to enter the game again gives the crowd a chance to boo: this is childish, but the players have to be he-men of the hairy-chested type and, though padded against physical calamity, they must have the hearts of lions as well as the speed of deer to earn a living on the flashing skates of this whirlwind kind of combat on a surface which certainly offers no featherbed to the fallen.

The effect of television on sport is remarkable because it turns forms of contest in which few once took any interest into spectacles of wide public concern and excitement. That is particularly true of swimming races whose winners used to live in a small world of their own and now are heroes and heroines of nation-wide renown. The astonishing thing is the speed with which fame of an almost global kind can be achieved in the aquatic contests. The Olympic Champions are often teen-agers. One would think that the swimmers' muscular power and capacity for endurance would increase until they were well into their twenties: but that does not happen. The boys and girls reach the top of their form and travel far and wide to compete in international events and in the Empire or Olympic Games at sixteen or seventeen. Miss Judy Grinham, a London girl who astonished the world with her prowess, retired before she came of age. Swimmers, it seems, are too old at twenty.

There has been a similar growth of public interest in athletics which may also be attributed to television with its power to give a wide intimacy to a sport that once seemed specialised and remote. Events that used to attract hundreds rather than thousands to the track-side, where the leading runners and jumpers could once be fairly described as " known to their own," are now watched at home by myriads, and sometimes by millions. What goes on at London's White City Stadium has nation-wide coverage. Thus the names and personalities of the champions are familiar to countless people who were hitherto unconcerned with the rivalries of the record-breakers and the split seconds of the timing they achieve. Both swimming indoors and athletics, out of doors but sometimes nocturnal and flood-lit, began to reach hosts of evening viewers, with the result that the names and personalities of Pirie, Bannister, Chataway, Shackleton, and others were no longer on the lips only of a clique. The big meetings and team matches, quite apart from the occasional high spots of the Olympic and Empire Games, are now very well publicised and a series of track events at the White City will be strongly supported. It has been discovered that transmitting part of a play to millions by television from the theatre may not use up the play's possible audience but can actually increase the box-office patronage of the public whose attention has been thus drawn with curiosity quickened. And so it is with most sports: the ability to watch them on the screen stimulates in many the desire to see them " on location," as the film-makers say.

An additional spurring of interest has come from the astonishing advance made in the skill and endurance of the runners in all countries, especially in the middle-distance and longer races. Forty years ago the covering of a mile in less than four minutes would have seemed a fantastically remote possibility. But such has been the improvement of methods of training and technique that running a mile at the rate of a minute for each quarter is no longer a surprise. At the White City one may expect on the great days to see a mile race in which several, if not all, of the entrants break the four-minute barrier. There is no sport in which the mastery of the masters has been more strikingly developed. Records are made only to be broken within a month or two. There must be an end to it, but it is a fair guess that the timing of the mile will soon be reduced to three minutes and fifty-five seconds—or even less.

Consequently, while certain games which I have mentioned have lost their sparkle, track athletics have risen sharply in their spectacular appeal and power to fascinate. One need not go out of London, except for some international events, to see the makers of the new world records. Many foreign teams come here for matches so that at the White City one is often attending what the statesmen would call a summit meeting. It is a wonderfully fine spectacle to see, in the last lap of a long race, one of the contestants suddenly pull out a staggering burst of speed and break away from the field with the flash of a hundred-yard sprinter, coming away from the others as though a cork had exploded from a bottle. The ancient Greeks celebrated and immortalised the prowess of their athletes with the highest honours of sculpture and of poetry. The runners' years of victory are inevitably brief: surely we owe to their prowess the preservative power of the arts. In the hour of triumph they have publicity enough: for the decades that follow there should be the odes of a British Pindar or the stone and bronze of inspired sculpture to counter time's sad erasure of their names.

The Inner Man

Whilst you are upon Earth, enjoy the good things that are here (to that end were they given) and be not melancholly.

John Selden

A dew-bite and breakfast, a stay-bite and dinner, a mummet and a crummet, and a bite after supper.

Anon.

10

IN any city of great size it should be possible to eat as you like, however exotically, if you have the money to pay for it. London does not fail on that score. In its various sectors it provides every kind of hotel and restaurant, from the majestical type which Arnold Bennett described in two of his novels as Grand Babylon and Imperial Palace to the minor guest house whose pride is to boast of " separate tables." (Boarding-house is a term no longer used, but it had a frankness not apparent in guest house where the visitor is not entertained for nothing: but there is a popular snobbery in these matters and many a feminine worker has to be called a hostess nowadays in whatever form of activity she is taking your money.) The best in London's catering kind is by no means cheap, but it is unlikely to be more expensive than what is offered elsewhere in establishments owning similar pomp of architecture and circumstance of service. On the whole the class of customers known as Ritzy can pay the same and get the same whatever capital they visit; the entertainment provided in the London Babylons will be up to the standards (and prices) customary in that category. Variety of choice is assured since many styles of national recipe and cooking can be accommodated where there are big kitchens and big staffs.

Then there are the West End restaurants, such as the Ivy and Caprice, which have a special appeal to people in the news and to those who read the news or want to be in the news. They have a cultivated standard of feeding as well as an attendance of gossip-column personalities among their regulars. In the luxury class (admittedly a rather loose

definition, since who shall decide where luxury begins?)
prices are based on the fact that many of the patrons are
" expense account " folk whose bills either go direct to the
business or are set against private income when tax relief is
being claimed. A more interesting point about the nourishment of any nation is what you can expect for a moderate
range of spending.

The intellectuals and aesthetes habitually prefer every
country to their own in matters of art and there is a similar
snobbery of the alien in estimates of food and flavour. It is
assumed as indisputable that all English food will be dreary
and that anything served on the other side of the Channel
will be wonderful. This assumption, which I challenge,
has now been much more widely tested since holidays
abroad have become a vogue with myriads of British people
who until recently regarded their own seaside as the summit
of their vacational ambition. With the inflationary flow of
money wage-earners who had hitherto regarded Calais or
Boulogne as their limit in Continental experience save up
for flights and voyages and may be discovered grilling their
bodies, sometimes to a painful extent, beside the coasts
called azure or discovering that the Danube is not always
as blue as it has been painted. Since the cost of living has
recently been lower in Spain than elsewhere and air travel
by charter plane can also be cheaply arranged, the Balearic
Islands and the Costa Brava have been cutting in substantially on Blackpool, Scarborough, Margate, Weston-
super-Mare and other British beaches for possession of the
holiday money. But there is now so much holiday money
that the home resorts will still be packed from the end of
June until the middle of September.

Thus those of the British who are accustomed to enliven
their food by pouring bottled sauces on top of it are made
aware that similar results in " pepping up " may be achieved
by inserting garlic and spices within it. They are being
introduced to a new range of flavours, but the number of

15—L

people afflicted with some gastric upheaval in the process appears to be considerable, and the risks should be borne in mind by those explorers of Europe who make an industrious search for national specialities on the menu. A friend of mine, recently returned from Spain, replied to my polite queries about his inner health by saying that he had kept well by observing three conditions. He never drank water; he never touched a salad; and he always went to the best hotels which had international standards and cuisines, thus enabling an escape from the greasy and oily Spanish dishes to which British livers are unaccustomed and may be rebellious. Another friend, who had stayed more thriftily in Majorca, said that nearly all his party had been internally smitten. At least we can claim on London's behalf that the milk and water are safe and that you can eat a salad without expecting your stomach to become a rumbling cavern of distress. That, it can be argued, is a negative kind of praise; but the measure of security implied is none the less important. No holiday is enjoyable which involves the embarrassments, and possible agonies, of a continual search for what the Americans so accurately call " a comfort station."

On the positive side, those of limited income, whether natives or travellers, can find in London all things for all palates; Chinese and Indian restaurants are plentiful and usually economical. The European nations have long been amply represented in Soho and still are, but this cosmopolitan corner has ceased, with very few exceptions, to be the resort of the student class or of the middle-class diner-out who has to count his shillings. There is another corner of international catering in Fitzroy Street, to the west of the Tottenham Court Road, where the costs and quality of a meal vary considerably. It has been complained that the London suburbs, with Chelsea excluded, have been dismally deficient in restaurants; but there are changes here. In my own area there are now several restaurants proclaiming their Indian, Spanish, Polish, or Italian dishes. They are not imposing or spacious but at least it is possible for the locals to feed locally without being limited to a tea-shop or café which closes early or to the kind of snack bar where baked beans are deemed the essential remedy for British hunger.

As to native offerings, there is proper reliance on the fact that British grass, nurtured by British weather, makes British meat as good as any in the world and far better than that raised in less moist and temperate zones. One cannot, of course, generalise about the probability of getting a tender and succulent steak or chop beyond saying that the chance of doing so is much better in London than in most other capitals. There are steak-houses advertising that their supply of beef comes from the East of Scotland which is famous for its livestock. The British are much addicted to the simple methods of the grill and there is no better method if the raw material be of the first class. The essential flavour is there: titivation is not needed. Nations who specialise in sauces and spices are forced to do so by the poor quality of the food on which they are working. It has been said of the French that they are compelled to be good cooks because their food is so bad; since the farmers are avaricious the meat is ill-fed. The English have not been under similar constraint because their herds have excellent pasture and their fish comes from the comparatively cold waters of northern Europe. These, as the Scandinavian fish-restaurants so admirably prove, yield sea-food of far higher quality than does the warmer Mediterranean. The blazing beaches of the coasts called Blue and Brave are kindly to the exterior of the human body and to the bathers in sea and sunshine, but they are less kind to the human interior, especially when fish is being served.

It must be admitted that the Londoner, like most of his race, is, apart from the " choosy " intellectuals, not acutely food-conscious. It was once sung of the Hundred-per-cent American,

"In art I pull no highbrow stuff,
I know what I like and that's enough."

Substitute victuals for art and that holds true of the average Briton and of the nourishment that he takes in the home or the restaurant. It must be remembered that during the last forty years the British have undergone ten years of bitter warfare including intense blockade by submarines; thus a mainly industrial nation, largely dependent on imported foods, had to put up with what it could get, which was often both scanty and unattractive. The available foods in the lean and hungry years were of a starchy kind and there had to be much dependence on the home-grown potato. This tuber can be a helpful form of stomach wadding to supplement a tiny sliver of meat. When young it can be delicious. But later in the year it is a lumpy article which needs to be chipped and fried to be in any way appetising. When fats are severely rationed this frying becomes impossible and an old, boiled potato can only be welcomed by those who are very empty and must fill themselves with something in order to keep going.

Those years of a diet limited in size and dreary in quality inevitably left the British with the notion that any food will do and it takes a long time to outlive that conception of catering. Moreover, the rationing went on for some years after the end of the last great war. But at last the customer was able to choose freely instead of having the shopkeeper's intimation that he was lucky to be served at all. London has now outlived the period of meek acceptance of anything that was going and the consequent disinclination to be fussy about food. So standards have risen sharply.

The eating habits of the British have undergone a sweeping alteration during the last sixty years. The reduction of quantity, at least among those who could afford to eat largely and lavishly, has been astonishing. When we look at the menu of an Edwardian banquet, or even of a private dinner party, we are staggered at the array of courses, with the entrées after the fish, the addition of game to joints of meat, and the partition of the huge list of dishes by a sorbet or water-ice which would stimulate the palate for renewed gustation. Such Roman feeding is unthinkable now: if we were forced to lose the habit by the pressure of the wars and by the labour problems involved in serving a Lucullan repast, that is nothing to regret. It used to be said by doctors, and no doubt truthfully said, that more people killed themselves by over-eating than by over-drinking. The wealthy who had enjoyed, or undergone, a London season with this kind of hospitality were accustomed to retire to native or foreign spas later on and submit themselves to liver-packs and other restoratives of normal bulk and vitality. There is little or none of that now.

When the wartime regulations put a strict limit to the number of courses they imposed a discipline which the free conditions of today have mitigated but by no means reversed. The fact that people are now more health-conscious than food-conscious and much more alarmed by the prospect of obesity than were their grandparents is another reason for the disappearance of the banquet. Even in prosperous homes there is not the labour to cope with a number of courses and there is always the influence of the high price to work against the gastric indulgence. Consequently the Londoner who takes a civilised interest in feeding discreetly is now an *à la carte* customer at his restaurant: he selects one main dish with a small preceding appetiser, smoked salmon if he can afford it or potted shrimps if he has to be careful, and possibly cheese after. Women often end with the main dish and go straight to the coffee.

The excellence of native fish has already been mentioned. It is true that London's fish has mostly to be brought up by rail or road and to go through the central fish-market of Billingsgate with some loss of primal freshness. The fish

will have even more flavour where it goes more directly
from the harbour to the kitchen and the table, as happens
in Scotland. None the less, I doubt whether any capital,
outside Copenhagen, where the fishboats land their cargo
actually outside the fish restaurants, has anything of better
flavour than English or Scottish salmon in the early part of
the year. Especially delicious are the sea-trout, which are
more delicate in taste than their larger cousins, the salmon.
These arrive around midsummer. The shellfish too can be
exceptionally good. The ancient Romans found English
oysters to be the best, and the oysters from the river mouths
near London in the Kent and Essex estuaries have not
betrayed the Roman estimation. The lobsters are brought
with sufficient speed from the coasts to London to have
retained in full their tang of the sea. Then there is the grilled
Dover sole, which, at its best, has few rivals in the categories
of white and flat fish.

The fact that so many London women go out to work in
offices has enormously increased the amount of feeding
away from home, especially at midday. Hence the number
of café-restaurants and snack bars to be seen everywhere.
In most big businesses there is a canteen, probably subsi-
dised by the firm and so able to provide a substantial meal
at a very moderate price. But it is natural to want a change
from the workaday premises during the luncheon break.
Consequently the canteen, though it offers a bargain, is not
attractive to all. Business firms frequently offer luncheon
vouchers as an additional payment to the ordinary wages
and salaries: these provide a modest escape from income
tax to the recipients, who, if they got the money as part of
their ordinary receipts, might have to pay tax on it. The
vouchers, for that reason, are limited in value, since otherwise the Chancellor of the Exchequer might prohibit the
practice altogether. But, modest as they are, they are a
considerable incentive to the office girl to go out at midday
to a sandwich bar or one of those small restaurants which

have personal names such as Pam's Pantry or Anne's Kitchen.

The male workers usually prefer the back room or upper room of a public house, where more substantial meals are provided, with drinks available, at very reasonable prices. The service is not to be described as dainty: the luncher can expect to be called " dear " by a buxom woman who has not studied the refinements of the waiter's craft and there may be somewhat limited space between the tables. But the patrons are not there in quest of daintiness: they would rather have Worcester sauce than daffodils on the table. The public house is not concerned to make much profit on its food; its primary function is to sell beer and spirits, and if good cheap catering brings more customers to the bar that is sufficient reason for laying on a three-course lunch at a price considerably less than that of a single course in more exalted surroundings. For round about five shillings a public-house luncher can do himself quite well; the meat, in my experience, is usually good and well cooked, but I must admit that the vegetables reveal a too common British reluctance to consider them as anything but routine extras, in whose preparation spending trouble is deemed an unnatural waste of energy or time.

Good, solid puddings are out of fashion as a result of the general eagerness to diet for the sake of one's bodily statistics. But those who still like a slab of apple pie or suet pudding will get them thrown in with a plate of soup and a cut from the joint at what is justly called " popular prices." But, as I said, there is no " class " about this kind of catering, just solid value for money. There is a genial type of slapdash service laid on by waiters or more probably waitresses with too many tables to serve. The prevailing spirit is that which Thackeray's Mr. Yellowplush described as " all lacy ally and easy pleasantry." Few of the public houses find it worth while to serve anything but sandwiches at night, since the labour costs would be too high for the

number of potential diners. It is a midday traffic. But there
are some exceptions to that both in the suburbs and the
centre of London. There is a notable one at the north-east
corner of Leicester Square where the ancient brewing house
of Whitbread has celebrated the founder's name with an
elegant type of bar below and restaurant above. The whole
house, with its curved front, makes a handsome exception to
the assortment of curious and contradictory building styles
which the industry of entertainment has grouped around
the Square's central statue of William Shakespeare as he
stands, serene and undismayed, amid the star-clustered
temples of the cinema.

That area of London has now become a centre of stool-
or-stand feeding at bars redolent with the fried onions in
which Hamburgers are always described as " smothered."
America's world conquest of Show Business has brought
in its train a victory for the popular American " eats "
whose savoury quality is not to be denied. I have thought,
when visiting the United States in the past, that the comparatively poor got a better bargain at their range of prices
than did the big spenders in the costly restaurants. The
young Londoner, who has made the journey " Up West,"
is obviously an addict of the sizzling hamburger, of which
there is abundant provision. The " burger " part of the
word has now become in Leicester Square the generic term
for any similar dish, whatever its contents. The snack bars
proclaim their succulent company of beefburgers, tongue-
burgers, cheeseburgers, and even beanburgers. It may surprise some of the patrons to discover that a hamburger
is not made of ham.

The replacement of the meal by the snack is a result of the
high cost of living. It is probably a delusion that better
value is obtained from eating sandwiches than by going to
one of the various types of Lyons' houses and getting a
regular meal. There is, however, a common belief that one
is saving money by sitting on a stool instead of at a table.

But it is quite easy to spend in a snack bar as much as would buy a square meal in a public house. However that may be, it is perfectly obvious that to perch over hamburgers and hot dogs is a very popular form of session in the neighbour-hood of Leicester Square, where several caterers, with a range of establishments, meet all tastes with savoury dishes whose presence, as I noted, eloquently proclaims itself to the nostrils as one passes by. The long-established firm of Lyons sticks to tables, chairs, and solid fare, whether it be in their self-service tea-shops, in those middle-price palaces called Corner Houses, or the marble halls of the Trocadero. The Corner Houses offer many kinds of meal in their separate and sumptuous departments, from the grill to the egg-and-bacon room and from the Brasserie to the " Wimpy." They have food shops in the main hall for the " take-it-away " customers; they are well fitted and clean and they are never extortionate.

There is the trouble with the Corner Houses that they are overwhelmingly popular: hence it may be difficult to find yourself a corner. But that speaks for good service: the Lyons public is not that of the snack-bar youngster type. It is made up of people who want a square deal and a good sit-down and know where to get them.

During past years there has been a great increase of coffee-drinking in London. Coffee became popular during the last war when tea was tightly rationed: it provided the mid-morning relief or stimulant which had previously been supplied by what is commonly called " char." That word seems to be a confusion of the old Chinese Tcha, an aristo-cratic tea, with the stronger Indian leaf which provides the English with their strong, black " cuppa," whose presence now seems indispensable in most offices, workshops, and wherever building workers are engaged. That it suits the requirements of charwomen, those props of London office life, has nothing to do with the derivation of the name. But

coffee has become a much more favoured rival to " char "
that it was a generation ago.

The coffee mainly used in London homes and business
premises is of the made-up and " instant " kind which can
be of good flavour as well as very convenient. In the snack
bars the apparatus known as Espresso turns out a coffee
which is usually consumed " white " and well sugared.
The coffee bar has taken the role in London life of a
students' gathering-place and is sometimes also, less fortunately, a rendezvous of rowdy youth. It is a curious fact,
established in many a police court, that the origins of
trouble are not in spirit-drinking among the adolescent but
in the coffee bars whence the sons of Belial emerge not
flushed with wine but flown with insolence and coffee.

But this does not mean that you will run into rowdiness
in the normal " Espresso." The coffee bar has largely
replaced the milk bar whose arrival in London in the
nineteen-thirties inflicted a considerable shock on those
regarding the word " bar " as properly associated with
alcohol alone. The presence of a milk bar in Fleet
Street struck a certain number of journalists to the heart.
One of them, the witty as well as percipient essayist Robert
Lynd, remarked to his companion on passing one of these
newcomers, " Look, James, just look at those milk-sodden
faces." Naturally the coffee bars vary in the quality of the
food they serve according to the kitchen space and the
managerial skill available. They can be excellent and very
cheap. For example, just before writing this, I had in one
of them an excellent three-course meal for three and sixpence. Admittedly, one had to sit rather cramped, but the
same fare would have cost at least three or four times as
much in a mid-London restaurant of no special renown.

The London public houses, whose midday meals I have
mentioned, are of such widely different kinds that it is
impossible to cope here with a subject on which whole
volumes have been written. There are the historic taverns,

THE GEORGE INN, SOUTHWARK

What remains is nearly 300 years old and can be said to have the
bouquet of its years. A good meal can be obtained there.

some of which such as the George in Southwark and the
Cheshire Cheese in Fleet Street have already been noted.
There are the East End and riverside taverns which many
like to visit. Such houses as the Prospect of Whitby at
Wapping and Charlie Brown's in Limehouse could hardly
be called normal places of London refreshment. They cater
for the sightseer as well as for the local with a thirst. A
small establishment, very central and not usually mentioned,
is the Red Lion in Duke of York's Street, running into St.
James's Square from the north. Within its tiny space it
presents an exquisite specimen of the old style of London
public-house adornment with its polished wood fittings
and glass with decorative scroll-work. This is indeed a
collector's piece. The artist John Piper has described with
the greatest admiration the wonderful patterns engraved
on bar doors, windows, and mirrors. In his view
" preservation is imperative, for its wealth of bevelled and
brilliant cut glass is almost unrivalled."

In some cities to visit the markets is a common exercise
of the tourist. In London it is not the markets themselves
that are attractive but their surroundings. In a vast conurbation a central market is an anachronism and a nuisance,
since it means that a huge amount of stuff has to be carted in
and out of areas already congested. That is particularly
true of the fruit and vegetable market in Covent Garden
just north of the Strand. As most of its produce is grown
in market gardens and on farms round London it would
seem much more reasonable to have dispersed markets on
the edges of the town. To these the local produce could be
taken and then sent into the shops of the regions instead of
adding to the vast traffic of trucks and lorries which con-
verge on the already crowded streets of the West Central
district. But conservatism prevails. There Covent Garden
has been and there it remains. The best that can be said of it
as an institution is that it brings a blaze of colour into the
drabness of the streets. On a dull winter day one's eyes

may be warmed by crates of golden oranges or of rubicund apples. Some of Andrew Marvell's "Thoughts in a Garden" have come into my head as I have passed on my way through the open spaces of the market or traversed the roofed-in area with their fruit shops and stalls.

> "What wondrous life is this I lead!
> Ripe apples drop about my head;
> The luscious clusters of the vine
> Upon my mouth do crush their wine;
> The nectarine and curious peach
> Into my hands themselves do reach;
> Stumbling on melons, as I pass,
> Ensnared with flowers, I fall on grass."

It must be admitted that, if I fall, it is not on grass: it is more likely to be a hard pavement with the accident caused by a squashed tomato or a banana skin. But the wanderer can move among the delicate yellow-green of melons and be ensnared into the purchase of flowers. When spring comes to London it shows its flags abundantly in Covent Garden.

The district began its life as the Convent Garden, a haunt of the monks of Westminster. The dissolution of the monasteries in the reign of Henry VIII made an end of that and the Earls of Bedford, later Dukes, were the beneficiaries. The fourth Earl had the good sense to employ Inigo Jones to lay out a part of his gains as a residential quarter with roofed arcades and these, known as the piazzas, were a prominent feature of London's elegance for many years and a strolling-ground of the fops of Restoration London. There is little sign of that now, but the church of St. Paul's to the west of the market is, though rebuilt in 1795, a striking reminder of Inigo Jones's London as well as of this region's connection with the world of plays and players.

Architecturally it is not admired. It was called a barn and still is so called by John Betjeman in his *Guide to English*

Parish Churches. Inigo Jones had remarked that, if it was a barn, it was the handsomest barn in Europe, to which it may be replied that Jones can hardly have seen every barn of so comprehensive a continent. As " the actors' church " it can at least be called a sanctuary of the barnstormers since many of the greatest players have begun with touring of the humblest kind. St. Paul's has received in its vaults the remains of masters of all the arts, among them Sir Peter Lely, the painter, Grinling Gibbons, the wood-carver, and William Wycherley, the dramatist. The ashes of Ellen Terry are also there. For the lovers and students of theatrical history that makes this church holy ground twice over.

A curious new fame has come to St. Paul's through Bernard Shaw's play *Pygmalion,* basis of the most popular musical of the nineteen-fifties, *My Fair Lady.* It was on the steps of the large eastern portico that Eliza Doolittle sold flowers and caught the ear of Professor Higgins, while the crowd of operagoers and playgoers sheltered from a down-pour and strove to get cabs home. There have been three theatres named after Covent Garden since 1732: the first, built in that year, was the sounding-board for Handel's oratorios as well as for the acting of all the great eighteenth-century leaders of the stage. Fire seemed to be an unavoid-able destroyer of theatres in those times. The first Covent Garden went up in flames in 1808 and the second in 1856; the present Opera House has fortunately survived its cen-tury, and those patrons of opera and ballet who go westward on their way home and have not found a taxi on a wet night can still shelter where the imaginary Eliza carried on the decorative commerce of " The Garden " and rose from the kerb to the drawing-room. Her Cockney accent and its cure have paid gigantic dividends to the Shaw estate and to the British Treasury which draws tax and surtax on its earnings.

Returning to our topic of food and its distribution, we

have next to proceed to two corners of the City of London. Billingsgate, to the east of London Bridge, has been a centre of fish marketing for a thousand years. Its name may be derived from a pre-Christian British King called Belin or from a Roman magnate called Belinus. It has survived to be a synonym for foul and abusive language. The place was noted as far back as Elizabethan times for the ribaldry of the oyster-wives. Their male colleagues kept up the reputation of the riverside porters and salesmen for their readiness with an oath or an obscenity. But there is no reason to suppose that the workers in other markets are tongue-tied when things go wrong. The flat caps worn by the fish-carriers have been an ancient badge of their calling. Efforts have been made to shift the market from so valuable a site on the edge of the City to premises farther east; but, as in the case of Covent Garden, conservatism has beaten considerations of economy and convenience. Billingsgate is one of London's immovables.

Here again there is an adjacent church of remarkable beauty, that of St. Magnus the Martyr. It has been established in the mind of poetry readers by T. S. Eliot with his reference to Lower Thames Street:

> " Where fishmen lounge at noon: where the walls
> Of Magnus Martyr hold
> Inexplicable splendour of Ionian white and gold."

It is a Wren church with one of the loftiest of the City spires; it soars almost as far into the sky as does the Monument, that fluted Doric column designed by Wren and erected in the sixteen-seventies to commemorate the Great Fire of 1666. (Those who enjoy upward movement, self-propelled, can mount the latter's 311 steps to gain a naturally comprehensive view of the outspread city and its river.) St. Magnus provides High Church services beneath its wonderfully complex tower with Ionic pilasters and lead cupola. The scent of incense counteracts the regional scent of fish.

The interior is inexplicably splendid, with more Ionic columns and fine examples of woodwork. If Billingsgate mutters and swears, St. Magnus is a most eloquent work of praise.

Mention of eloquence brings to mind the quaint pieces of the English language that linger in the markets. The Covent Garden porters have their cotchell, which is a bundle of vegetables. Their earnings are large in these times, but they get a bonus too since they can have a cotchell free. The only available explanation of the term is that a coshery was once a free feast in Ireland. An Irish porter may have introduced his idea of a cotchery with subsequent modification of the word and benefaction to his fellows. Billingsgate had its bummarees. These were middlemen in the fish trade and people of some wealth and consequence in the eighteenth century. Since then the term has passed on to the porters and is in use at the meat market in Smithfield too. Not long ago the Smithfield men objected to the survival of this ancient noun which they described with the adjective " obnoxious." Presumably they were linking it with the word " bum," which in America means a tramp and in England a bailiff's man sent in to seize household property in return for unpaid debts. A bum is also slang for a bottom. If bummarees think themselves put in the bum class by this description they have cause to complain; but the title is, in fact, historic and honorific.

Smithfield Market lies north of Holborn and south of Aldersgate on the eastern verge of the City. Like the other markets it has been there for hundreds of years; thereabouts was held the great Bartholomew's Fair in which, every August, the sale of cloth was accompanied with popular revels. Ben Jonson's play of *Bartholomew Fair*, occasionally revived, gives us a rich theatrical panorama of the mountebanks, pedlars, puppet shows, and general " high jinks " which were to be found in this district along with the cozeners who exploited it and the Puritans who denounced it. Smithfield was also a long-established horse and cattle market and a place of execution for human beings as well as for the butchers' livestock. Scots visitors can here honour the name of their militant patriot, William Wallace, since there is a tablet on the wall of St. Bartholomew's Hospital commemorating his execution by the English.

At Smithfield one would have to amend the lines of Marvell already quoted to "Stumbling on sirloins as I pass." The array of carcasses must be a vegetarian's nightmare. Markets do not appear to be good for the temper. Billingsgate has been notorious for its language and Smithfield of recent years has been notorious for the nature of what are politely called "industrial relations." The Smithfield men are continually voicing their grievances and threatening or insisting on strikes. Whether one calls them bummarees or meat operatives they never seem to stop grumbling. Many a middle-class business man or civil servant would be glad of the money they earn.

Once more food and faith go together: and in this case medicine is another companion. Smithfield has its great hospital of St. Bartholomew, which, linked originally with an Augustinian priory, served body and soul together. It was refounded as a hospital only by King Henry VIII after the priory's suppression. "Bart's" has handsome buildings, with a Great Hall by James Gibbs, erected in the seventeen-thirties, and well added to by Thomas Hardwick early in the following century. The chief physician of "Bart's" from 1609–43 was Dr. William Harvey, famous for his conclusive proof of the circulation of the blood. (He was not its discoverer since it was mentioned by Shakespeare in *Coriolanus* before Harvey's famous exposition in 1616.) Another phrase of Shakespeare's, "When blood is their argument," seems generally applicable to the meaty Smithfield area. Famous for its surgeons, its medical college, museum and library, and sometimes for the vigorous expertness of its students in playing Rugby football, Bart's

16—L

has had as notable a part in London medical life as the old Cloth Fair played in its commerce and its carnivals.

There are two Smithfield churches, St. Bartholomew the Less, approached by way of the hospital, and St. Bartholomew the Great, on the east of the market. The latter's brick tower of the seventeenth century has England's oldest ring of bells; the size is very great for a parish church and rather suggests an abbey. John Betjeman, who lives near by in Cloth Fair, describes the interior as " vast, dark, and Romanesque." " Charmingly the perpendicular tomb of Rahere, founder of the great hospital, and a perpendicular watching window in the triforium opposite are inserted between rugged Norman columns." Here " the centuries kiss and commingle " and the result is massive, impressive, and not a fane in which joy is an immediate emotion.

The whole district echoes with great names. Milton hid here after the Restoration, Hogarth was born here, and, if one moves northward to St. John's Gate, there is the old priory which became the office of the Elizabethan Master of the Revels. In the person of Edmund Tilney he was a stern censor of plays, more vigilant for political reference and propaganda than for moral offences. The old building subsequently reverted to the Order of St. John of Jerusalem, whose successors are the members of the St. John Ambulance Brigade, continuing yielders of good service. Beyond that is the Charterhouse, whose chronicles are extensive and dear to readers of Thackeray. By the time that a perambulation of the Smithfield area has carried one into Clerkenwell, where Shakespeare sent his plays for vetting and Lenin once edited a paper called *The Spark*, the wanderer will surely have acquired sufficient thirst and appetite to be thinking more of cosseting the inner man than of taking further courses in the chronicles and curios of London life.

I I

After-Word

To cheer but not inebriate.

Bishop Berkeley

11

ONDON is too big for words, certainly too big for the
number of words that can be contained in a single
book or indeed in half a dozen books. It presents a
menu of the gigantic size that one is handed in very smart
restaurants; one must select from abundance, feed *à la carte,*
and leave much untasted. It can at once be said that my
choice of London features has led to the omission of many
important aspects and themes. There has been, for example,
very little about the square mile of the City itself. It is a
fascinating subject, this hub of the conurbation, the continuing settlement of the original Londinium and of the
walled fortress of the Romans. Present excavation digs
into pre-Christian faiths and can discover a temple of
Mithras, the Persian god whom the legions of the garrison
preferred to the official and Olympian deities. London is
like one of those parchments which, being scarce and
precious, had to be scribbled on over and over again. The
more the scrutiny, the more is the inducement to further
search for underlying treasure.

To one writing in the year 1959, the City was obviously
in such a state of drastic reconstruction that judgments on
its new look would be unfair until the whole face had been
lifted. The remoulding is on a gigantic scale. Millions of
pounds are being invested in the upthrust of new business
mansions. (Palace is too regal a word for these monsters and
premises seems too petty a description.) After a leisurely
start due to the after-war shortages, there has been no
change so large and so swift since the City rose again from
the ashes of the Great Fire of 1666. In a few years it will be
fair to risk an opinion on what we have achieved in the way

of architecture, amenity, and communications. The last of
these three is not the least important, since we have reached
a way of living in which vast motive power and capacity
for speed are combined with a maddening immobility in and
around our towns. The age of fantastic speed in the air has
become the age of fantastically slow motion on urban
ground. The thoroughfare is now a place one cannot get
through. A man can fly jet-propelled to Rome in the time
that it will take him to drive, in the highest-powered car,
from the Tower of London to London Airport. How, in
the London of tomorrow, shall we be coping with that
absurdity?

The City poses all sorts of questions that cannot yet be
answered. It is not alone in that; everywhere the conurbation becomes one vast traffic block and the problem of
getting in and out of central areas plagues all big towns
increasingly. The middle of London has its own particular problems. Can it be made residential again? Is it
possible for more people to " live over the shop "?
Could the City be made more domestic, thus saving its
workers the nuisance, expense, and exhaustion of long daily
travel? I recently saw and heard some television interviews
with the few people who have a home in the square mile;
they all seemed to like it, especially the surprising tranquillity of the evenings and weekends when the day's turmoil
is over. Perhaps the City, offering flats as well as offices,
will cease to be a nest only for caretakers. Meanwhile how
are the daily incomers and outgoers, multiplied by many
thousands when the new offices are taken up and fully
staffed, to make their journeys with endurable conditions
of travel?

One thing seems certain. The City will retain the
symbols, ritual, and pageantry of its ancient life at the
Guildhall, the Mansion House, and in the halls of the
historic craft and merchant companies. That rich piece of
mummery (and of nonsense if you insist on the practical

view) the Lord Mayor's Show in November, no longer holds up the life of the town through the middle of a busy weekday. It is properly arranged for Saturdays when it will cause less traffic trouble and when the schoolchildren will be free to line the streets and to enjoy this curious promenade in which the latest inventions are paraded among the medievalism of coach and horses making it seem that Dick Whittington drives again. The City will continue to show pride in its ancientry and will refuse to take away its baubles because they happen to be old. The remaining churches of the seventeenth and eighteenth centuries will be seen like jewels embedded in the rocks. The companies will administer their affairs and their heritage of charities and the liverymen will dine upon occasion amid their silver treasures in what is left of their truly noble halls. The Common Council, with perhaps a rather larger electorate, will govern its republic, so small in size and so huge in wealth, and administer its strange legacy of woods and forests, such as Epping to the east and Burnham Beeches to the west.

Nothing will end that. The Londoner, like most Englishmen, is an obstinate ritualist in civic matters. He is accustomed to mayors strangely and colourfully robed and furred and wearing chains of office. There is a common phrase about things broken or discarded which describes them as being " knocked into a cocked hat." But the last thing to be knocked out will be the cocked hats of our City rulers and " worshipful persons." Nor will the traditional ceremonial and costumery be considered pathetic and even ridiculous amid a mass of architecture which has left tradition far behind. These things have so well survived the pressure of time and the smiles of youth that one cannot see them fading from the city modernised.

The future may arrive in better shape than the apprehensive now imagine. Probably in time we shall see the river sensibly used for public transport, a welcome renewal of ancient practice. The river banks may be rescued from squalor and at night, with the aid of modern lighting, make the water a silvery snake as it winds through the many miles from the western suburbs to the Port and the estuary. New conceptions of amenity and entertainment will be forthcoming. We have to realise that the best use of leisure must be considered as the logical consequence of the new office machinery. There is no advantage in doing our business arithmetic by press-button methods if we still have as many people spending as much time in minding the competent inventions as were engaged in doing their own slower handiwork. The age of automation demands that the people in control of it shall not be automata, but capable of using their freedom from old drudgeries. If there is more leisure, then we must see that our cities are places in which it can be spent in a civilised way. Is it Utopian to envisage a London in which the press-button ingenuities have been used to make a more ample life in a city of ample enjoyments?

It is strange in this age of fear to remember that the composition of Utopias was the common practice of fifty and sixty years ago. Before he surveyed " The Shape of Things to Come," a younger and happier H. G. Wells poured Utopias out of his fertile brain and planned a radically altered world with confident anticipation. It seemed then that man had only to apply his reasoning to his inventive powers and to the new resources at his command in order to win a world of serenity, governed by good sense, with its hates and panics gone. Into that liberal optimism of freedoms swiftly broadening out crashed the two world wars and the new despotisms, the denial of reason amid a tumult of fears, and the frustration of all Utopian belief. There was the terror of the new weapons, tools mental as well as military, since by the application of the new mass-media millions could be turned into the patient acceptors of any wicked rubbish talked to them and of any disciplines imposed on them. The darkness spread when it was realised that even the greatest victories for freedom in battle could be transient and brittle. What had become of " the war to end war "? It seemed an idle task to write any more Utopias. The cacotopia or hell-spot of George Orwell's *1984* was the kind of prophesy that suited the pessimism of the period.

The future of any city is the future of the world. If peace goes, all goes. But if dread of the new engines of destruction can force men out of their old combative moods and the fatalistic acceptance of slaughter as the inevitable end of international disagreement, the prospect has infinite promise. If we could at last get the nations to stop snarling and rocket-rattling (sabres being somewhat out of date) and divert the vast expenditure of brains and bullion now devoted to armaments to the remaking of our towns, with due regard to the saving of our countryside, the future is even brighter than it was in the years of the Wellsian Utopias. We have far more money to spend and far better machinery to employ. Material advantages, it is true, guarantee nothing unless there are the confidence, the energy, and the resolution to use them. Those qualities may surely be evident and prominent once we are free of the inhibiting apprehensions natural to an age of fear.

The application of taste together with a new audacity to the design for urban living is something that could happen and happen not so far ahead. All bad dreams do not come true. Vast stretches of the featureless and dreary in all our towns could be swept away without spending more than we are now devoting to armaments which are out of date a few months after they have been so cunningly and so expensively devised. This new London would have many problems of civic education to solve. If we are on the verge of a Leisure State, with an age of under-employment as the natural product of an age of automation and with the labour so shared that none are overworked while others are workless altogether, the business of filling the time sensibly has got to be learned.

A Leisure State full of yawning loafers would be a hideous society in which to live. If all that our technical skills can achieve is to make a world for television to exploit, a paradise for arm-chair sitters who have not even the energy to be arm-chair critics, progress has few attractions for those who see happiness in terms of activity, at least while age and health permit the use of all one's faculties. People must discover how to employ their machines, as the ancient Athenians employed their slave-labour, turning the ease of their life to the free exercise of their capacities. It is possible to foresee a London in which recreation, a word often debased to cover the silliest forms of time-killing, has its full meaning, the remaking of the self, the achievement of a personal renewal. In such a city the doing of things for oneself would be as natural as the sluggish acceptance of provided services.

It is a poor condition of life in which we have to keep championing and rescuing the arts as though we were righteously maintaining abnormal articles for people's good. "Do-gooders" would be out of work in a sound society because much would be instinctively done which has now to be urged with uplifting appeals and sedulous campaigning. The creators of the best of the old England and of old London were not continually lectured on "the place of the architect in contemporary society," nor were they put through courses on the nature of beauty. They kept their minds open to foreign examples: they adapted their materials to the spot and the building to its purpose. Their Gothic expressed the wonder of their worship; their Classic proclaimed their sense of reason and proportion. They took their crafts in their natural stride and when they worked on a cathedral, abbey, or church, they were no more governed by abstract theorising about beauty than Shakespeare was governed by lectures on the nature of poetry and the principles of dramatic composition. The fatal change came when building was accepted as something naturally dull or even ugly and therefore in need of embellishment—fearful word—to make it attractive. Beauty, like happiness, is a by-product and is the companion of activities freely and unselfconsciously pursued.

So, if we stop fussing about beauty and can build to-morrow's London as something seemly and serviceable, it will be its own adornment, proving that a good living-place is mainly founded on a basis of good sense. All depends on the lifting of the cosmic fears. With that stifling cloud dispersed, the planner, with our inventions, our wealth, and our techniques at his command, could visualise and realise a city as desirable as that sung by the poets of old and charted by the Utopians of half a century ago. We must not let the Orwellian nightmare hold us in thrall for ever. In a pacified world London could " wake up and dream " and so, while recapturing its medieval spirit of creation and exploiting the riches and resources of today, become in both senses of the adjective indeed a capital city.

Index